BERBER&Q

THE COOKBOOK

THE COOKBOOK

BERBER & Q

JOSH KATZ

EBURY
PRESS

CONTENTS

On 24 April 2015 Berber & Q opened its doors to the public for the first time, white smoke billowing from our open mangal onto a dimly lit Haggerston backstreet.

We were born in an old taxi repair shop, housed in the most beautiful converted railway arch I'd ever seen. I remember the first moment we saw her, exposed brick as far as the eyes could see, dark, cavernous, dripping in grease but packed with character. It was love at first sight. We had, for some time, been harbouring designs for a hazy, fucked-up barbecue joint, hidden down some neighbourhood alley, shrouded in mystery from the outside, bursting with energy from within. Arch 338 on Acton Mews ticked all the boxes.

Within a few weeks of opening, queues had begun to snake outside our door and down the little mews. The warm red glow of hospitality and heady smell of cumin-scented barbecue emanating from inside our arch seemed to draw local East Londoners in. Groups of mates surged in to huddle around massive tables, eating with their hands from communal trays piled high with Technicolor barbecue, spilling punchy cocktails before emerging half-cut and meat-drunk to free up space for the ever-expanding crowd outside. This was how we dreamed it would be.

Droves have kept coming ever since. Every so often I make sure to stand back and take it all in. Berber & Q has a magical spirit and energy to it that is difficult to capture or express properly in words. It's a combination of our beautiful arch, our beautiful team, but most importantly, our beautiful customers, who have always let us be what we always wanted to be without judgement or reservation. We will be forever grateful for this.

INTRODUCTION

My path to owning a North African and Middle Eastern-influenced barbecue joint has not been paved with clarity and a well-informed sense of direction. I've always loved barbecue, but I haven't always known *how* to barbecue.

I don't hail from Texas. I didn't spend my school summer holidays working at my local barbecue joint. I've been to Turkey. Several times. And I've even followed the grill 'ustas' (masters) around like a bad smell. But I can't claim to be one of them. Not by a long shot. I've never lived on a farm, nor reared my own herd of needy pigs. And I sure-as-shit have never had to hunt for my food. The closest I've ever come to foraging in the wild was in the bagel queue at Daniel's Bakery on a Sunday morning. (Believe me, it can get pretty primitive in there. Especially if you were responsible for taking the last sesame-seeded chollah.)

I don't come from good barbecuing stock. I grew up in a Jewish household, the youngest child to South African parents, in the leafy enclave of Hampstead Garden Suburb. The beating heart of privileged Jewish North West London, it's not an area renowned for its entrenched barbecue culture, save for a few kosher grill houses in nearby Golders Green such as the legendary Solly's, which threw down a mean lamb shawarma but some decidedly average grilled meat skewers.

I think my parents had probably hoped for me to be a banker, or possibly a doctor. Maybe even both, at the same time. I on the other hand had always loved food, and harboured dreams of running restaurants. This was in no small part down to them. Food was always a *thing* in our house.

Whilst other kids my age were spending their pocket money on music, fashion accessories and trainers, I was buying dim sum at Local Friends, a Chinese restaurant in Golders Green. I'd go there on the way home from school for char sui bao (barbecued pork bun) and some prawn cheung fun.

I quickly graduated to taking trips across town to West London's Edgware Road, with its array of Lebanese and Persian grill houses. By the time we were old enough to drive, my mates and I had discovered apple shisha, and would regularly head down on a Saturday night to smoke flavoured tobacco into the early hours. We thought we were so cool, but in truth, I only ever went for the food. I loved the lamb shawarma from Ranoush Juice, and the hummus beiruty and fattoush from the legendary (though recently closed) Beirut Express. Soon I was commuting across town in the other direction, to Green Lanes' Turkish grill houses, where I'd introduce my mates to mixed mezze and shared meat platters.

For a long time I refused to seriously consider a profession in the hospitality industry. Back when I was finishing school and deciding what to do with my life, that world was only just starting to garner its current sex appeal. The restaurant business had a bad rep for long hours and low pay. Not much, other than people's perceptions of it, has changed.

So I did what everyone else was doing and enrolled in university, emerging still without much clue as to what I wanted to do. I began a career in marketing for a small design agency in Covent Garden, a more conventional career path for me, but try as I might I couldn't get into it. When the time came to make a change, it felt right to pursue my love for food and restaurants professionally.

I started my apprenticeship at the eponymous Galvin Bistrot de Luxe, an acclaimed French bistro on Baker Street owned by the Galvin brothers, Jeff and Chris. It was a tough, bruising experience. I was 'in the shit' from the minute I arrived until I left. I stuck it out for 18 months, just to prove wrong those who thought I'd only last two weeks. At no point did I really enjoy cooking French food, but I endured out of stubborn resistance.

I moved myself on and found work at Ottolenghi in Notting Hill. At the time it was only just starting to make waves. I had no idea of the seismic impact that Yotam Ottolenghi and Sami Tamimi would go on to make in the world of cookery, helping to shape and define the way we eat at home. I also had no idea of the effect it would have on my own career, how it would shape and define how and what I like to cook, and how it would open doors for me through association.

I loved everything about my time at Ottolenghi – the team, the people I met, many of whom are my friends or colleagues still to this day, and the sense of family spirit that was generated amongst the staff. But most of all I loved the food. Big, bold flavours, not too complicated, but always seasoned correctly. They taught me about colours, texture and balance, about touching all of the different parts of the taste receptors, and about how to make food look spectacular in an unrefined, lavish kind of way.

It was during the latter stages of my time at Ottolenghi that I first met my now business partner and dear friend Mattia Bianchi, who was working front-of-house. He was, as he still is today, a walking, talking set of contradictions. He has an unquenchable greed for food but never puts on weight. He has an ungainly physique, incredibly tall and skinny, with flailing limbs like a clumsy giraffe, but he glides across the restaurant floor with the grace of a cheetah. Above all, he has an unassuming air completely lacking in pretence, with a sense of cool that he radiates without even trying. Just don't tell him I said that.

I met many fantastic people over the course of my two years at Ottolenghi but was especially close to Mattia. In 2010 we both moved on together to take the next step in our respective careers, helping to launch Made In Camden, a new restaurant at the iconic Roundhouse in Chalk Farm. From that moment on we began hatching plans to open our own restaurant. We had to wait until 2015 for the opportunity.

THE BEGINNING

I am a huge fan of American barbecue. I've played around with it at the edges since long before I became a chef, without ever going all in. I was sitting in Fette Sau, one my favourite barbecue joints in Williamsburg, Brooklyn, when I had my light bulb moment and first conceived the idea for Berber & Q. At the time, I had no notion of what kind of restaurant I wanted to open. But I knew that I wanted it to reflect and promote the laid-back unpretentious attitude I associated with American barbecue.

What occurred to me, as I ploughed my way through my oversized tray of smoked meats, were the obvious commonalities between American and Arabic barbecue culture. There's a shared emphasis on communal feasting from a central platter or tray of meats, which has a familial and relaxed feel to it that I am drawn to. There are pickles, used to cut through the richness of the meat. There's bread and sauces, from hot sauce to harissa. And there are uncomplicated sides. In fact, the only real difference I could observe was the way in which meat is cooked. American barbecue takes inexpensive large joints and smokes them low and slow, until the fat and collagen melt and they all but fall apart, where Arabic barbecue tends to take inexpensive cuts and grill them quickly, close to a bed of charcoal.

I felt there was an opportunity to bring all of these threads together and to present them, uniquely, at the same table. I wanted to take all that I loved from both cultures and styles of barbecue and sit them side by side. I saw American craft beer next to skewered Turkish kebabs, trays of smoked meat doused in Moroccan harissa atop Arabic flatbread; fried chicken and tahini.

We never intended for Berber & Q to be an authentic representation of the cuisines or culinary cultures we were so heavily influenced by. Let's be honest, by its very nature, a restaurant owned by Jewish Londoners and an Italian Catholic, serving Arabic-inspired American barbecue food out of an arch in East London, was never going to win any awards for authenticity.

We set out to be deliberately inauthentic, and proudly so. This is what is true to us. Our backgrounds have been forged in multicultural London. We've been influenced by the array of ethnic and cultural diversity that defines our city.

Berber and Q could only ever have been born in East London, which I consider the beating heart of London's cultural melting pot. Our restaurant sits just up the road from the BYO Vietnamese spots, down from all the Turkish mangals to which we are so heavily indebted, and surrounded by steel drum Caribbean takeaways.

An old head chef of mine once told me that he considered himself a perfectionist seeking perfection in every single plate of food he put out. It's a line I often hear banded around the industry.

The search for perfection is not *my* food philosophy. I find it too constrictive. It strips away the carefree and therapeutic aspects of cookery that made me enjoy it in the first place. I've wasted enough time in my life seeking perfection to know how hard it is to find. Like a mirage, it always seems to disappear the closer you get. Instead I'm okay with imperfections. They're what make us human.

The way I cook is an extension of this philosophy. At Berber & Q we don't 'brunoise' and rarely 'chiffonade', instead we roughly chop and shred. We burn things, on purpose, or lightly char them round the edges. We actively seek these imperfections because they define our style. We don't do precise but we always do things right. Our food is simple, honest and always punches above its weight. We do loud colours, and big, bold flavours, underpinned by solid technique that is neither fancy nor overly fussy.

This is what drew me to the food of North Africa and the Middle East, and to the barbecue. Berber & Q is our expression of this food philosophy.

OUR PHILOSOPHY

GETTING STARTED

The recipes in this book are intended only as a guide, not as hard-and-fast rules to live your life or die your death by.

Cookery, much like life, is an imperfect science. Ingredients vary in size and composition. Some cauliflowers are bigger than others and will take longer to parboil as a result. Barbecue brings added layers of complexity. Each fire you light will be different to the last, as will the set of conditions in which you barbecue, whether with gas, charcoal or wood.

The truth is, there are so many different variables in cookery, and even more in barbecue. Recipes will always require a degree of interpretation or adaptation to suit a given situation. Try not to let yourself be paralysed by this fact but instead allow yourself to be liberated by it.

With all this said and done, here are some philosophies of mine that I think you might find helpful.

Be a jazz musician in the kitchen. Trust your instincts. Learn how to improvise and be brave.

Cooking times are guidelines. They are designed to steer, but they are not definitive instructions. Learn to feel when vegetables are tender, or when a piece of fish is cooked, by touch, or by taste, through trial and error.

Taste everything. Adjust where necessary. If you feel you need to add more salt, do so. If you want to add chilli flakes, go for it. Never be confined by the parameters of a given recipe. If you prefer one cheese to another, or another fish, swap it out. Some of my best recipes I've stumbled on accidentally.

Actively burn shit. It's something that I learnt from the godfather of fire cookery, Francis Mallmann (only he'd express it far more eloquently). It brings a certain flavour and smokiness. We burn our onions in the fire. We char our bread to add to salads. We blacken our aubergines. But don't burn everything. Meat, for the most part, rarely ever benefits from being burnt.

Vegetables should be leading ladies (never the quirky best friend). At Berber & Q we take our vegetables very seriously. They are a main component of any meal, with equal status to our meats, not a sideshow.

Make mistakes. Learn from them and go again. Always go again. We only ever learn from the mistakes we make. It's how we get better.

Relax. It will make you a better cook. Put on some music. Pour yourself a glass of wine; take your clothes off. Actually probably don't do the last one – it contravenes a number of health and safety laws. The point is, do whatever you fancy. But, whatever you do, have fun.

STAR INGREDIENTS

Some ingredients I always try to have kicking around my larder.

Biber salcasi. A hot red pepper paste, like tomato purée but with more depth to it. Get it from Turkish greengrocers. An unsung hero.

Tahini. Top grade tahini is essential for what we do. Go for Middle Eastern, Arabic, Lebanese, Palestinian or Israeli varieties. Ethiopian is the best.

Flaked sea salt. Salt is the single most important ingredient in cookery. The Maldon variety is more expensive than table salt, so I don't use it in a sauce or a braise where it gets mixed in. But at the end, it is really great for the pops of savoury power.

Cumin and turmeric. In fact, all spices. Make sure that they're fresh, as spices lose their punch over time. Every true Berber & Q scholar should take a field trip to the Arabic greengrocers on the Edgware Road.

Date syrup and pomegranate molasses. American barbecue dishes will use a lot of cane molasses. We sub in a date syrup or pomegranate molasses to bring the Middle Eastern touch. Use in dressings and sauces.

Garlic. I like to grate my garlic using a coarse Microplane because I find it packs the strongest punch. It's not for everyone. Chopping with a knife yields a far milder result. Just be sure to chop it finely, preferably with the addition of salt to help it break down to a purée. Never buy pre-minced.

Flavoured oils. Many of the recipes in this book call for the use of garlic oil (page 260). I like to have a number of different flavoured oils in my fridge, including chilli, shallot and herb oil. They're super easy to make and are endlessly versatile, adding an extra layer of taste to everyday dressings, marinades and condiments. But they aren't essential by any means, and can be easily substituted with normal or extra virgin olive oil.

DIRECT VERSUS INDIRECT GRILLING

Learning the difference between direct and indirect grilling is a critical lesson and essential starting point for any budding barbecue enthusiast.

The main difference between the two is neatly illustrated by looking at American and Turkish barbecue side by side.

Turkish grill houses build a bed of burning coal embers and cook the skewered meat very close to the heat source, directly over the radiant heat that's being emitted. The distance between fuel and protein is rarely more than 7–10cm, sometimes closer. It is a technique best suited for cuts that cook quickly. Almost every grilled meat on a Turkish menu will cook in under 10 minutes. Typically you will direct grill at high, searing temperatures from 180°C and beyond.

American barbecue, on the other hand, involves barbecuing larger joints of meat that need to be cooked for longer periods over a lower temperature. It's what is often referred to as barbecuing 'low-and-slow' or smoking. Here, the protein is cooked indirectly, offset from the heat source, which will either be in another chamber altogether, or on the opposite side of the same cooking vessel. The meat cooks by convection heat circulating around the grill or smoker, much in the same way an oven works. Typically you will indirectly grill between temperatures of 110°C and 160°C, with 'low-and-slow' smoking occurring at the bottom end of this scale (110°C and 130°C), and what I like to refer to as barbecue roasting between 130°C and 160°C.

As a child experimenting with barbecue in my parents' garden, it took me a while to discover indirect grilling. Like most people, I fought to grill everything at the same time whilst simultaneously trying to manage the temperature of burning coals. Invariably meat would burn on the outside before being cooked all the way through, or cook faster than other pieces.

It all felt very chaotic and stressful. But once I'd discovered that I could build my bed of coals banked to one side and cook my meat on the opposite side with the lid down, where it would cook indirectly without fear or risk of immediate burning, it changed everything.

Suddenly I could swap items out, moving them back and forth between different heat zones so as to manage all the items that I was grilling simultaneously. I could keep some warm whilst I finished others off.

It occurred to me that a barbecue is really just another oven. Once I'd understood this elementary principle, I started to ask myself what else could I cook indirectly? Everything that I would normally cook in a domestic oven I could now barbecue instead, imparting smokiness into my food.

The recipes in this book call for either single zone, direct grilling or a two-zone set-up for indirect grilling, all illustrated below. It's worth noting at this point that I would always advocate a two-zone set-up over a single-zone one. It provides you with so much more flexibility in how you cook, allowing both direct and indirect cooking at the same time, but also giving you space on your grill where you can pull meat off to if the fire is too hot, or rest the meat whilst you grill the vegetables.

SINGLE-ZONE SET-UP FOR DIRECT GRILLING

This is the simplest set-up and involves building a large bed of burning embers, usually at a distance of between 7cm and 15cm directly below the grill rack itself. The coals can either be distributed evenly across the charcoal grate, or be built up more heavily in one area to create different grilling zones and enable you to cook at different temperatures. Open the vents at the bottom if you have them.

TWO-ZONE SET-UP FOR INDIRECT GRILLING

A two-zone set-up for indirect grilling is slightly more complicated.

Bank your coals on the charcoal grate to one side of your barbecue. Place the grill grate over the charcoals and have a water pan, filled with water about 2.5cm or so deep, set directly above the charcoal. This is intended to add moisture to your smoke, but it's entirely optional. Place your meat on the opposite side to the charcoal. You can place a second pan under the meat, again filled with water about 2.5cm or so deep, which will collect dripping meat juices and fat. This will prevent flare-ups in your barbecue.

If your barbecue is old school and doesn't come with its own, it's worth investing in a thermometer probe that can gauge the internal temperature.

Direct Grilling   **Indirect Grilling**

HOW TO BUILD A FIRE

I believe we are all intrinsically connected to fire. The ability to control fire was, after all, a turning point in human evolution. We have built fire since our very beginning – it is what identifies us as human – for warmth, protection and as a means of cooking food. It has allowed us to change our diet, to survive cooler temperatures and in turn to geographically disperse across the planet.

And yet controlling fire for the purposes of cooking is an activity that most people may never have undertaken. Modern life strips away our need for it. This is our loss. It's an important aspect of who we are and we should reclaim it.

Building a fire is nowhere near as intimidating as people perceive it to be. But, like any relationship, getting to know fire properly, how it burns and behaves, so you can use it to your advantage, takes time, diligence and some work.

The type of fire you build is determined by what you're cooking, how you plan to cook it, what piece of equipment you're barbecuing on, and what fuel source you're using. Ultimately, learning what type of fire to build for any given set of circumstances is a journey of discovery. It's part of the fun, challenge and skill of learning how to barbecue. Here are some guidelines for getting started.

WOOD VERSUS CHARCOAL

The first thing to do is ascertain what fuel source you'll be using. Most domestic barbecuing uses charcoal, as it's more readily available. Wood brings more flavour and smokiness to the party, but it burns out much quicker. Charcoal, on the other hand, burns for longer and brings more heat, but has less flavour. This is important to note because it determines usage. Think of charcoal as your gas, and wood as your seasoning.

STARTING AND TENDING TO A FIRE FOR DIRECT GRILLING

I'll only ever barbecue with wood exclusively if I'm cooking direct only, for a short period of time. In this instance, I'll always build my wood fire with firelight and kindling followed by larger twigs and sticks and then logs. I arrange my logs in rows of three, evenly spaced in between, and sit three logs on top perpendicular to the first row. I'll add one more row to the top, parallel to the first row, before lighting the whole thing up. If you've built your fire correctly, the whole stack will go up in a blaze, but given time (20–25 minutes depending on the wood) it will burn down to a proper bed of coals that are perfect for grilling over.

If I'm building a charcoal fire for direct grilling I use a chimney starter, packed full with briquettes, and light firelight or newspaper underneath. Within 20–30 minutes you will have a bed of burning coals to empty into your barbecue.

Whether I'm using wood or charcoal, there are basic rules I always adhere to:

- Never grill off flame. It will leave a black residue of soot that will cling to your food and taint it with an acrid taste. Wait until the flames have burnt away and you're left with a glowing bed of burning embers.

- Always set aside an area of your fire or grill for topping up with additional fuel. This will ensure you have a constant supply of incoming coals. You will need two distinct zones within your set-up. One for cooking over, the other for adding more coal or wood.

- Use a fire poker or shovel to move the embers around, building them up in areas where you're looking for more heat, or distributing them outwards when you're burning too high.

- If you're using a barbecue with vents at the bottom, play around and see how the airflow impacts upon your burn. Adjust according to requirements. If you need more throttle, open up all the way.

STARTING AND TENDING FOR INDIRECT SMOKING/ROASTING

If I'm in for the long haul, cooking low-and-slow over several hours or more, I don't want to be building up my fire every half an hour, so I always opt for a bed of good-quality slow-burning charcoal briquettes and feed it with wood chunks intermittently to add the smoky flavour I'm looking for.

Make sure the vents in your barbecue are open and set a small bed of charcoal alight (7–10 briquettes) using a chimney starter or a blowtorch. Top the burning coals with a good pile of unlit briquettes, followed by a handful of wood chunks. Put the lid on and once the desired internal temperature has been reached close off the vents and add your meat.

The process of monitoring and maintaining the temperature in your barbecue is one that demands practice. Essentially you have two main forms of control. You can shut off (choke) or open up the air vents, or add more lit coals as the temperature starts to drop off. As a general rule, you will need to add five lit charcoal briquettes every hour or so to maintain steady temperature, but of course there are many external factors at play (such as outdoor temperature and wind), so this rule is not hard and fast.

SOURCING

The process of correctly barbecuing meat starts with sourcing the best you can find. Ask your butcher where it came from, how it was farmed, what it was fed. You're looking for sustainably reared meat. Better still, buy direct from the farm if you have an avenue to do so.

Rare heritage breeds, particularly with beef and pork, are a luxury worth one's salt if your money can stretch that far. They will yield a far superior product because of the care and craft that's gone into the rearing.

PREPARATION

There are endless debates within the world of barbecue as to the best methods of meat preparation. Ignore them. My feeling is that it's best to figure out your own position through trial and error.

BRINING

The process of salting meat helps to keep it moist and juicy, specifically by drawing moisture to its surface, protecting it from drying out and overcooking whilst you wait for the meat to cook sufficiently at its centre.

How you apply the salt, whether with a wet brine, a saline solution or a rub, will really depend on individual preference.

I tend to wet-brine pork and game birds, as I find both are in greatest danger of drying out during the cook. Just be sure not to brine your meat for too long and if in doubt give it less time rather than more. I like to use yoghurt as a tenderiser for chicken. And I mostly dry-brine lamb or beef using a rub.

MARINATING

Many of the recipes call for marinating the meat in advance. I'm a big fan of marinades, both to tenderise meat and to add an extra layer of flavour. As a general rule of thumb, the longer you can leave the meat to marinate the better. If time is precious, don't be put off. A long marinade is ideal, not essential.

TEMPERING

Ideally you should let your meat come up to room temperature before cooking it. This is to get the centre of the meat up to the same temperature as the surface, which prevents the surface from overcooking and drying out whilst waiting for the centre of the cut to be cooked properly. Allow smaller cuts of meat to sit, covered, for up to 30 minutes, and up to an hour for larger cuts and whole joints.

BARBECUING

Here are some principles to keep in mind when barbecuing.

MAILLARD REACTION

The Maillard reaction, so-named after the French scientist Louis Maillard, who undertook a study on the browning of meat way back when, occurs when the surface of food comes into contact with dry heat, causing a reaction between naturally occurring sugars and amino acids that generates browning or caramelisation. In simple barbecue terms, it's what happens when meat develops its crunchy, richly flavoured mahogany-brown surface that keeps us coming back for more. No matter the cut or the technique, the end goal is always the same – we want the meat surface to have a deep caramelised crust.

REVERSE-SEARING AND TWO-STAGE COOKING

One of the major problems we face when barbecuing is the danger of meat drying out and overcooking at its surface before being cooked to adequate 'doneness' at its centre. Reverse-searing is a technique to help overcome this and involves cooking or smoking meat indirectly at a lower heat so that you give it the opportunity to gently come up to temperature at its core, before finishing it directly over burning embers at a far higher temperature to achieve the coloured exterior that is so desirable. This is also referred to as two-stage cooking.

Reverse-searing is considered most suitable for thick cuts of steak such as rib-eye, or particularly large chops, butterflied leg of lamb, whole chickens or boned chicken joints.

LOW-AND-SLOW, BARBECUE-ROASTING AND MANGAL GRILLING

Low-and-slow smoking involves cooking large joints of meat indirectly (see two-zone set-up for indirect grilling, page 17) at very low temperatures, usually in the range of 110–130°C, for a long period of time. Most large joints of meat are suited to this style of barbecue but I tend to use it when the goal is to take the internal temperature very high, to 88°C and beyond, until the collagen breaks down and the meat all but falls apart. Examples include beef brisket or short rib, pork shoulder or ribs, lamb shoulder or shank.

In the restaurant we use a commercial woodsmoker, but your barbecue at home will be fine (see Barbecuing Devices, page 26).

Barbecue roasting occurs when your barbecue is heated to a higher temperature, usually in the range of 130–160°C. I like to employ this technique to roast my meat indirectly (see two-zone set-up for indirect grilling, page 17), as one would use an oven, only imparting the unmistakable taste of smoke.

The technique is great for slow-roasting large joints of meat, often on the bone, such as pork belly or a loin of pork, as well as a leg of lamb, whole chicken and large cuts of beef such as rib-eye.

Unsurprisingly the cook time is shorter than with low-and-slow and I tend to pull red meat out somewhere between 50°C and 60°C, depending on how I want my meat to be cooked, or 68°C and 70°C for chicken.

Mangal grilling is akin to grilling direct. Here the meat is cooked very close to the charcoal over searing heat and turned regularly. It would be rare to direct grill anything that takes longer than 12–15 minutes to cook, with the exception of some thick cuts of steak. In general, direct grilling is a good technique for small or thinner cuts, such as skewered kebabs, offal or chops, and butterflied birds.

In the restaurant we use a big open mangal (grill) for the purposes of direct grilling, but at home you can direct grill off any of the devices used for two-zone barbecuing (see Barbecuing Devices, page 26), or indeed just a fire pit with a cast-iron grill on legs.

SOUTH AMERICAN BARBECUE

Worth mentioning is the barbecue technique employed in parts of South America, specifically Argentina and Uruguay, as well as parts of Southern America, which doesn't fall into any of these categories but instead borrows from all three. Whole animals, or entire joints, are hung or positioned at a significant distance from an open burning fire (usually wood), to roast very slowly over a gentle heat, until golden brown and cooked to the desired level. This can often take 8–12 hours. It is a labour of love that pays in dividends.

RESTING

Resting is a subject of fierce debate amongst barbecuing aficionados. Some see it as a critical step in correctly grilling a piece of meat, one often overlooked, whilst others believe it to be detrimental to the finished product.

I'm a fan of the rest. For meat that has been directly grilled, or barbecue-roasted at higher temperatures for shorter periods of time, I find that resting the meat after it has finished cooking gives it the opportunity to relax, encouraging the meat juices to redistribute evenly across the whole cut and improving texture. It's worth noting that resting does not apply to smoking low-and-slow, where the temperature is so low that the meat is effectively resting as it cooks.

As a general but vague rule of thumb I tend to rest meat for half its cook time, turning it halfway through so that it can rest evenly on both sides. This rule tends to apply to direct grilling of steaks, chops or large joints of beef or lamb, but does not hold up in all instances.

CARVING

Always carve against the grain. It will make the meat so much easier to chew. The grain is usually pretty visible, but if in doubt you'll definitely be able to see once you've made the first slice. Readjust if you got it wrong the first time.

HOW TO BARBECUE MEAT

Chimney Starter

Welding Gloves

Cast Iron Pans

Meat Thermometer

Coal Shovel

Heavy Duty Tongs

Barbecue Brush

HEAVY-DUTY BARBECUE TONGS

These will become an extension of your arm. Like a good pair of shoes, you need to find a pair that feels comfortable. For me, the longer the better.

THERMOMETER PROBES

With enough time chalked up behind a grill barbecuing, you will learn how to feel for when your meat is 'done'. But this tends to be a skill reserved for experts and doesn't really help for low-and-slow-cooked joints of meat. A thermometer probe enables you to get an accurate read on your meat.

I like to use two different types of probe – a Thermopen and a Maverick Dual Probe. The latter comes with two probes, one for leaving in the meat as it cooks and a second for gauging the temperature of your barbecue. It transmits the temperature readings to a handheld device, which is particularly useful for barbecuing large joints indirect, as it enables you to go about other duties from afar whilst keeping an eye on how your meat is cooking.

CAST-IRON PANS

These absorb heat beautifully, distributing it evenly across the surface. They never bend or warp, no matter how hot they might get, which makes them perfect for cooking on or over fire and virtually indestructible. And contrary to popular belief, maintenance is straightforward and relatively effortless. Scrub after use. Keep dry and well oiled. Treat with love and care. The end.

Look out for Lodge, which is my favourite brand to use, but there are plenty of other reputable manufacturers to choose from.

WELDING GLOVES

Welding gloves are readily available online for next to nothing. Invest in a pair or five. You'll be grateful to have them, believe me.

GRILL BRUSH

Always keep your grill grate well brushed after use. You'll be amazed how quickly it will build up with tar, making it more difficult to cook and to clean. I don't believe that grill grates need to be scrubbed clean too often, but they should be kept free from the excessive build-up of charred debris.

COAL SHOVEL OR TRENCH SHOVEL AND FIRE POKER

Both of these tools are useful for manoeuvring hot coals around, or getting rid of them at the end of a cook. They'll also make you look like you actually know what you're doing in front of your mates. When in doubt, just shovel the coals around aimlessly for a few seconds. It normally does the trick.

METAL SKEWERS

Kebab skewers can be found in most Turkish or Middle Eastern grocers of notable size. Or else buy them online. I keep a variety, in all different shapes and sizes.

CHIMNEY STARTER

A Weber chimney starter (or any other brand for that matter) is a great little device for getting your coals burning real quick.

OTHER BITS AND PIECES...

- Heavy-duty meat turner or spatula

- Firelights

- Ash and charcoal bin

- Bricks for resting your grill or burning hot items on

- Heavy-duty barbecue apron

BARBECUING DEVICES

KETTLE BBQ

A Weber Original Kettle Charcoal Grill is a brilliant entry-level barbecue to get a handle on barbecuing techniques such as two-zone cooking, low-and-slow smoking and direct grilling. It's the simplest of designs, with vents at the bottom and in the lid to control the airflow and thus the temperature. The main advantage of a Weber Kettle is price, which is not at all prohibitive, but its downside is insulation. It doesn't hold temperature very well, or for all that long, meaning you'll have to spend a good amount of time playing with the vents and your fire to learn how to control the internal temperature. In short, it's great for quick smokes, but will require more attention when it comes to low-and-slow.

DRUM BARREL SMOKER

A drum barrel smoker is essentially a vertical oil drum with a charcoal grate at the bottom and a grill grate at the top, separated by a water pan, which sits in between the two. It's a handy piece of kit with similar upsides and downsides to a kettle, but the one main advantage being its configuration, which enables you to hang meat and utilise its depth, as opposed to being confined to the width available on the grill grate. This ultimately means they have a bigger capacity. The provision and position of a water pan also helps to distinctly separate out the meat from the heat source. I'd recommend a Mac ProQ Elite.

CERAMIC EGG

A ceramic egg barbecue such as a Big Green Egg is by far the most sophisticated barbecue available for dedicated barbecuing enthusiasts. The ceramic insulates and distributes heat brilliantly, meaning the egg will hold its temperature for many hours before you need to fiddle with the controls. The convenience of being able to step away from your fire for several hours and get on with other things comes at a price. It's really a matter of how dedicated you are as to whether the price is justified.

CHAPTER 01

MEZZE

BURNT SPRING ONIONS
WITH GREEN TAHINA

When in doubt, throw some spring onions on the barbecue and eat them fresh off the grill with little more than a drizzle of oil and some flaked salt thrown on top. This recipe adds herbed tahini to bring some depth and creaminess to the dish.

SERVES 2–4

GREEN TAHINA SAUCE

handful each of picked flat-leaf parsley, basil and rocket leaves

100ml water

juice of 1 lemon, plus extra to taste

100g tahini paste

2 confit garlic, ground to a paste using a mortar and pestle, or else use 1 minced garlic clove as a substitute

1 tsp salt

1 tsp extra virgin olive oil

SPRING ONIONS

4 large spring onions, cut in half lengthways

2 tbsp olive oil

50g Green Tahina Sauce (above)

1 tbsp Hazelnut Dukkah (optional) (page 242)

1 tbsp lemon juice, plus extra to finish

Garlic Oil (page 260) or extra virgin olive oil, to drizzle

FOR THE GREEN TAHINA SAUCE

Blend the herbs and water in a food processor until smooth.

Combine the lemon juice, tahini and confit garlic together in a bowl or food processor, adding a small amount of the herbed water and whisking or blending to combine. At first the tahini will thicken to a rough cement-like paste, but it will loosen as you gradually pour in and combine the remaining herbed water. Season with salt, and whisk in the extra virgin olive oil and some more lemon juice to taste as required. This will make more green tahina than is necessary for the recipe, but if stored properly in the fridge it will keep for up to three days and make a great dip or accompanying sauce for most grilled meats and fish.

FOR THE SPRING ONIONS

Brush the spring onion halves with olive oil and season with salt and pepper. Set a barbecue up for single-zone direct grilling over medium-high heat and grill the spring onions until softened and charred, no more than 1–1½ minutes on each side. Alternatively, lay the spring onions on a wire rack and blacken them under your stove grill until coloured and soft.

Remove the spring onions from the grill and serve on top of the green tahina sauce, garnished with a sprinkling of hazelnut dukkah (if using), a final squeeze of lemon juice and drizzle of garlic oil for good measure. Eat immediately.

CARDAMOM-CURED HAKE CRUDO
WITH PINK PEPPERCORNS & PEACH

The curing salt in this recipe can be used for any firm white fish. I've used hake here, really just because I like it, but feel free to substitute your fish of preference. You might need to adjust the curing time, depending on the fish you've chosen and its thickness.

SERVES 4–6

250g skinless, boneless hake loin in one piece (ask your fishmonger)

CARDAMOM CURING SALT

25g sea salt crystals

1½ tbsp caster sugar

½ tbsp pink peppercorns

½ tsp coriander seeds

½ tsp fennel seeds

2 cardamom pods

½ tsp dried chamomile

GARNISH AND SERVE

2 tbsp extra virgin olive oil (the best quality you can afford)

1 peach, destoned and cut into thin segments, 0.5cm thick

1 tbsp pink peppercorns, roughly crushed

¼ preserved lemon, rind only, very finely chopped

1 tbsp Confit Chilli Salsa (page 260) or 1 red chilli, finely chopped

½ tsp finely chopped dill

2 tbsp soured cream (optional)

2 spring onions, green parts only, finely sliced (optional)

FOR THE CARDAMOM CURING SALT

Combine all the cardamom curing salt ingredients in a mortar and pestle and grind together. Don't be too fanatical – it's simply a case of bruising the spices and seeds to release and infuse their flavour.

This curing salt can be made in advance and stored in an airtight container, where it will keep for up to 6 months.

FOR THE HAKE

Rub the hake all over with the curing salt and leave at room temperature for 30–45 minutes to allow the salt and sugar to dissolve. Wrap the hake in clingfilm, followed by tin foil, and place in a container in the fridge. Allow the fish to cure for 2–3 days, turning it over at least once a day.

TO GARNISH AND SERVE

Remove the hake from its wrapping and rinse under cold water briefly to remove any excess salt on the surface. Pat the hake dry with kitchen paper.

Using a very sharp knife, slice the hake as thinly as you can, trying to slice it in one long continuous motion so as not to tear the fish as you slice.

Lay the hake slices on a serving platter and drizzle with the olive oil. Intermittently layer the peach segments in between the slices of hake and garnish with pink peppercorns, the chopped preserved lemon rind, confit chilli salsa and dill.

I like to serve the dressed hake crudo with some soured cream and sliced spring onions strewn over the top, but these are both optional.

PUMPKIN BORANI
WITH MINT YOGHURT & ALEPPO CHILLI BUTTER

This mezze is a tribute to one of my favourite joints in London – the Afghan restaurant Ariana II in Kilburn. It's their second restaurant, the original hailing from the upper West side of Manhattan. It always seemed like a strange choice of location for a second outpost to me. Even the most fervent and devoted fans of Kilburn High Road must admit it's a far cry from uptown Manhattan. But then the restaurant is always busy, so look who had the last laugh. Plus, they make the most outrageously good kadoo (pumpkin) buranee. I can eat that stuff with a spoon.

SERVES 8

MINT YOGHURT
50g full-fat natural yoghurt
½ garlic clove, minced
½ tbsp dried mint
1 tbsp extra virgin olive oil
¾ tsp salt
zest and juice of ½ lime

PUMPKIN
60ml olive oil
2 banana shallots, finely chopped
1 tbsp ground turmeric
1 tsp dried chilli flakes
1 small pumpkin, blackened over the fire until tender, peeled and flesh removed (see note)
1½ tbsp tomato paste
juice of 1 lemon
1½ tbsp runny honey

ALEPPO CHILLI BUTTER
40g unsalted butter
1 garlic clove
1 tbsp Aleppo chilli flakes (also known as pul biber or red pepper flakes) or use smoked paprika with a pinch of dried chilli flakes

GARNISH
2 tbsp mint yoghurt
1 tbsp dried mint
picked dill fronds

FOR THE MINT YOGHURT
Combine all the ingredients together in bowl. Season according to taste and refrigerate until required.

FOR THE PUMPKIN
Heat half the olive oil in a heavy-based non-reactive saucepan over medium heat and fry the shallots until coloured but not burnt.

Add the turmeric and chilli flakes and continue to cook for 1–2 minutes before stirring through the pumpkin flesh. Sauté the pumpkin flesh for 2–3 minutes, breaking it into smaller pieces with a wooden spoon as it warms.

Fold in the tomato paste, lemon juice and honey, and continue to cook over medium-low heat. Stir continuously to prevent the pumpkin catching and burning on the bottom, and cook for 8–10 minutes until the mixture has darkened in colour and any excess moisture has evaporated. Season with salt and pepper according to taste.

FOR THE ALEPPO CHILLI BUTTER
Whilst the pumpkin borani is cooking, melt the butter in a small saucepan over medium-low heat. Add the garlic and soften for a few minutes, being careful not to allow the garlic to burn. Whisk the butter gently as it cooks, until it darkens and turns a nutty golden brown, then add the chilli flakes and immediately remove the pan from the heat.

TO GARNISH AND SERVE
Serve the pumpkin mixture still warm, with mint yoghurt spooned over the top, the chilli butter drizzled over the yoghurt and the dried mint and picked dill leaves dotted around the plate.

● ●
NOTE
The pumpkin can also be roasted whole in an oven preheated to 180°C/160°C Fan/Gas mark 4 and cooked until tender to a knife, before having the flesh scooped out ready to be used.

BURNT ONIONS
WITH POMEGRANATE MOLASSES

It was whilst staying on a kibbutz in northern Israel at the age of 15 that I first encountered onions being burnt with their skins on, next to the fire. Once the onions were cooked, the teenagers who had built the bonfire would peel them and eat them whole, biting straight into the vegetable almost as one would eat an apple. It felt to me at the time like some sort of peculiar, backward ritual of the deprived. Didn't they have something more exciting to cook on the fire than a simple onion? And couldn't you add something to it? I politely declined the offer to eat one.

As it turns out, the joke was on me. Burnt onions are now easily one of my favourite things to cook on the barbecue. They have a natural sweetness that is drawn out by intense heat, and a sponge-like composition, enabling them to absorb the smokiness of the burnt wood. I was definitely late to the party on this one. Still, I'd recommend some olive oil and seasoning as a bare minimum. There are limits to how much I will concede that I might have been wrong.

SERVES 2–4

2 medium, sweet onions (ideally Roscoff, if available), skin left on

1½ tbsp pomegranate molasses

1 tsp Dijon mustard

50ml olive oil, plus extra to finish

1 clove of garlic, finely grated

1 tbsp finely chopped lemon thyme leaves

generous pinch of Aleppo chilli flakes (also known as pul biber or red pepper flakes) or use dried chilli flakes

Start a fire in your barbecue pit and prepare a bed of burning embers.

The onions can be cooked in one of three ways, according to preference. You can skewer the onions whole by piercing them through the centre-point with a thick, heavy metal skewer and grill them directly over the coals without the support of a grill rack in the manner of a Turkish grill chef. In the absence of such a skewer, the onions can be cooked directly on the grill rack above the burning coals, turned frequently, until blackened all over. Alternatively, position the onions offset slightly at a distance of 15–20cm from the burning coals, and turn them regularly as they cook.

The outside skin of the onions will blacken and burn, but don't be put off, this is intentional. It will serve as a protective coat for the inner layers, which will steam within and soften through the cooking process. Whilst the onions are cooking, whisk together the pomegranate molasses (thinned out a little with a drop of warm water if particularly thick) and Dijon mustard, followed by the olive oil to emulsify.

When the onions are tender if pierced with a knife all the way through, remove from the barbecue and, once cool enough to handle, peel off the blackened outer layers.

Roughly chop the onion flesh into 2.5cm pieces. Season with salt and black pepper to taste and toss, whilst still warm, in the pomegranate molasses dressing with the grated garlic. Garnish with lemon thyme and chilli flakes, and serve immediately, finished with a final drizzle of some more olive oil.

BERBER & Q HUMMUS

It's my dream that one day world peace will be officially ushered in with the ceremonial sharing of a huge bowl of hummus, communally eaten by all the world leaders sitting around a large banquet table. Stranger things have happened. Just ask the Virgin Mary.

   The irony being that I fear said hummus would have been the cause of the war in the first place. It has a power to divide every bit as forceful as its ability to unite.

   Which chickpeas should be used? Do you blend in a machine, or pound by hand? Do you add olive oil to the blended hummus, or as a drizzle over the top? These philosophical questions of love and life dominate the conversations of many in the Middle East – I doubt there will be a resolution, but if there is, I trust it will be settled over a bowl of silky-smooth tahini-laden good stuff.

SERVES 4–6

250g dried chickpeas

½ tsp bicarbonate of soda

1 onion, cut in half

1 carrot, peeled and cut into two

6 garlic cloves, 4 peeled and left whole, 2 peeled and finely chopped or grated

200g tahini paste

40ml lemon juice

1 tsp ground cumin

2–3 tbsp Tahina Sauce (page 262)

50ml extra virgin olive oil

few pinches of sweet paprika and za'atar

1 tbsp chopped flat-leaf parsley

warm pita bread, to serve

Yemenite Dynamite (optional) (page 256), to serve

1 egg, hard-boiled and cut into 1cm thick slices (optional)

Soak the chickpeas in a large pot of water overnight or for up to 6 hours. Drain once soaked and return to the pot, covered comfortably with more water.

Set the pot over a high heat on the stove and bring to the boil, removing any scum that rises to the surface. Add the bicarbonate of soda – the chickpeas will bubble and froth almost instantly. Skim the froth from the surface, lower the heat to a gentle simmer, add the onion, carrot and whole garlic cloves, and cook, skimming the surface scum periodically, until the chickpeas have completely softened and are all but falling apart. This can take up to 2 hours and sometimes even longer. Keep an eye on the water level in your pot, and top up if needs be. Be patient, you need the chickpeas to be completely soft and to fall apart easily with the lightest of pressure. Once cooked, turn off the heat, season with ½ tbsp salt and set aside for 30 minutes or so.

Drain the chickpeas, reserving the cooking liquor for later use. Pick out the carrot and onion halves; transfer all but a few tablespoons of the chickpeas to a food processor (reserving those for garnish), add the tahini, lemon juice, grated garlic and cumin and blitz, ladling the cooking liquor back into the processor gradually until the desired consistency is achieved. The hummus must be as smooth as your food processor will permit. Bear in mind that the hummus will thicken considerably once cooled and refrigerated. Taste for seasoning – it may need some more salt or lemon juice.

Transfer the hummus to a serving plate and spread around its perimeter using the back of a spoon. Spoon the tahini sauce in the middle, topped with the reserved chickpeas, dressed in olive oil and seasoned. Dot the paprika and za'atar around the plate as you deem fit. Sprinkle parsley on top and finish with a very generous drizzle of the best olive oil you can buy. I like mine to be swimming in olive oil, but this comes down to personal preference, I suppose.

Serve with warmed pita, or bread of just about any description. Some Yemenite hot sauce (page 256) wouldn't go amiss, if you happen to have some spare lying around. I like to add a sliced hard-boiled egg, but it's not for everyone.

SPICY MARINATED OLIVES

Marinating olives is such a simple, stress-free way of elevating the humble, salty fruit into something a bit more special.

MAKES 500G

2 red chillies, finely chopped

3 garlic cloves, minced

100ml extra virgin olive oil

500g mixed olives (Kalamata, Moroccan, green)

1 preserved lemon, rind only, chopped

1 tbsp coriander seeds, toasted

1 tbsp fennel seeds, toasted

1 tbsp Aleppo chilli flakes (also known as pul biber or red pepper flakes) or use 1 tsp dried chilli flakes

1½ tbsp roughly chopped flat-leaf parsley

1 tbsp roughly chopped dill

In a large bowl, mix all the ingredients together, cover and refrigerate overnight to allow the olives to marinate. Transfer to a jar and keep refrigerated for up to 10 days.

• •

MIXED SPICED NUTS

These are great as a bar snack, dotted around your home for when your guests arrive. There's not much else I can say about nuts that's of any interest. They kind of are what they are.

MAKES 450G

½ tsp cumin seeds

½ tsp fennel seeds

120g peanuts

80g hazelnuts

90g whole almonds

20g cashews

50g pumpkin seeds

50g sunflower seeds

50g soft brown sugar

20g egg whites, lightly whipped

½ red chilli, deseeded and very finely chopped

2 garlic cloves, very finely chopped

2 tsp cayenne pepper

1 tsp Aleppo chilli flakes or use ½ tsp dried chilli flakes

1 tsp flaked sea salt

½ tbsp za'atar

Preheat the oven to 130°C/110°C Fan/Gas mark 1.

Toast the cumin and fennel seeds in a frying pan over medium-high heat until just smoking and fragrant. Transfer to a mortar and pestle and crush.

Line a baking tray with parchment paper.

Mix all the ingredients, except the za'atar, together in a bowl and spread over the baking tray.

Cook for 1 hour, stirring every 15–20 minutes to make sure the edges don't burn, until the nuts are deep golden brown.

About 10 minutes before removing the nuts from the oven, sprinkle the za'atar over the top.

Remove from the oven and allow to cool, stirring from time to time to prevent the nuts from sticking together in large clumps.

TWICE-COOKED SMOKY AUBERGINE
WITH EGG & WALNUTS

Round the corner from where I live is a Persian restaurant of great culinary distinction but dubious character. For legal reasons it shall remain nameless. Four of the last five times I've tried to order takeaway from them I've been informed, with different explanations each time, that this, in fact, would not be possible (why even bother to answer the phone I ask?). The last, and final attempt, I was told that their chef was, regrettably, in hospital. It was like I was living out a sketch from *Fawlty Towers*. I drew a line in the sand and moved my custom on to newer pastures.

But it was here that I was first introduced to the wonder of mirza ghasemi – an Iranian dish of grilled and sautéed aubergine bound together by egg. This is my attempt to recreate it.

SERVES 4–6

2 large aubergines

2 tbsp olive oil

1 shallot, finely chopped

2 garlic cloves, finely chopped

1 tsp ground cumin

½ tsp ground turmeric

1½ tbsp tomato paste

200g tomatoes, peeled, deseeded and roughly chopped

1 tbsp dried chilli flakes

2 eggs, beaten

1 tbsp lemon juice

20g walnuts, toasted and finely chopped

small handful of roughly chopped coriander

extra virgin olive oil, to serve

flatbread, to serve

Preheat the oven to 180°C/160°C Fan/Gas mark 4 or set a barbecue up for indirect two-zone grilling.

Pierce the aubergines several times with a fork or skewer and place on the grill rack, offset from the coals, with the lid of the barbecue on. Smoke the aubergine for 25–30 minutes until it starts to collapse in on itself. If using an oven, set the aubergine in a roasting tray and roast for 40–45 minutes until completely softened. Set aside until cool enough to handle.

Slice the aubergines in half lengthways through the stem, scoop out the flesh to a chopping board and roughly chop until coarse and chunky.

Warm the olive oil in a frying pan over medium heat and fry the shallot for 5–7 minutes, until golden brown. Turn down the heat to low, add the garlic, cumin and turmeric, and fry for a few minutes. Add the chopped aubergine to the pan. Cook for 10–15 minutes, stirring frequently, then add the tomato paste, followed by the chopped tomatoes and chilli flakes. Continue to cook for a further 10–15 minutes so that the sauce can come together, reduce and thicken slightly. Fold the beaten eggs through the mix and stir well to ensure they cook in the residual heat of the aubergine. Remove from the heat, season to taste and add the lemon juice, walnuts and coriander.

Finish the dish with a customary drizzle of extra virgin olive oil over the top and serve whilst still warm with flatbread or pita.

GRILLED HALLOUMI
WITH FRIED EGG, OREGANO & CAPER DRESSING

'Must be with fried eggs' was the comment made by Roger Marks, the Israeli father of a close family friend, on an Instagram photo I posted of grilled halloumi. Turns out he was right. This recipe is dedicated to him.

SERVES 2–4

OREGANO & CAPER DRESSING

1 tsp Dijon mustard

2 tbsp lemon juice

100ml extra virgin olive oil

1 heaped tbsp finely chopped oregano

1 garlic clove, minced

1 small red chilli, finely chopped

2 heaped tbsp capers, drained and rinsed

2 tbsp roughly chopped coriander

pinch of coarse ground black pepper

HALLOUMI

250g halloumi cheese, cut lengthways into 1cm slices

vegetable oil, for frying

1 medium free-range egg

picked coriander leaves, to garnish

FOR THE OREGANO AND CAPER DRESSING

Combine the mustard and lemon juice in a small bowl and slowly whisk in the extra virgin olive oil to emulsify. Add the remaining ingredients and stir to combine. Set to one side until required.

FOR THE HALLOUMI

Set a cast-iron ridged skillet over high and heat until smoking, or set a barbecue up for single-zone direct grilling.

Grill the halloumi on both sides to ensure it's nicely scored and heated through. At the same time, heat the vegetable oil in a frying pan and fry the egg, sunny-side up. Season with salt and pepper.

Transfer the cheese to a plate, lay the egg on top and spoon over the dressing. Serve immediately, garnished with some picked coriander leaves.

CRÈME FRAÎCHE & DILL OIL
WITH BLACKENED KEBAB SAUCE

Crème fraîche is such an understated, useful ingredient. I can eat it on its own with little more than some seasoning, a drizzle of oil and some pita to mop it all up. It's such an easy go-to dip but is so often overlooked in favour for more complicated alternatives.

The recipe here calls for blackened chilli kebab sauce, as I find the heat of a good chilli sauce counters brilliantly with the cooling creaminess of the crème fraîche. But the limits to what you can do with this dip creatively are bound only by your imagination. Just make sure to season the crème fraîche properly, to douse it liberally with lots of extra virgin olive oil and to serve it with crusty bread or pita, steaming hot and straight from the oven. (Pictured overleaf).

SERVES 2–4

DILL OIL
1 tbsp extra virgin olive oil
½ tbsp very finely chopped dill

CRÈME FRAÎCHE
150g crème fraîche
flaked sea salt (such as Maldon)
1 tbsp Blackened Chilli Kebab
  Sauce (page 256)
½ Scotch Bonnet or red chilli, very
  thinly sliced
1 tsp chopped coriander
4–5 picked dill fronds
pita bread, warmed in the oven
  or on the grill

FOR THE DILL OIL
Put the extra virgin olive oil and chopped dill in a small bowl and stir well to combine.

FOR THE CRÈME FRAÎCHE
Using the back of a large spoon, press the crème fraîche around the plate in a circular motion so that it's well distributed, but leave some contours and height in parts for a pleasing overall aesthetic.

Season the crème fraîche generously with salt and pepper, and drizzle the kebab sauce over the top, followed by a liberal lug of dill oil – you really can't have too much here, so be generous.

Garnish with the thinly sliced chillies, freshly chopped coriander and picked dill fronds. Serve with warmed pita bread.

CONFIT CHERRY TOMATOES
WITH HONEYED FETA HAYDARI & PICKLED WILD THYME (ZA'ATAR)

Confit tomatoes, cherry or otherwise, are an item that I like to have in reserve in my fridge. Delicate, sweet and intense in flavour, they work particularly well in salads, but also as a garnish to most grilled fish and vegetables, as well as chicken. They make for a fast and simple mezze, spooned onto a plate as is or paired with a creamy side, such as a whipped feta haydari, some labneh or crème fraîche. The lightly infused confit oil makes an excellent base for most dressings, or a substitute to normal olive oil when drizzling over just about anything. (Pictured overleaf).

SERVES 4

CONFIT CHERRY TOMATOES

350g cherry tomatoes, peeled, deseeded and quartered

1 tbsp salt

1 tsp pepper

3 sprigs of thyme

2 sprigs of oregano

1 sprig of rosemary

2 bay leaves

2 dried red chillies

3 garlic cloves, whole

olive oil, to cover

FETA HAYDARI

180g feta

2 Turkish green chilli peppers

60g crème fraîche

3 tbsp extra virgin olive oil

1 tbsp lemon juice

1 tsp Aleppo chilli flakes or use 1 tsp dried chilli flakes

1 tsp finely chopped dill

GARNISH AND SERVE

1 tbsp honey, thinned a little with a drop of warmed water

10–12 Confit Cherry Tomatoes (above)

pickled thyme fronds (optional)

1 tbsp Chilli Pangrattato (page 241)

1 tbsp finely chopped mint

extra virgin olive oil

toasted flatbread

FOR THE CONFIT CHERRY TOMATOES
Preheat the oven to 150°C/130°C Fan/Gas mark 2.

Score the underside of each tomato, making a small cross with a serrated knife.

Bring a saucepan of water to the boil over high heat. Have a bowl of iced water sitting next to you. Working in batches, blanch the tomatoes for 15–20 seconds, and transfer with a slotted spoon to the iced water to be refreshed and help to loosen the tomato skins. Peel the tomatoes and place them in a deep roasting tray or cast-iron pan.

Season with salt and pepper, and add the herbs and aromatics. Pour over the olive oil, enough to submerge the tomatoes, and tightly cover with tin foil.

Put the tomatoes in the oven to confit for 25–30 minutes, until softened but not overcooked. You don't want the integrity of the tomato's shape to be compromised; they should remain whole and be plump and juicy. Cool completely, and store submerged in the oil, in a shallow but wide container, where they will keep refrigerated for up to 3 weeks.

FOR THE FETA HAYDARI
Soak the feta in a bowl of water for roughly 15 minutes to remove any excess salt. Drain and repeat.

Blacken the chillies all over on a barbecue grill, or directly over a gas flame on the stovetop. Transfer to a bowl and cover tightly with clingfilm so they can sweat in their own residual steam. This will make the chillies easier to peel. Cut off the stalk, scrape out the seeds and roughly chop the peeled chillies.

Process the feta in a blender with the crème fraîche, olive oil, lemon juice and chilli flakes until smooth. Check for seasoning; the feta should be salty enough but add some salt if necessary. Transfer to a bowl and stir through the chopped green chillies and dill.

TO GARNISH AND SERVE
Drizzle the feta haydari with honey, and serve accompanied by the confit cherry tomatoes, a handful of picked wild thyme (if using), chilli pangrattato and the mint strewn over the top. A generous drizzle of olive oil or the confit cherry tomato oil is obligatory. Serve with toasted flatbread.

YELLOWTAIL CARPACCIO
WITH BURNT LEEK DRESSING & PEACH

I like to use yellowtail for this recipe but concede that it's not always that easy to get hold of. Most reputable fishmongers can source it for you if you plead with them long and hard enough, but you may need to order it in advance. If you're the spontaneous type who doesn't have the time or headspace for forward planning, you can substitute yellowtail with more commonplace tuna. Just make sure it's as fresh as possible.

SERVES 4

BURNT LEEK DRESSING
½ leek
4 tbsp extra virgin olive oil
½ shallot, finely sliced
4 tbsp cabernet sauvignon red
  wine vinegar

YELLOWTAIL CARPACCIO
320g yellowtail fillet (or other tuna
  fillet), skin removed (ask your
  fishmonger)
extra virgin olive oil (the best
  quality you can afford)
flaked sea salt (such as Maldon)
1 tsp thinly sliced green chilli
1 tbsp pomegranate seeds
few picked oregano leaves
grated zest of ½ lemon

FOR THE BURNT LEEK DRESSING
Preheat the oven to 250°C/230°C Fan/Gas mark 9. Separate the leek out into individual leaves and place on a baking tray. Transfer to the oven to incinerate, which should take between 8–10 minutes. Cool the leek to room temperature, transfer to a spice grinder and blitz to a fine powder.

Heat 1 tablespoon of olive oil in a small saucepan over medium-high heat and sweat the shallot until softened and translucent but not coloured. Add the vinegar and simmer to reduce by two-thirds. Transfer to a food processor, add the burnt leek and the remaining olive oil and blend until smooth.

FOR THE YELLOWTAIL CARPACCIO
Thinly slice the yellowtail at a steep angle with a very sharp slicing knife and arrange on a serving plate. Drizzle with extra virgin olive oil, season with some flakes of salt on each piece and dress with a few tablespoons of leek dressing spooned over the fish. Garnish the fish with some pomegranate seeds scattered around the plate, some sliced green chilli, oregano leaves and grated lemon zest. Serve immediately.

BEEF TARTARE (KIBBEH NAYEH)
WITH COURGETTE, BULGUR & HONEY MUSTARD

Kibbeh nayeh (or kubbeniya) is usually prepared with ground lean lamb meat, passed through a mincer at least twice and bound with water and bulgur wheat until it forms a meaty paste. It tastes better than it sounds, believe me.

I like to hand chop the meat, and we use beef tenderloin, so in many ways this recipe is more like a Middle Eastern steak tartare than an authentic kibbeh nayeh, but, to coin a phrase from the great Walter Sobchak, 'Are we going to split hairs here?'

SERVES 4

50g fine bulgur, rinsed and drained

300g beef fillet or rump, trimmed of any fat

1 green chilli, finely diced

1 shallot, finely chopped

2 tbsp Harissa (page 259) or shop-bought

small handful of finely chopped basil and mint leaves

½ courgette, very finely diced

grated zest of 1 lemon

1 tbsp capers, drained and rinsed

1½ tbsp pine nuts, toasted

extra virgin olive oil

1 egg yolk

SERVE
2 tbsp honey mustard

pickles of choice

flatbread or toasted challah, to serve

Soak the bulgur in cold water (to cover) for 5–7 minutes. Drain, tip into a tea towel and squeeze out as much excess liquid as you can.

Using a very sharp knife, dice the beef fillet as fine as you can. I cut thin slices from the fillet, each slice into strips, and then line 4–5 strips up in a row to cut into dice.

In a large bowl, combine the beef, chilli, shallot, harissa, herbs, courgette, lemon zest, capers, soaked bulgar and pine nuts, and mix well. Season to taste with salt and black pepper.

Spoon the beef onto a serving plate, drizzle with olive oil, and make a well in the centre in which to drop the egg yolk. Serve accompanied by some mustard, pickles of choice and some flatbread or challah.

GRILLED TURKISH CHILLI PEPPERS
WITH OREGANO & FETA

Turkish peppers can be difficult to find. They're long and green with a distinct flavour that is not quite as sweet as your everyday bell pepper. They're sold in any self-respecting Turkish greengrocer. If you don't have one of those nearby, you should consider a house move. Or possibly just try another recipe from this book, which might prove a more practical solution.

SERVES 2–4

4 Turkish green chilli peppers

2 tbsp Garlic Oil (page 260) or olive oil

1 tbsp lemon juice

½ tbsp salt

½ tsp coarse ground black pepper

1 garlic clove, thinly sliced

picked oregano leaves

2 tbsp crumbled feta

Blacken the chilli peppers on a barbecue grill, or directly over the gas flame on a stovetop. Once charred and softened, transfer the hot peppers to a bowl and cover with clingfilm. Allow to cool slightly, then peel the peppers, being sure to leave them whole with the stalks intact.

Run a knife along the peppers lengthways from bottom to top, stopping just before the stalk. Be careful not to cut through both sides of the pepper. Splay the peppers on a serving plate, flattened out with the stalks pointing upwards. Drizzle with oil and lemon juice, season with the salt and pepper, scatter over the garlic slices and oregano leaves and crumble the feta around the whole dish. Serve at room temperature.

GRATED BEETROOT SALATIM
WITH CUMIN LABNEH BALLS, WALNUT & MINT

Across North Africa and Middle Eastern cuisine beetroot is commonplace, often served as a small starting mezze, dressed with little more than some mint, cinnamon and olive oil. This dish draws on this for inspiration, adding the creaminess of some cumin labneh and some crunch from the addition of walnut.

SERVES 2–4
(MAKES 20 BALLS)

CUMIN LABNEH BALLS

Extra virgin olive oil

2–3 tbsp cumin seeds, toasted and lightly crushed

100g Labneh (page 261)

BEETROOT SALATIM

250g raw beetroot, grated using the coarse side of a box grater

50g Tahina Sauce (page 262)

25ml date syrup

25ml red wine vinegar

pinch of ground cinnamon

1 tbsp toasted walnuts, roughly chopped

1 tbsp finely chopped mint

10 picked dill fronds

4 Cumin Labneh Balls (see above)

extra virgin olive oil, to drizzle

Candied Orange Peel, to garnish (page 188)

FOR THE CUMIN LABNEH BALLS

Set a small bowl with some olive oil to one side, for rubbing through your hands to keep them well lubricated. You won't need more than 3–4 tablespoons. Place the cumin seeds on a baking tray and spread out to form a thin layer.

Keeping your hands well oiled at all times, roll the labneh into balls, about the size of a marble, and transfer them to a baking tray to be rolled and coated in the cumin. Once all the labneh has been rolled and coated, transfer to a small container, cover with extra virgin olive oil and refrigerate until required.

Kept in this way these labneh balls will keep refrigerated for several weeks, and can be used as a component for all sorts of salads, as well as a great garnish for some fish and meat.

FOR THE BEETROOT SALATIM

Combine the grated beetroot in a large bowl with the tahina sauce, date syrup and red wine vinegar. Mix well until incorporated. Add a pinch of cinnamon and salt and pepper to taste.

To serve the mezze, spread the beetroot on a plate and top with the toasted walnuts, chopped mint, picked dill fronds, the cumin labneh balls dotted around the plate, a drizzle of olive oil and the strips of candied orange peel.

MARINATED RED PEPPERS
WITH ANCHOVY & OLIVES

Red peppers and anchovies were meant to go together like melon and ham. The saltiness of the anchovy balances the sweetness of a good roasted pepper. Try to buy the best anchovies you can find. Substandard anchovies detract from a dish as much as good ones can enhance it. (Pictured on pages 54–55).

SERVES 2–4

2 red peppers

1½ tbsp salt

2 tbsp olive oil, or Garlic Oil (page 260)

3 anchovies, pounded to a paste in a mortar and pestle

1 tbsp Harissa (page 259) or shop-bought

1 tsp ground cumin

2 tbsp red wine vinegar

8–10 Kalamata olives, pitted and halved

1 tbsp roughly chopped coriander

Blacken the red peppers on a barbecue grill, or directly over the gas flame on the stovetop, until charred and softened, then transfer to a bowl. Cover with cling film and cool. Peel, quarter and deseed the peppers, removing any remaining white membrane. Place the pepper quarters between sheets of kitchen paper and push down to absorb as much excess liquid as possible. Salt the peppers on both sides and roll them up tightly like a rug. Set aside for 2 hours.

Unroll the peppers and press again with kitchen paper to remove any excess liquid. Heat the oil in a non-stick frying pan over medium heat and fry the peppers for a few minutes. Add the anchovies, harissa and cumin, and continue to sauté for a further minute. Pour in the vinegar, increase the heat and reduce until almost all the liquid has evaporated. Throw in the olives and chopped coriander, give them a toss in the pan and remove from the heat.

Allow the peppers to marinate for 30 minutes before serving at room temperature. Check for seasoning before serving.

The peppers can be refrigerated for several days, during which the flavours will intensify and improve.

M'SABAHA (MARINATED CHICKPEAS)
WITH TAHINA & YEMENITE HOT SAUCE

Humums Abu Hasan serves the best hummus I've found in Israel, or anywhere else in the world for that matter (don't all shout at me at once). It always comes laden with silky-soft mesabaha (stewed, marinated chickpeas), a quartered onion (your guess is as good as mine) and some green chilli sauce.

The chickpeas are a dish all by themselves. I like them swimming in tahina with a blast of Yemenite dynamite to keep things fiery. (Pictured overleaf).

SERVES 2–4

MARINATED CHICKPEAS

100g dried chickpeas, soaked in water overnight

½ tsp bicarbonate of soda

1 onion, cut in half lengthways

1 head of garlic, cut in half horizontally

3 sprigs of oregano or lemon thyme

3 tbsp lemon juice, or more to taste

50ml olive oil

1 tsp ground cumin

1 tbsp finely chopped coriander

1 tbsp finely chopped flat-leaf parsley

GARNISH AND SERVE

100g Tahina Sauce (page 262)

2 tbsp Yemenite Dynamite (S'chug) (page 256)

extra virgin olive oil

pinch of ground cumin (optional)

pita bread, warmed in the oven or on the grill

FOR THE MARINATED CHICKPEAS

Drain the soaked chickpeas and transfer to a large saucepan. Cover with water and bring to the boil over high heat. Skim away any foam that surfaces and add the bicarbonate of soda. Lower the heat to a gentle simmer, add the onion, garlic and oregano, and continue to cook until the chickpeas have softened but retain their shape; about 1½–2 hours, but this can vary depending on their age.

Transfer the chickpeas to a bowl using a perforated spoon or sieve, retaining the cooking liquor for later use. Remove the herb sprigs where possible, and dress whilst piping hot with the lemon juice, olive oil and 2–3 tablespoons of the reserved cooking liquor. Add the cumin, chopped herbs and season to taste with salt and pepper. The chickpeas need to be quite citric and sharp, so add more lemon juice if required.

TO SERVE AND GARNISH

Serve the chickpeas atop the tahina sauce, garnished with the Yemenite hot sauce, a generous lug of extra virgin olive oil and an extra pinch of ground cumin if you feel like it. Serve immediately with warmed pita.

LABNEH, PISTACHIO DUKKAH & PRESERVED LEMON PICKLE
WITH HERB OIL & SHALLOTS

Labneh is a type of soft cheese, made by straining the whey out of yoghurt until the desired consistency has been achieved. We hang our yoghurt tied up in muslin cloth, ideally in the fridge, with a bowl positioned underneath to capture the escaping fluid, for anything between 8–48 hours depending on how soft or hard we want the end product to be. In the absence of muslin, you can get away with a couple of overlapping jay cloths pulled together and tied at the top with some string.

Labneh is a wonderfully versatile ingredient, which can be used as a dip, a spread in sandwiches or on toast, as a component in salads, or as a garnish to meat and fish. You can get creative with it as well, adding various flavours or elements to it, either before straining the yoghurt, or afterwards. The crunch of the pistachio dukkah works brilliantly with the creaminess of the labneh in this recipe, and the sharpness from the quick preserved lemon ties it all together. Any of the dukkah recipes provided in the larder section (see page 242) would also work, so pick your favourite if pistachio ain't your vibe. (Pictured overleaf).

SERVES 2–4

LABNEH
100g Labneh (page 261)

1 garlic clove, finely grated

½ tbsp dried mint

2 tbsp Herb Oil (page 264) or olive oil

about 20 strands of Quick-preserved Lemon Pickle (page 251)

1 tbsp Pistachio Dukkah (page 242)

½ shallot, sliced finely (preferably using a mandoline) into rings

10–12 picked dill fronds

1 green chilli, sliced

½ tsp za'atar

SERVE
pita bread, warmed in the oven or on the grill, or a crusty loaf of bread

FOR THE LABNEH
Mix the labneh in a small bowl with the garlic and dried mint until well combined.

Using the back of a large spoon, spread the labneh around the perimeter of a small, shallow bowl, and season all over with salt and pepper. Drizzle the herb oil generously around the whole plate, and garnish with the quick-preserved lemon pickle, strewn at random around the outside.

Sprinkle the pistachio dukkah over the top and place the shallot rings, picked dill fronds and sliced green chilli at intermittent intervals around the plate.

Season with za'atar and finish with a final drizzle of olive oil if you like.

Serve immediately, with warmed pita fresh off the grill, or simply a crusty loaf of white country bread.

BLACKENED AUBERGINE BABA

Baba ghanoush is a gift from the culinary gods, adored by one and all. I like to use Turkish aubergines where possible, which are long, thin and have a more intense flavour than their plump and more rounded Dutch cousins – though the latter are eminently more available. You can really give it to them on the grill. They can take it, and will reward you for it with a punchy smokiness.

If you're the resourceful type, peel off but retain the charred skin. Dry it out in the oven at a low temperature (110°C) and then blitz it in a food processor or spice grinder with some salt and ground cumin. You've just made yourself a blackened aubergine rub and it tastes pretty intense. You can dust it over the top of crème fraîche or labneh to make a great dip, or to garnish grilled fish, adding an extra dimension of smoky goodness.

SERVES 2–4

AUBERGINE BABA

1 medium-sized aubergine

2 garlic cloves, finely chopped

grated zest of 1 lemon, plus the juice of ½

¾ tbsp tahini paste

50ml extra virgin olive oil

generous pinch of Aleppo chilli flakes (also known as pul biber or red pepper flakes) or dried chilli flakes

GARNISH AND SERVE

1 tsp pomegranate seeds

3–4 walnuts, roughly chopped

4–5 picked dill fronds

pita bread, lightly brushed with oil and warmed in the oven or on the grill

FOR THE AUBERGINE BABA

Preheat the oven to 180°C/160°C Fan/Gas mark 4, or set a barbecue up for two-zone, indirect grilling (page 17).

Pierce the aubergine 5–6 times with a knife or a skewer and roast in the oven on a roasting tray, or, ideally, directly on the grill rack in your barbecue, offset from the coals with the lid on. It will take 30–45 minutes for the aubergine to blacken and soften, though it might take less in your barbecue depending on the strength of your fire, so keep an eye on it. Remove from the heat source once cooked all the way through, and set aside until it's cool enough to handle.

Cut the aubergine in half lengthways through the stem. Scoop out the flesh as carefully as you can onto a chopping board, and try and retain the skin in its shape and form for later use. Add the garlic to the aubergine flesh, and chop until a chunky purée has formed. Don't be too diligent in your chopping – a few chunks make for a more texturally interesting baba.

Transfer the aubergine mix to a large bowl and add the lemon zest and juice, the tahini paste and 30ml of the olive oil, and stir thoroughly to combine. Season with chilli flakes, salt and black pepper, then taste. Add more lemon juice or seasoning as required.

TO GARNISH AND SERVE

Spoon the baba back into the empty aubergine skins on a small serving plate, spreading it out slightly with the back of a spoon. Drizzle the remaining olive oil over the top and garnish with pomegranate seeds, walnuts and picked dill fronds. Serve with warmed pita bread.

MARINATED CHICKEN LIVERS

Chicken livers aren't for everyone. In fact, arguably, they aren't for anyone. I can count the number of people I know who actually like chicken livers with two fingers, and I'm one of them. This recipe is for the other one. You know who you are.

SERVES 2

400g chicken livers, cleaned and trimmed
500ml whole milk
1 tsp ground cumin
½ tsp ground allspice
¼ tsp ground nutmeg
60ml extra virgin olive oil
1 garlic clove, finely chopped
small knob of unsalted butter
juice of ½ lemon
1 tbsp finely chopped flat-leaf parsley
crusty bread or pita bread, to serve

Soak the chicken livers in a bowl of milk for 1 hour, to draw out impurities and soften the metallic taste that can sometimes accompany liver.

Drain the livers and pat dry before mixing them with the ground cumin, allspice, nutmeg, 30ml of olive oil and garlic in a small bowl to marinate for up to 4 hours in the fridge.

Wipe the excess marinade from the livers and pat dry again. Warm a large sauté or frying pan over medium heat until searing hot, add the remaining olive oil and the butter and throw in the chicken livers. Don't overcrowd the pan.

Sear the chicken livers for 4 minutes, toss in the pan to colour both sides, until tender to the touch and cooked to pink or blushing. Remove from the heat source, season and immediately add the lemon juice and chopped parsley straight to the pan, tossing the contents to coat in the sauce. Serve immediately, with your bread of choice.

IMAM BAYILDI
WITH CURD CHEESE & CRISPY CAPERS

Imam bayildi literally translates as 'the imam fainted', after legend has it that, upon being presented with this dish by the royal kitchen, the great imam fainted, such was his pleasure. I have to admit, nobody fainted when I presented this to my friends. My mate Dave looked a little queasy, but he tells me that was down to the late-night kebab he'd had. You win some you lose some, as they say.

SERVES 4

GARLIC YOGHURT
150g full-fat natural yoghurt
2 garlic cloves, very finely chopped
½ tbsp lemon juice
2 tbsp extra virgin olive oil

AUBERGINES
12 baby aubergines
2 tbsp salt
50ml olive oil, plus extra to drizzle
2 tbsp Çökelek curd cheese, or goat's cheese
4 tbsp garlic yoghurt
1 tbsp finely chopped flat-leaf parsley
2 tbsp Crispy Capers (optional) (page 240)

TOMATO SAUCE
100ml olive oil
2 banana shallots, finely diced
3 garlic cloves, thinly sliced
1 red chilli, finely sliced
1 tsp smoked paprika
½ tsp ground cumin
1 tsp Aleppo chilli flakes or use ½ tsp dried chilli flakes
1 tbsp hot red pepper paste (biber salcasi)
80ml water
1 x 400g chopped tomatoes
1 tbsp lemon juice
1 tbsp date syrup
½ tsp pomegranate molasses

FOR THE GARLIC YOGHURT
In a small bowl, combine the yoghurt, garlic and lemon juice. Whisk in the extra virgin olive oil and season to taste.

FOR THE AUBERGINES
Start by peeling 3–4 strips out of each aubergine, from the top to the base. Cut a slit in each aubergine lengthways from the base to within a few centimetres of the top, being careful not to cut through the stalk. Gently ease the aubergine open and score the flesh with a sharp knife. Spread the salt generously into one side and squeeze the aubergine together. Repeat with all the aubergines, and set them in a colander or sieve over a sink or bowl to drain for no less than 30 minutes and up to 1 hour.

FOR THE TOMATO SAUCE
Meanwhile, make the sauce. Heat 60ml of olive oil in a heavy-based saucepan over medium-low heat and sweat the shallots, garlic and chilli until softened and translucent but not coloured. Stir in the spices and hot red pepper paste and continue to cook for a few minutes. Pour in the water and stir to combine.

Add the chopped tomatoes, lemon juice, date syrup and pomegranate molasses. Bring to the boil over high heat, turn down the heat to low and simmer the sauce until reduced by half and intensified in flavour. The sauce should be sticky and rich, sweet and not too acidic. Season the sauce with salt and pepper according to taste.

TO FINISH THE AUBERGINES
Preheat the oven to 180°C/160°C Fan/Gas mark 3. Heat the olive oil in a non-stick frying pan over medium heat and fry the aubergines on all sides until golden brown. Remove from the pan and place on kitchen paper to absorb any excess oil. Cool the aubergines until they can be handled.

Sandwich the curd cheese into the slits of the aubergine, along with some of the tomato sauce, and press the top half of the aubergine down tightly. Arrange neatly in a small baking dish, and spoon over the remaining sauce. Bake for 15 minutes until softened and the sauce is bubbling hot. Allow to cool.

Serve the aubergines on top of the garlic yoghurt, with the parsley and crispy capers (if using) strewn over the top and any sauce spooned over.

TWICE-FRIED ARTICHOKES
WITH LABNEH & CHILLI

Much like mothers-in-law, artichokes involve a bit of hard work and preparation. There's just no getting away from it. I like to twice-fry mine, because I find it makes them extra crispy, much in the same way you'd double-fry handcut chips.

Labneh is a beautiful, creamy foil to the crunch of the fried 'choke. If you don't have any, crème fraîche will suffice. A good squeeze of lemon is obligatory. (Pictured overleaf).

SERVES 4–6

1kg baby artichokes

acidulated water (water with 2–3 lemon halves squeezed into it)

about 1.5 litres sunflower oil, for frying

flaked sea salt (such as Maldon)

GARNISH AND SERVE

100g labneh (page 261)

1 tbsp Aleppo chilli flakes (also known as pul biber or red pepper flakes) or use 1 tsp dried chilli flakes

2 red chillies, thinly sliced

3 tbsp chives, finely sliced

1 lemon, quartered

Prepare the artichokes. Cut off the top half of each artichoke and discard.

Peel away the tough, outer layers until the softer centre has been reached. Spoon out and discard any of the hairy choke that might be inside the heart. Trim or peel back the tough outer layer of the stem that connects to the heart. Cut the artichoke in half lengthways through the stem. As you go, throw the trimmed artichokes into a bowl of acidulated water to stop them discolouring.

Pour enough sunflower oil into a wide frying pan to come about 2.5cm up the sides. Set the pan over medium heat until the oil reaches 120°C when probed with a thermometer.

Drain the artichokes and pat dry with kitchen paper. Fry the artichokes for 12–15 minutes, stirring frequently, until tender. Remove the artichokes with a perforated spoon and drain on kitchen paper.

Turn the heat up to high and heat the oil to 180°C. Flash-fry the artichokes for 30 seconds until crisp and deep golden brown in colour. Don't overcrowd the pan – rather fry in batches.

Lift the artichokes from the oil with a perforated spoon and drain well on kitchen paper. Season liberally with flakes of salt and a few grinds of black pepper.

Spread the labneh out on a serving plate and sprinkle with the chilli flakes. Top with the fried artichokes and garnish with sliced red chilli and chives. Serve immediately, whilst piping hot, accompanied by some lemon wedges for squeezing over the top.

FRIED WHITEBAIT
WITH CUMIN SALT & HARISSA AIOLI

Frozen whitebait will suffice. But fresh is almost always best when it comes to seafood, with the exception (possibly) of octopus or squid.

Make sure your oil is up to temperature before frying. Soggy whitebait is as depressing as listening to Adele with a nasty hangover. You always end up crying. (Pictured overleaf).

SERVES 4–6

450g whitebait, fresh or use prepared frozen and defrosted

about 2 litres sunflower or vegetable oil, for deep-frying

220g plain flour

1 tsp paprika

1½ tbsp ground cumin

½ tsp cayenne pepper

1 tbsp salt

1½ tbsp finely chopped flat-leaf parsley

1 lemon, quartered, to serve

150g Harissa Aioli (page 264), to serve

1½ tbsp coarse sea salt and 1½ tbsp freshly ground cumin, mixed together

Wash, drain and pat-dry the whitebait on kitchen paper.

Heat enough oil to deep-fry the whitebait in a heavy-based pan (or a wok) to 190°C, making sure the pan is no more than half full.

Combine the flour, paprika, cumin, cayenne pepper and salt in a bowl. Dredge the whitebait in the flour until well coated and shake off any excess.

Working in batches, deep-fry the fish for 3–4 minutes, until crunchy and golden brown, being sure to bring the oil back to temperature after frying each batch.

Transfer the whitebait to some kitchen paper to soak up any excess oil, toss gently with the chopped parsley and serve immediately, still piping hot, garnished with lemon wedges and accompanied by some harissa aioli and a pile of cumin salt for dipping.

FRESH TOMATOES & PRESERVED LEMON
WITH TAHINA SAUCE

Fresh tomatoes. Tahini. Sometimes, in fact often, this is all you need in life. And when it's not, it's usually for one of two (and often both) reasons. Your tomatoes aren't good enough. Or...your tahini isn't good enough.

SERVES 4

200g cherry tomatoes, quartered

½ shallot, finely chopped

1 tbsp chopped flat-leaf parsley

1 tsp green chilli, finely chopped

¼ tsp ground cumin

2 tbsp extra virgin olive oil, plus extra to drizzle

1 tbsp lemon juice

1 garlic clove, finely grated

½ preserved lemon, pulp only

80g Tahina Sauce (page 262)

Combine the tomatoes, shallot, parsley, chilli, cumin, olive oil and lemon juice in a bowl and mix well. Season to taste; be generous with black pepper – a key ingredient in any decent tomato salad.

Mix the grated garlic and preserved lemon pulp together to form a chunky paste or relish.

Make a bed out of the tahina sauce, spoon the dressed tomatoes on top and garnish with the preserved lemon and garlic relish. Finish, as always, with a customary drizzle of olive oil.

HARISSA HOT WINGS
WITH PICKLED CHILLIES & PEANUTS

Grilled chicken wings are a staple on the menu of most Middle Eastern grill restaurants, usually in the mezze section as a hot starter, always grilled to crisp and served with toum (garlic sauce). They're not to be confused with Buffalo wings, a staple on the menu of many American barbecue joints, usually deep-fried and rolled in hot sauce.

This recipe is a bastardisation of both these influences, using a sweet and spicy glaze to baste and coat a smoked and then grilled wing.

I like to cut my wings in half and remove the wing tip. It makes for a more manageable way of eating them. But the Turks just whack them on as is, so this is entirely up to you.

SERVES 2

WINGS RUB
- 1 tbsp Aleppo chilli flakes (also known as pul biber or red pepper flakes) or use 1 tsp dried chilli flakes
- 2 tbsp smoked paprika
- ½ tbsp garlic granules or powder
- ½ tsp ground cumin
- 1 tbsp soft dark brown sugar
- 1 tsp fine salt
- ½ tsp coarse ground black pepper

HARISSA HOT SAUCE
- 2 spring onions, halved lengthways
- 1 tbsp extra virgin olive oil or Garlic Oil (page 260)
- ½ tsp salt
- 6 tbsp harissa (preferably rose harissa), shop-bought
- 4 tbsp runny honey
- 2 tbsp lemon juice
- 1 tbsp red wine vinegar (or Red Chilli Vinegar, page 263)
- 1 tbsp roughly chopped coriander

WINGS
- 6 two-bone chicken wings, cut in half, wing tip removed
- 4 tbsp olive oil or Garlic Oil (page 260)

FOR THE WINGS RUB
Combine all the ingredients in a small bowl and mix well.

FOR THE HARISSA HOT SAUCE
Preheat the grill to medium-high.

Brush the spring onion halves with the garlic oil, season with the salt and a grind of black pepper, lay them on a wire rack and blacken them under the grill until softened, about 3–5 minutes. Remove from the grill and cool until they can be handled. Place the harissa, honey, lemon juice and vinegar in a small saucepan, whisk to combine and bring to a simmer over medium heat. Turn the heat down to medium-low and simmer for 7–10 minutes so as to thicken and reduce the liquid to a glaze-like consistency. Put the spring onions, coriander and harissa sauce in a food processor and blend to an even, coarse texture. Season and set aside at room temperature until required.

FOR THE WINGS
Toss the wings in the rub, making sure it is evenly distributed and each wing is well coated.

Set a barbecue up for two-zone indirect grilling (page 17), ensuring you're cooking at a barbecue temperature of around 180°C, and arrange the wings in a single layer on the grill rack with no burning coals underneath, set up for reverse-searing (page 21). You can add some soaked wood chips as well to the burning coals. Close the vents off at the bottom but allow the lid's vents to remain partially open. Put the lid on the barbecue and smoke for 15–20 minutes until the internal temperature when measured with a thermometer probe reads between 70–75°C. Remove the lid from the barbecue and use tongs to transfer the wings for reverse-searing so that they are directly grilling over the hot coals. Nicely char the outside of the wings to ensure they have good colour and remove from the grill.

Toss the wings in the reheated harissa hot sauce with 2 tablespoons of olive oil.

continues overleaf...

1 spring onion, green parts only, thinly sliced

1 tbsp Aleppo chilli flakes (also known as pul biber or red pepper flakes) or use 1 tsp dried chilli flakes

1 tbsp unsalted peanuts, toasted and roughly chopped

1 tbsp coriander, roughly chopped

1 tsp Pickled Chillies (optional) (page 251)

SERVE (OPTIONAL)

Whipped Feta (page 261)

TO GARNISH AND SERVE

Arrange on a serving platter, topped with the sliced spring onion, chilli flakes, peanuts, coriander and pickled chillies (if using). Finish with a drizzle of the remaining oil over the top. These wings are great with a side serving of whipped feta, which balances the heat with a lovely saltiness and adds a gentle cooling effect to the whole experience.

● ●

ALTERNATIVE METHOD

The wings can always be seared on the outside over the fire until nicely charred, and then transferred to a roasting tray, covered with tin foil and cooked in an oven preheated to 180°C/160°C Fan/Gas mark 4 for 15–20 minutes, or until an internal temperature of 70°C is reached.

CHAPTER 02

SMOKED CHICKEN THIGHS
WITH SAFFRON & ORANGE BLOSSOM CARAMEL, HAZELNUT DUKKAH & BASIL

Chicken thighs on the bone are a great starting point for any budding barbecue enthusiast keen to start a relationship with fire and outdoor cookery. They are quite forgiving to fluctuations in temperature; they cook relatively quickly; and are also inexpensive, which makes them a useful beginner's ingredient for playing around with whilst you learn about the properties of your barbecue and of fire, and how to control the temperature of both.

These smoked chicken thighs are great as a snack for when the boys (or girls) come round to watch the game. Make a bucketload and pass them round.

SERVES 4

SAFFRON ORANGE CARAMEL

180ml freshly squeezed orange juice, strained

200g caster sugar

100ml saffron water (a generous pinch of saffron soaked in 100ml boiling water and left to infuse for 15 minutes)

1 tbsp orange blossom flower water

CHICKEN THIGHS

8 chicken thighs, on the bone ·

75g Everyday Chicken Rub (page 243)

GARNISH

picked basil leaves, ripped

generous pinch Aleppo chilli flakes (also known as pul biber or red pepper flakes) or use 1 tsp dried chilli flakes

2 tbsp Hazelnut Dukkah (page 242)

FOR THE SAFFRON ORANGE CARAMEL

Combine the orange juice, sugar and saffron water in a heavy-based saucepan and cook over medium-high heat until a caramel has formed with the consistency of a loose honey. Resist the urge to dip your finger in to test this. It won't forgive you easily.

Remove from the heat and stir in the orange blossom flower water.

FOR THE CHICKEN THIGHS

Toss the thighs in the rub, making sure each thigh is well coated and the spice mix is evenly distributed.

Set a barbecue up for smoking using two-zone indirect grilling (see page 17) with an internal temperature of between 130°C and 150°C. Arrange the thighs in a single layer on the grill rack with no burning coals underneath, set up for reverse-searing. Add some woodchips to the burning coals, put the lid on the barbecue and smoke for 40–45 minutes, or until the internal temperature when measured with a thermometer probe reads ideally between 70°C and 75°C (or above). In the absence of a probe, cut into the meat to the bone and check the juices run clear.

Remove the lid from the barbecue and use tongs to transfer the thighs for reverse-searing (page 21) so that they are directly grilling over the hot coals. Start to baste the chicken thighs in the caramel, turning regularly and continuing to baste on each side. Pour approximately the last quarter of the caramel into a heavy-based cast-iron pan and place on the grill next to the thighs, allowing the caramel to bubble and thicken. Nicely char the outside of the thighs to ensure they are well coloured and the skins have crisped up, then transfer to the cast-iron pan. Cook for a final 1–2 minutes in the reducing caramel, spooning the sauce over the thighs as you go.

TO GARNISH

Remove the pan from the grill, throw some ripped basil over to wilt in the residual heat, and garnish with chilli flakes and hazelnut dukkah. Serve immediately.

LAMB CIS KEBAB

This is a straightforward recipe that benefits from giving the lamb sufficient time to marinate properly. Yoghurt and grated onion are used in Middle Eastern and Indian cookery to tenderise the meat – a trick that works remarkably well.

This kebab should be served with sauces, salads, pickles and flatbread, so that you can rip and dip and make little wraps.

SERVES 2–4

LAMB CIS KEBAB

2 tbsp hot red pepper paste (biber salcasi)

80g full-fat natural yoghurt

2 tbsp olive oil

1 tsp sweet paprika

2 garlic cloves, grated

½ onion, grated

800g diced lamb shoulder, cut into 2.5cm pieces and trimmed of any sinew

8 thin metal skewers, 35–40cm long

Garlic Oil (page 260) or olive oil, for brushing the meat

PARSLEY, ONION AND SUMAC SALAD

handful of picked flat-leaf parsley leaves

½ white onion, thinly sliced

1 tbsp pomegranate seeds

1½ tbsp olive oil

generous pinch of ground sumac

SERVE (OPTIONAL)

flatbread, brushed with an onion wedge and warmed on the grill

1 lemon, quartered into wedges

Green Tahina Sauce (page 30)

Blackened Chilli Kebab Sauce (page 256)

Mixed Grilled Vegetables (page 171)

FOR THE LAMB CIS KEBAB

Put the hot red pepper paste, yoghurt, olive oil, paprika, garlic and grated onion in a bowl and mix thoroughly. Add the lamb and use your hands to massage the marinade into the meat. Pack tightly into a resealable bag, or keep in the bowl covered with clingfilm, and refrigerate for 4–6 hours or preferably overnight.

Set a barbecue up for single-zone, direct grilling (page 17) – ensuring that you are cooking on hot embers.

When the fire is ready, thread the meat on to the metal skewers and season generously with salt and pepper on both sides of the skewer.

FOR THE PARSLEY ONION AND SUMAC SALAD

Combine the parsley and onion in a bowl with the pomegranate seeds, and dress with olive oil and sumac. Season to taste.

TO FINISH THE CIS KEBAB

Grill the kebabs for about 3 minutes on each side until coloured and cooked through, brushing intermittently with garlic oil (if using) as the kebabs cook.

TO SERVE

Remove to a serving platter and serve with warmed flatbread, lemon wedges and condiments of choice. I like to use green tahina and blackened chilli kebab sauce here, but to be honest these kebabs are good with just about any of the sauces in the larder section (see Chapter 7, page 238). Take your pick. A nice, sharp salad works well to counter the meat, as well as some customary grilled Turkish chillies, tomatoes and onions.

BARBECUE-ROASTED RIB-EYE
WITH CUMIN BUTTER & BURNT ONION SALAD

Rib-eye is an expensive cut of meat that's great for any occasion where you can justify its expense. Ask your butcher for the steak to be cut from the fore-rib with the entire rib bone left in. I've heard this called the 'Piedmontese axe handle' over in the States, but it's more commonly known as the tomahawk steak here. Both names are brilliant and conjure images in my mind of the Wild West.

Due to its size, a tomahawk steak is perfectly suited to being barbecue-roasted indirectly to medium-rare (55–58°C), before being reverse-seared directly over the burning coals to colour up at the surface and caramelise (also known as the Maillard reaction, see page 21).

SERVES 3–4

CUMIN BUTTER
4 tbsp unsalted butter, softened
1 tbsp whole cumin seeds, ground
1½ tsp sweet paprika
pinch of cayenne pepper
1 tbsp grated lemon zest

BURNT ONION, PARSLEY
AND SALGAM SALAD
300ml salgam (turnip juice)
100ml pomegranate molasses
1 medium white onion, peeled and quartered through the root
1 red onion, peeled and quartered through the root
2 tbsp olive oil
small bunch of picked flat-leaf parsley leaves
1 tbsp pomegranate seeds
½ tsp ground sumac

RIB-EYE
1 rib-eye steak, bone-in, weighing approximately 2.5kg
olive oil, for brushing
flaked sea salt and black pepper

SERVE (OPTIONAL)
Cumin Salt (page 61)
Pickled Red Onion (page 252)
4–5 Turkish chillies, blackened on the grill

FOR THE CUMIN BUTTER
Put all the ingredients in a bowl and mix until incorporated and smooth. Roll into a clingfilm-wrapped sausage and set aside in the fridge to solidify.

FOR THE BURNT ONION AND PARSLEY SALAD
Reduce the salgam in a saucepan over medium-high heat by two-thirds, about 30–35 minutes. Whisk in the molasses and simmer to reduce for 3–5 minutes, until the dressing has a glaze-like consistency. Check for seasoning and adjust according to taste. It should be the right balance of sweet, salty and sour.

Blacken the onions on a grill until well charred and softened. Separate the onion petals and put in a small bowl. Dress in the olive oil and season to taste.

Add the parsley to the onions and throw in the pomegranate seeds and sumac. Toss the salad with the salgam dressing just prior to serving. The amount of dressing needed is according to taste, so start with half and then add more.

FOR THE RIB-EYE
Stand the rib-eye at room temperature for 30 minutes to an hour before grilling. Brush with olive oil on both sides and season generously with salt and pepper.

Set a barbecue up for two-zone indirect grilling (page 17) with an internal barbecue temperature of between 150–170°C. Barbecue-roast the steak until cooked to the desired doneness. I would recommend taking it no further than 55°C for a cut of such grandeur, but this is up to you. It should take approximately 45 minutes, but use the internal temperature of the meat as your guide rather than time. Finish by reverse-searing the meat directly over the hot coals until well scored, turning at a 45-degree angle to get a criss-cross pattern.

Remove from the barbecue and rest, wrapped in clingfilm and covered with tin foil, for 10–15 minutes, flipping once halfway through. A good rest is crucial.

TO SERVE
Serve the rib-eye sliced, on a large serving platter, seasoned with more salt and pepper, topped with the cumin butter and accompanied by the burnt onion salad. I like to add some cumin salt for dipping the meat, as well as some pickled red onion and blackened Turkish chillies.

BUTTERFLIED LEG OF LAMB
WITH GREEN CHARMOULA DRESSING & CHARRED AUBERGINE

Leg of lamb is a regal cut of meat, which, when butterflied, can be barbecued to temperature within an hour. Given that the joint is not tied in this recipe, it won't cook uniformly all the way through and some thinner parts of it will be more well done than at its thickest point in the centre, which should be medium-rare. That's fine though, because a leg of lamb can easily feed eight to ten of your friends and often more, and there will always be some who prefer their meat more cooked.

Serve the meat sliced and spread out across a large platter. It may cool slightly as you prepare it, but the leg is the only cut of lamb that will forgive you for not being served piping hot.

SERVES 8–10

LEG OF LAMB

6 garlic cloves

zest of 2 lemons

2 tbsp finely chopped lemon thyme leaves

2 tbsp finely chopped rosemary leaves

180ml olive oil

1 small bunch of spring onions, thinly sliced, white parts only (green parts reserved for Charmoula Dressing, see below)

2kg leg of lamb, boned and butterflied, trimmed of fat and skin (ask your butcher)

3 aubergines, sliced to 1cm rounds

SERVE

Green Charmoula (page 130)

Mejaderah (page 186)

200g Garlic Yoghurt (page 59)

Turkish Shepherd's Salad (optional) (page 174)

FOR THE LEG OF LAMB

Grate 5 garlic cloves and the lemon zest into a bowl and add the herbs, 100ml of olive oil and the white part of the spring onions. Pour the marinade all over the lamb and work it deep into the flesh using your hands. Season generously with salt and black pepper.

Set aside, covered and refrigerated, for 4–6 hours or preferably overnight.

Take the lamb leg out of the fridge an hour or so before you intend to cook it so that it can come to room temperature.

Set a barbecue up for two-zone, indirect grilling (page 17) with a target temperature of between 140–160°C.

Barbecue roast the butterflied lamb for roughly 1½ hours, turning regularly, until the internal temperature when probed with a thermometer reaches around 55°C for medium rare, or higher as per personal preference. Remember that the meat will continue to cook once removed from the heat source, so pull it off just before it reaches the optimum temperature. Finish by reverse-searing the meat directly over the hot coals until well browned, turning at a 45-degree angle to get a lovely criss-cross pattern effect.

Transfer to a chopping board, cover with tin foil and rest for 20–25 minutes.

Whilst the lamb is resting, grate or finely chop the last garlic clove and mix with the remaining 80ml of olive oil. Brush the aubergine slices on both sides liberally with the oil and season with salt and black pepper. Heat a cast-iron pan on the fire or stovetop, brush with more oil and char the aubergine for 3–5 minutes on each side, until well browned and softened.

Thinly slice the lamb across the grain and transfer to a serving platter. Flake some salt and black pepper over the meat and serve with the green charmoula over the entire platter.

TO SERVE

Serve the lamb and aubergine accompanied with some mejaderah and garlic yoghurt. A fresh, sharp salad such as a Turkish shepherd's salad would be a welcome addition to balance the richness of the meat and rice.

BARBECUED PORK LOIN CHOP
WITH ALMOND SALSA, PICKLED WALNUTS & GLAZED FIGS

A good pork chop, when cooked correctly, is hard to beat. The margins for error are quite fine, however, and the difference between one that's been grilled to perfectly blushing pink and a chop that's overcooked and dry is vast. I always like to brine pork meat where possible, as it helps to keep the whole affair moist. It also helps to widen that margin for error, if only slightly.

Make sure you source the best possible pork for this recipe. This sounds obvious, but some cuts of pork are more forgiving than others. A good layer of fat between the skin and meat is essential. Look for meat with a deep and almost ruby shade of pink that's well marbled and layered with fat.

Score the pork chop through the fat – this prevents it from shrinking, causing the meat to curl. Pickled walnuts are available from most large supermarkets. We use Opies.

SERVES 4

MASTER BRINE

300g table salt

250ml just-boiled water, plus
   4 litres water

200g caster sugar

PORK LOIN CHOPS

4 pork loin chops, bone-in, 2.5cm
   thick, about 300–350g each

flaked sea salt (such as Maldon)

1 lemon, quartered

ALMOND SALSA

½ tbsp orange blossom water

grated zest of ½ orange

1½ tsp runny honey

40ml sherry vinegar

pinch of caster sugar

50ml extra virgin olive oil

150g almonds, toasted and finely
   chopped

1 tbsp chopped mint

SAFFRON OIL

large pinch of saffron

1 tbsp finely chopped lemon thyme
   leaves

1 garlic clove, grated

60ml extra virgin olive oil

FOR THE MASTER BRINE

Add the salt to the hot water and stir to dissolve, forming a sludge-like consistency. Top up with the 4 litres of water. Add the sugar and stir to combine.

FOR THE PORK LOIN CHOPS

Submerge the pork chops in the brine and set aside for 4–6 hours.

FOR THE ALMOND SALSA

Combine the orange blossom water, orange zest, honey, vinegar and sugar in a bowl and whisk together. Gradually pour in the olive oil and whisk to emulsify. Pour the dressing over the almonds and fold through the chopped mint. Season to taste with salt and black pepper and set aside until required.

FOR THE SAFFRON OIL

Combine the ingredients in a small bowl and refrigerate for 4–6 hours, or ideally overnight, until thick and cloudy or preferably solidified.

TO FINISH THE PORK CHOPS

Remove the chops from the brine and pat dry with some kitchen paper. Score the fat on the chop by making several incisions along its length. This will prevent the chop from curling up when it hits the heat.

Spoon some of the solidified saffron oil onto each chop, season well with salt and black pepper and bring to room temperature.

Set a barbecue up for single-zone, direct grilling (page 17) – ensuring that you are cooking directly over medium-high embers.

Grill the chops, skin-side down, to crisp up the skin and render out some fat. Grill them on all sides, until the fat is golden and they are caramelised and scored all over. Remove when medium to the touch, or between 53°C and 55°C when probed with a thermometer (about 10–12 minutes).

Transfer the chops to a serving platter and leave to rest for half the cooking

SERVE

4 figs, cut in half

2 tbsp caster sugar

100g pickled walnuts, roughly chopped and mixed with 1 tbsp extra virgin olive oil and 1 tsp pomegranate molasses

olive oil

time, flipping them over once halfway through. Whilst the meat is resting, sprinkle the fig halves with sugar and caramelise them under a grill.

TO SERVE

I like to detach the loin or eye of the chop from the bone and slice it across the grain into 5–6 slices. Season each slice with salt and black pepper and return the slices to reconfigure the loin in its original position. Spoon the almond salsa over the top, and serve alongside the caramelised fig halves and pickled walnuts. Finish with a liberal drizzle of olive oil.

HONEYED BARBECUE PORK BELLY
WITH FILFELCHUMA & PINEAPPLE SALSA

There are so many different cuts of pork, each with a unique set of characteristics that require their own method of barbecuing or cooking. From the creamy loin chop that needs quick grilling, to the meaty shoulder that should be slow-smoked and pulled. From the soft and gelatinous cheek that must be braised, to the crispy tail that needs to be fried. I could go on.

The belly is my guilty pleasure. It can be slowly braised until it pulls apart, cured to make bacon or barbecue-roasted until soft and tender. There are chops to be slow-grilled, ribs to be smoked and crackling to be devoured. This recipe uses a combination of these techniques, slow-braising the belly until meltingly tender and then finishing it on the grill for some smoky barbecued goodness.

Filfelchuma, a Libyan condiment similar to harissa, provides a fiery garnish juxtaposed against the sweet pineapple salsa.

SERVES 12

BRINE
500ml just-boiled water, plus
  8 litres water
600g table salt
400g caster sugar

PORK BELLY
1 x 4–4.5kg pork belly, boned
200g Pork Rub (page 247)
4–5 Turkish chilli peppers
2 large onions, sliced into
  2cm rounds
150ml runny honey
300ml water
100ml white wine
2 dried bay leaves
3 tbsp Filfelchuma (page 260),
  or Harissa (page 259) or
  shop-bought
½ bunch of thyme sprigs

FOR THE BRINE

In a container large enough to hold the pork belly (a saucepan works well), add the salt to the hot water and stir to dissolve, forming a sludge-like consistency. Top up with the remaining water, then add the sugar and stir to combine. Submerge the pork belly in the brine and leave in the fridge overnight.

TO COOK THE PORK BELLY

Preheat the oven to 130°C/110°C Fan/Gas mark 1.

Remove the pork belly from the brine and pat dry. Score both sides of the belly with a sharp knife in a crosshatch pattern, up to 0.5cm deep. Rub the pork all over generously with the rub.

Scatter the chilli peppers in a roasting tray or casserole dish large enough to accommodate the pork belly, and lay the onion slices as a bed upon which the pork will sit. Transfer the pork, skin-side down, on top of the onion and drizzle half the honey directly over it and the remaining half into the pan. Add the water and white wine, followed by the bay leaves, filfelchuma and thyme. Cover tightly with a double layer of tin foil, making sure to crimp the foil along the edge of the roasting tray. Transfer to the oven and cook for 2 hours, basting periodically with the juices, before turning the pork over to cook for a further 3 hours, until tender and all but pulling apart with the lightest of pressure.

Once cooked, carefully lift the pork from the roasting tray and transfer it to rest on a cooling rack. Strain the cooking liquor through a fine sieve into a heavy-based saucepan. Place over high heat and simmer to reduce to a thickened sauce with a glaze-like consistency thick enough to coat the back of a wooden spoon. Cool and refrigerate.

Wrap the pork in clingfilm and return it to the cooling rack, set over a shallow tray, pressed with a heavy weight overnight in the refrigerator. I use a roasting tray filled with water as a press, but heavy tins should also work just fine.

continues overleaf...

PINEAPPLE SALSA

1 pineapple, peeled, cored and cut into wedges

olive oil

100g sugar

80ml cider vinegar

2 tbsp orange juice

1 star anise

1 cinnamon stick

1 tsp cayenne pepper

1½ tsp ground cumin

pinch of salt

4–5 spring onions, green parts only

2 tbsp roughly chopped coriander

SERVE

Filfelchuma (page 260)

The next day, take the pork belly out of the fridge and allow it to come back to room temperature. Set a barbecue up for single-zone direct grilling (page 17) over medium-high heat.

FOR THE PINEAPPLE SALSA

Roll the pineapple in olive oil and season with salt and pepper. Grill the pineapple directly over hot embers, until well charred all over. Remove from the grill and hack into rough pieces.

Combine the sugar, vinegar and orange juice in a small saucepan and place over medium-high heat to dissolve the sugar. Add the star anise, cinnamon stick, cayenne and cumin as well as the pineapple chunks, and continue to cook over low heat for 12–15 minutes, until the liquid has thickened. The salsa should be quite dry. Season with salt to taste and leave to cool a little. Fold the spring onion greens and coriander through the mix once nearly cool.

TO FINISH THE PORK BELLY

Slice the pork into 2.5cm thick slabs. Reheat the glaze. Grill the pork belly slices on both sides, brushing continually and generously with the glaze until well charred and warmed through.

TO SERVE

Serve the pork with some filfelchuma, pineapple salsa and bread.

SLOW-SMOKED LAMB BREAST
WITH APRICOT, PISTACHIO & MERGUEZ STUFFING

Stuffed and rolled lamb breast can be a bit of a time-consuming faff, but those willing to undertake this will be rewarded with one of the most unctuous and satisfying joints of smoked meat.

The stuffing absorbs the meat juices from both the lamb and the merguez, ensuring you get a double hit of meaty goodness. (Pictured overleaf).

SERVES 6

ROSE HARISSA YOGHURT
250g Greek yoghurt
3 tbsp Rose Harissa or Harissa (page 259) or shop-bought

APRICOT AND MERGUEZ STUFFING
250g merguez sausage
1 red onion, finely chopped
olive oil, for frying (if needed)
60g dried apricots, finely chopped
60g pistachio nuts, toasted and finely chopped
2 tbsp finely chopped flat-leaf parsley
1 garlic clove, finely chopped
30g dried white breadcrumbs

LAMB BREAST
2–3 large spring green leaves, stems discarded
1 lamb breast (about 1.2kg), boned and skinned
3 tbsp Harissa (page 259) or shop-bought

FOR THE ROSE HARISSA YOGHURT
Combine the yoghurt and rose harissa in a bowl and stir well. Season to taste with salt and black pepper and set aside until required.

FOR THE APRICOT AND MERGUEZ STUFFING
Warm a frying pan over medium-high heat on the stove, then remove the merguez sausage meat from its casing and fry for 6–8 minutes, until browned, breaking it up with a wooden spoon. Lift the meat from the pan with a slotted spoon and set to one side.

Return the pan to the stove and fry the onion in the merguez juices over medium-low heat until softened and translucent, about 10–12 minutes. (You might need to add some olive oil if the juices left behind were scant.) Season with salt and pepper to taste. Add the dried apricots and pistachios to the pan and cook for a few minutes to soften. Remove the pan from the heat and fold through the parsley, garlic, breadcrumbs and merguez along with any accompanying fat.

FOR THE LAMB BREAST
Bring a large pan of salted water to the boil over high heat and blanch the spring greens for 30 seconds, refreshing in an iced water bath to stop the cooking process. Drain them and squeeze tightly to remove any excess water.

Season the lamb breast liberally with salt and black pepper on both sides and then lay it flat, skin-side down, on a chopping board. Brush half the harissa over the meat and place the greens on top, spreading them out thinly and evenly to cover the entire flesh. Press the stuffing onto the meat and neatly roll the breast up from the short end, so that the skin-side is on the outside (use both hands as you roll, trying to keep all the stuffing encased in the spiral). Tie the lamb breast with kitchen string, making 5–6 tight, evenly spaced knots.

Set a barbecue up for smoking using two-zone indirect grilling (page 17), and try and hit (and maintain) a temperature zone between 110°C and 130°C.

Smoke the lamb breast, with the lid on, for 5–6 hours, or until the internal temperature reaches between 85°C and 88°C when probed with a thermometer. Remove from the heat and rest, wrapped in clingfilm, for 20 minutes.

Alternatively, cook the lamb in the oven. First seal the lamb in a frying pan over a medium-high heat until coloured on all sides. Preheat the oven to 150°C/130°C Fan/Gas mark 2 and transfer to a roasting tray. Cook for approximately 2 hours, tossed periodically in the cooking juices, until tender and falling apart. Rest for 15–20 minutes before serving.

Carve the lamb using a sharp knife and serve with the rose harissa yoghurt.

IZMIR KOFTE
WITH WHITE BEAN SALAD & QUICK PICKLED RED CABBAGE

The key to a good kofte, as with a hamburger, is a generous ratio of fat to lean meat. I aim for no less than 30 per cent fat. This has the benefit of adding flavour (since fat tastes good), whilst keeping the koftes juicy by lubricating the meat as it cooks and melts.

Try, if possible, to avoid buying pre-prepared mince. Invariably it tends to be a far leaner cut and more finely ground than is desirable, with a drier end result. Instead, pick out some meat from the counter (I like to use chuck, brisket or short rib in any combination) and ask your butcher to grind the meat for you, using a coarse setting.

SERVES 4–6

IZMIR KOFTE

1½ tsp cumin seeds

1 tsp coriander seeds

½ tsp ground allspice

800g minced beef, preferably a 50:50 combination of chuck and short-rib, 20–30% fat, coarsely ground (ask your butcher)

½ onion, finely chopped

2 large garlic clove, finely chopped

1 tbsp finely chopped flat-leaf parsley

1 tsp lemon thyme leaves, finely chopped

generous pinch of Aleppo chilli flakes (also known as pul biber or red pepper flakes) or use dried chilli flakes

1 tbsp salt

½ tsp coarse ground black pepper

WHITE BEAN AND
ONION SALAD

1 medium white onion, very finely sliced

400g tin white beans, drained

2 tbsp chopped flat-leaf parsley

50ml extra virgin olive oil

2 tbsp white wine vinegar

FOR THE IZMIR KOFTE

Heat a heavy-based pan over medium-high heat and toast the cumin and coriander seeds until just lightly smoking and fragrant. Transfer to a spice grinder and blitz to a fine powder.

Combine the spices, minced beef and remaining ingredients in a bowl, and knead gently to combine. You don't want to overwork the meat and knock out the air pockets that naturally occur within the mince. These will keep the koftes moist, so do your best to keep the meat light and airy, rather than compact or compressed. Shape the mix into oval patties (roughly 60–70g each) and set aside in the refrigerator, covered, to firm up until required.

FOR THE WHITE BEAN AND ONION SALAD

Combine the onion, white beans and parsley in a small bowl and dress with the oil and vinegar. Season with salt to taste.

FOR THE QUICK-PICKLED CABBAGE

Cut the cabbage in half, remove the core, and shred the cabbage as thinly as possible. I like to use a mandoline but in the absence of one a sharp knife and some useful knife skills will suffice. Salt the cabbage liberally in a bowl, mixing well with your hands, and set in a colander over the sink, pressed down with a suitable weight such as a bowl filled with water or heavy cans or bottles. Leave to soften for up to 1 hour, then rinse under cold water. Combine the cabbage with the lemon juice and extra virgin olive oil in a mixing bowl and toss well.

TO FINISH THE IZMIR KOFTE

I like to reverse-sear (page 21) my koftes, which may not be the conventional method of cooking minced patties but it works well for me. If you prefer to cook these directly over the coals, by all means do so.

Set a barbecue up for two-zone indirect grilling (page 17) with an internal barbecue temperature of around 180°C, and arrange the koftes in a single layer on the grill rack with no burning coals underneath, set up for reverse-searing. Place the lid on the barbecue and cook the koftes until the internal thermometer has reached 60°C when probed with a thermometer. Flick the

QUICK-PICKLED RED CABBAGE
½ head of red cabbage
1 tbsp salt
3 tbsp lemon juice
2 tbsp extra virgin olive oil

SERVE
4 Turkish chilli peppers, blackened
   on the grill
Blackened Chilli Kebab Sauce (page
   256) or Acili Ezme (page 258)
full-fat natural yoghurt
crusty bread

koftes across to the opposite side of the grill so they are cooking directly on top of the searing coals, and char them quickly, no more than a couple of minutes, on both sides, to add colour and caramelisation. Transfer to a plate and rest somewhere warm for a few minutes, turning halfway through the resting process.

TO SERVE
Serve immediately, with some blackened Turkish chilli peppers fresh off the grill, the white bean and onion salad, the quick-pickled red cabbage and some blackened chillli kebab sauce or acili ezme (page 258). Yoghurt should be used as a coolant, along with a crusty loaf of bread to mop everything up with.

JERUSALEM GRILL
WITH TURMERIC & LEMON THYME BUTTER

Offal, of any kind, can be a hard sell. No matter how much our waiters and waitresses would talk it up, our Jerusalem mixed grill would often fall on deaf ears. A shame, because it's a wondrous dish of rich, meaty organs bound by the sharpness of lemon and the yellow tinge of turmeric butter.

   The dish is said to have originated in Jerusalem's Mahane Yehuda market, as a means of getting rid of the cheaper and unwanted offcuts from the ubiquitous chicken. Word spread. Soon everyone was claiming possession of it – an all too familiar argument in this part of the world.

SERVES 4

TURMERIC AND LEMON
   THYME BUTTER

40g unsalted butter, softened to
   room temperature

1 garlic clove, grated

1½ tsp ground turmeric

1 tbsp lemon juice

1 tbsp lemon thyme leaves, finely
   chopped

JERUSALEM GRILL

2 large onions, thinly sliced into
   rings

1 tbsp caster sugar

1 tbsp olive oil

200g chicken hearts, cut in half
   lengthways

250g trimmed chicken livers

250g trimmed lamb liver

GARNISH AND SERVE

1½ tbsp cumin seeds, roughly
   crushed

2 tbsp finely chopped flat-leaf
   parsley

juice of ½ lemon

50g Tahina Sauce (page 262)

Herb Salad (page 263)

Mango pickle or Amba Yoghurt
   (optional) (page 133)

pita bread

FOR THE TURMERIC AND LEMON THYME BUTTER
Whisk all the ingredients together well by hand in a small bowl until thoroughly incorporated.

FOR THE JERUSALEM GRILL
Dust the onion rings on one side with half the sugar. Set a wide, heavy-based frying pan over high heat until smoking hot, and lay the rings flat, in a single layer, sugar-side down. Sprinkle the remaining sugar on the onions as the bottom side caramelises. Sear until golden brown, turning just once, for 2–3 minutes on each side. Season and set aside. Wipe the pan clean with kitchen paper.

Heat the pan or frying pan over medium-high heat, until nearly smoking. Add the oil, followed by the chicken hearts, and sear for 2–3 minutes.

Add the chicken and lamb livers to the pan, followed by the turmeric and lemon thyme butter and the seared onions. Fry the livers for 4–5 minutes, tossing in the pan to colour the livers on both sides and coat in the butter. Remove from the heat when the livers are tender to the touch; they should be pink and blushing.

TO GARNISH AND SERVE
Season the meat with salt and black pepper, sprinkle over the cumin seeds and garnish with the parsley. Taste and add lemon juice if required.

Serve the Jerusalem grill straight from the pan, still sizzling, with some tahina sauce, herb salad, mango pickle and some pita bread.

VEAL CHOP
WITH PRESERVED LEMON OIL, ZA'ATAR & CONFIT GARLIC

This is a simple recipe that plays to the strength of the main ingredient. A veal chop is a beautiful cut of meat, both delicate and creamy, that needs only the lightest of helping hands – a drizzle of oil perfumed with preserved lemon, some sweet, golden confit garlic and a good sprinkle of za'atar.

I'd recommend always trying to source British veal wherever possible, since British law ensures that calves are reared to higher standards than some of their EU counterparts. Look for meat that's less white and more pink or rose, since this a good indication of better nutrition and welfare.

I like to serve this chop with a fresh tomato salad (page 64) and potatoes of choice.

SERVES 4

VEAL CHOPS

4 tbsp olive oil

1 tbsp chopped lemon thyme leaves

2 garlic cloves, grated

grated zest of 1 lemon

4 veal chops, about 3.5cm thick

PRESERVED LEMON OIL

80ml extra virgin olive oil

1 preserved lemons, pulp only, chopped

1 tbsp lemon juice

1 tbsp chopped lemon thyme leaves

GARNISH AND SERVE

1 lemon, quartered

2 tbsp za'atar

16 Confit Garlic Cloves (page 260)

Crispy Capers (optional) (page 240)

FOR THE VEAL CHOPS

Put the olive oil, lemon thyme, garlic and lemon zest in a small bowl and stir well. Add the veal chops and season with salt and pepper. Set aside to marinate, refrigerated, for 2–4 hours or preferably overnight.

FOR THE PRESERVED LEMON OIL

Combine all the ingredients together in a bowl and mix well. Set aside in the fridge to solidify whilst the meat is marinating.

TO FINISH THE VEAL CHOPS

Remove the veal from the fridge and scrape the marinade from the meat.

Set a barbecue up for direct grilling (page 17) over medium-high.

Grill the chops for 5–6 minutes (for medium at 60°C) on either side or longer if you prefer your meat to be cooked more thoroughly. Turn the chops at 45 degrees halfway through the cooking of both sides to form a crosshatch pattern. Cook on the fat-side standing upright for 1–2 minutes, just to render the fat slightly.

Transfer to a plate and leave to rest for a few minutes, turning once halfway through. Blacken the lemon quarters on the grill whilst the meat is resting.

TO GARNISH AND SERVE

Serve with a dollop of preserved lemon oil on top, garnished with za'atar, confit garlic cloves, crispy capers (if using) and a blackened lemon wedge.

CHICKEN, PISTACHIO & DILL KOFTE

Skewering koftes is not for the faint-hearted. Here are some tips to get you through your ordeal.
1. Don't be afraid to make a mess of it.
2. If you make a mess, use pre-soaked bamboo skewers to mould smaller, sausage-shaped koftes.
3. If you make a mess of that, consider making patties as you would for a hamburger, flattened out between the palms of your hands, without any skewer at all. It will still taste great.
4. If you make a mess of this last one, consider giving up on the recipe and maybe think about moving on with your life altogether. You need a new hobby.

SERVES 6

CHICKEN KOFTE

1 tbsp olive oil

2 shallots, finely diced

1 large garlic clove, minced

800g chicken mince

2 tbsp finely chopped dill

1 tbsp finely chopped coriander

3 tbsp pistachios, toasted and finely chopped

2 tbsp hot red pepper paste (biber salcasi), or tomato paste

1 tbsp Aleppo chilli flakes or use 1 tsp dried chilli flakes

grated zest of 1 lemon

1 red chilli, deseeded and finely chopped

1½ tbsp salt

1 tsp coarse ground black pepper

6 flat metal skewers, approximately 2cm wide and 35–40cm long

GARNISH AND SERVE

1 tbsp olive oil (or Garlic Oil, page 260)

1 lemon, to serve, cut into wedges

Tahina Corn Remoulade (page 262)

picked flat-leaf parsley and dill leaves

2 large onions, quartered and blackened on the grill

6 Turkish chilli peppers, blackened on the grill

FOR THE CHICKEN KOFTE

Heat the olive oil in a frying pan over medium heat and sauté the shallots and garlic until softened and translucent but not coloured. Remove from the heat and cool.

Put all the ingredients in a large bowl and knead together with your hands until well combined. Rest in the refrigerator for 1 hour, or ideally 3–4 hours.

Remove the chicken from the refrigerator and divide into 6 balls (about the size of a tennis ball). Keeping a small bowl of tepid water by your side, wet your hands and form the meat around six flat 2.5cm wide metal kebab skewers. Gently squash each ball around the skewer, and, working from top to bottom, lightly press and massage the meat with your fingers so that it spreads across the skewer and is distributed as evenly as possible. Use the tepid water to keep your hands moist throughout, which will help you to shape the meat and prevent the mixture from sticking to your hands. Once completed, put the skewers back in the refrigerator for a further hour whilst you make the tahina corn remoulade.

TO FINISH THE CHICKEN

Set a barbecue up for single-zone, direct grilling (page 17) – ensuring that you are cooking over medium-hot embers.

Grill the skewers for 4–5 minutes on both sides until well coloured and cooked all the way through.

TO GARNISH AND SERVE

Remove the chicken and transfer to a serving platter. Brush with olive oil, squeeze over lemon juice and serve with the tahina corn remoulade. Strew the parsley and dill leaves on top along with the remaining blackened corn kernels. Serve with flatbreads or pita lightly grilled, and mixed grilled peppers and onions.

CHEESEBURGER KOFTE KEBAB
WITH KEBAB SALSA (ACILI EZME)

This recipe is from Shaun Whitmore, our hugely talented head chef at Berber & Q Grill House.

Not our most authentic recipe, by any means, but a fusion of the American and Middle Eastern cuisines and cultures that we love in equal measure. It's also just a bit of fun.

Serve it to your non-Turkish friends. Turkish people may never forgive you for bastardising a national treasure as universally adored as their holy kofte.

SERVES 4

KOFTE KEBAB

500g aged beef steak trim (ask your butcher) or minced beef

100g aged beef fat (ask your butcher)

1 tbsp smoked paprika

1 tbsp ground cumin

1½ tbsp ground coriander

1 tbsp Aleppo chilli flakes (also known as pul biber or red pepper flakes) or 1 tsp dried chilli flakes

¾ tbsp coarse ground black pepper

7 garlic cloves, peeled

8 slices of American cheese

4 flat metal skewers, 2.5cm wide and 35–40cm long

GARNISH AND SERVE

4 laffa breads, or flatbreads

olive oil

1 head of baby gem, ripped or cut into random pieces

50g shredded red cabbage

100g Kebab Salsa (Acili Ezme) (page 258)

100ml Toum (Garlic Sauce) (page 261)

50g Bread and Butter Pickles (page 254)

1 red onion, thinly sliced

pinch of ground sumac

FOR THE KOFTE KEBAB

Dice the meat and fat into cubes and combine with the dry spices and the garlic in a bowl. Use a meat grinder, fitted with a coarse plate, to grind the beef. (In the absence of a grinder, mix the spices with a minced blend of meat from your butcher, ensuring the garlic is crushed or minced.)

Portion the kofte mix into 4 balls, roughly 150g each, and, keeping a small bowl of tepid water by your side, wet your hands and form the meat around the metal skewers. Gently squash each ball around the skewer, and, working from top to bottom, lightly press and massage the meat with your fingers so that it spreads and is distributed as evenly as possible. Use the tepid water to keep your hands moist throughout, which will help you to shape the meat and prevent the mixture from sticking to your hands. Once all the skewers are completed, put them back in the refrigerator for an hour to set.

Set a barbecue up for single-zone direct grilling (page 17) over medium-high heat and grill the koftes for about 7–10 minutes, turning every so often to ensure they are well coloured on both sides and cooked through. When the koftes are almost ready, place the cheese on top to melt through.

TO GARNISH AND SERVE

Brush the laffas with a little olive oil mixed with a drop of water, and warm through briefly on the grill. They can be placed directly on top of the skewers if there isn't sufficient room on the barbecue grill.

Assemble the kebabs as you deem fit, but we like to start with the ripped baby gem and red cabbage as a base, followed by the kofte, then the kebab salsa and toum drizzled all over. Garnish the kebab with bread and butter pickles and some thinly sliced red onion, and finish with a pinch of sumac.

MINUTE STEAK YOGURTLU
WITH TOMATO GRAVY & ALEPPO CHILLI BUTTER

Yogurtlu is a wonderfully rich Turkish dish of grilled meat served atop kebab bread on a bed of tomato sauce and yoghurt, drizzled with melted butter. It should never be confused with iskender, which is also a wonderfully rich Turkish dish of grilled meat served atop kebab bread on a bed of tomato sauce and yoghurt, drizzled with melted butter. Go figure.

I like to use minute steak as a gourmet substitute for the thin shavings of cheap doner meat often used. It's both very quick and easy to prepare. But in truth just about any meat could work here. If you're short on time, you can forgo the marinade – it will still taste fantastic.

SERVES 2–4

MINUTE STEAK MARINADE

1 onion, coarsely grated, plus ½ onion for brushing

80ml extra virgin olive oil

1 tbsp lemon thyme, finely chopped

grated zest of 1 lemon

1 tsp smoked paprika

1 tsp flaked sea salt

¼ tsp coarse ground black pepper

6 x 100g sirloin steaks (approximately 0.5cm thick – ask your butcher), pounded flat with a meat mallet

flatbreads (1cm thick or less)

olive oil, for brushing

TOMATO GRAVY

2 tbsp olive oil

1 onion, finely chopped

2 garlic cloves, grated

1 tbsp Confit Chilli Salsa (page 260) or 2 tsp dried hot chilli flakes

3 tbsp tomato paste

2 tbsp hot red pepper paste (also known as biber salcasi)

2 tbsp Red Chilli Vinegar (page 263) or use red wine vinegar

1 x 400g tin plum tomatoes

1 tsp runny honey

FOR THE MINUTE STEAK MARINADE

Combine all of the ingredients together in a bowl. Add the steak and massage the marinade into the meat with your hands. Cover and refrigerate for 4–6 hours or preferably overnight.

FOR THE TOMATO GRAVY

Heat the olive oil in a heavy-based saucepan over medium-low heat before adding the onion and cooking until softened and translucent but not coloured, about 5–7 minutes. Stir in the garlic and confit chilli salsa and continue to fry for a few minutes. Add the tomato and hot red pepper pastes and fry for a further 1–2 minutes. Pour in the vinegar and turn the heat up high to reduce the liquid by half. Add the tinned tomatoes, bring to a boil, turn the heat down to its lowest setting and let the sauce simmer for 35–40 minutes, until thickened. Towards the end of the cooking time, stir in the honey and season with salt and pepper to taste. Set aside until ready to use. The sauce can be kept for up to 3 days in the fridge, where the flavour will intensify and improve.

FOR THE ALEPPO CHILLI BUTTER

Melt the butter over medium-low heat in a small pan, then add the garlic and fry, allowing the garlic to soften (be careful not to burn it). Whisk the butter gently as it cooks, until it darkens and caramelises to a nutty golden brown, about 3–5 minutes. Add the chilli flakes right at the end and remove the pan from the heat. Keep warm until ready to use.

TO FINISH THE MINUTE STEAK

Set a barbecue up for single-zone, direct grilling (page 17) – ensuring that you are cooking over hot embers. Remove the marinating steaks from the fridge, so they can come to room temperature.

Reheat the tomato gravy (if needed) in a heavy-based cast-iron pan placed on the edge of the barbecue. Rub the flatbreads with the open side of half an onion, brush with olive oil and grill on both sides. Set to one side or the edge of the barbecue whilst you cook the meat. Alternatively, if you feel comfortable doing so, and your barbecue is big enough to accommodate it, fulfil this task at the same time as cooking the meat so that the bread comes fresh off the grill.

continues overleaf...

ALEPPO CHILLI BUTTER

40g unsalted butter

1 garlic clove, finely chopped

1 tbsp Aleppo chilli flakes (also
known as pul biber or red
pepper flakes) or use 1 tbsp
smoked paprika with a pinch of
dried chilli flakes

GARNISH AND SERVE

4 tbsp full-fat natural yoghurt

picked flat-leaf parsley leaves

1 shallot, sliced as thinly as
possible into rings

Pickled Turkish Chillies (optional)
(page 255), or shop-bought

Flash-grill the minute steaks quickly on both sides over burning hot embers,
brushing with oil as you go. Transfer the meat to the tomato gravy pan and
finish briefly in the sauce, spooning the tomato gravy over the steaks as it
bubbles and cooks. Remove from the heat and serve immediately.

TO GARNISH AND SERVE

Place the grilled flatbreads on the base of a serving platter followed by a
generous amount of the tomato gravy. Lay the steaks, each chopped into 2 or
3 pieces, on top and spoon the yoghurt over them followed by the Aleppo chilli
butter. Garnish with parsley and shallot rings. As always, add a final drizzle of
olive oil for gloss and serve with pickled Turkish chillies if available.

LAMB BELLY RIBS
WITH SPICY SICHUAN RUB & RED PEPPER KETCHUP

Lamb belly ribs are often deemed an undesirable offcut and tossed aside as scrag, or for stock, which I find peculiar. For me, and the entire population of Turkey seemingly, they are one of most sought-after cuts. What they lack in lean meat they more than make up for in flavourful, melt-in-your-mouth fat. Ask your butcher for the whole lamb breast, ribs removed but retained.

Stuff, roll and slow-cook the breast as per page 83, and flash grill the ribs directly over the coals, so that they almost touch the burning embers. Two dishes for the price of one.

SERVES 2–4

SPICY SICHUAN RUB
1 tbsp Sichuan peppercorns
1 tbsp cumin seeds
1 tsp fennel seeds
1 star anise
2 cardamom pods
½ tsp cloves
½ cinnamon stick
1 tbsp caster sugar
½ tbsp salt
1 tbsp cayenne pepper
½ tbsp smoked paprika
¼ tsp garlic granules or powder

RED PEPPER KETCHUP
3 red peppers
60g white wine vinegar
60g caster sugar

LAMB RIBS
12–15 lamb ribs (approximately 1kg), cut to individual ribs (ask your butcher)
1 tbsp olive oil

FOR THE SPICY SICHUAN RUB
Place the Sichuan peppercorns, cumin and fennel seeds, star anise, cardamom pods, cloves and cinnamon in a heavy-based frying pan, preferably a cast-iron one. Toast the seeds and spices over medium heat until smoking and fragrant but not burnt. Remove from the heat and transfer to a bowl, adding the sugar, salt, cayenne pepper, paprika and garlic powder. Blend the spice mix to a powder using a spice or coffee grinder, or mortar and pestle. Set aside until required. The rub can be stored in an airtight container for up to 10 days.

FOR THE RED PEPPER KETCHUP
Blacken the peppers on a grill or naked flame on the stovetop, until charred all over. Transfer to a bowl and cover tightly with clingfilm. Alternatively, use a resealable sandwich bag. Set aside for 10–15 minutes so that the peppers can sweat in their own residual steam, making them easier to peel.

Warm the vinegar in a saucepan over medium heat and stir the sugar into it to dissolve.

Peel, deseed and roughly chop the peppers. Transfer to a food processor and blitz with the vinegar liquid until smooth. Season with salt to taste.

FOR THE LAMB RIBS
Set a barbecue up for single-zone, direct grilling (page 17) – ensuring that you are cooking on hot embers.

At this point you can choose to skewer the ribs as they would in a Turkish mangal – using 2 thin metal skewers running through either end of each rib, until you have connected 6 or 7 ribs at a time, and then repeat the process for the remaining ribs with a second set of skewers. Alternatively, simply place each rib individually on the grill rack and cook for 7–10 minutes, turning frequently, until the fat has crisped and charred and the meat has cooked through.

Remove the ribs from the grill and toss together generously with the spice mix in a large bowl. Each rib needs to be heavily coated all over in spices.

TO SERVE
Serve immediately, still piping hot, with the red pepper ketchup – this will counter the heat of the Sichuan peppercorns with a sweet acidity.

SMOKED BEEF BRISKET
WITH CARDAMOM RICE, BROAD BEANS & BURNT BUTTER YOGHURT

Beef brisket is often lauded as one of the most challenging cuts of meat to barbecue, and the true test of a pit-master's skill level. Revered across the Southern states of America, its reputation is not without foundation: a temperamental cut of meat that makes you work for your money.

It's essentially a tough cut of meat, taken from the front breast of the cow, which the animal engages endlessly for the purposes of feeding from the cud. It's therefore quite lean, lacking the quantity of fat found in other muscles, which otherwise help to lubricate the meat as it cooks, keeping everything lovely and moist. Beef brisket demands to be cooked low 'n' slow, as it can easily dry out when smoked at higher or fluctuating temperatures.

It's not unusual for it to take up to 18 hours to cook, during which time the internal temperature of your barbecue needs to be maintained steadily between 110°C and 125°C. In the absence of a commercial smoker, one which you can set the temperature of and leave, this is no mean feat and not for the faint-hearted. It requires your time, dedication and, most importantly of all, practice. But for those who persevere, this can be one of the most rewarding recipes that you will cook, as much for its unbelievable taste and melt-in-your-mouth texture as for the challenge accomplished.

Source great beef, the best you can, aged and hung to a deep mahogany red, with a high fat content that's blushing golden yellow. Life is too short to waste time smoking poor-quality brisket.

SERVES 10–12

SMOKED BEEF BRISKET
4kg beef brisket, point end (ask your butcher)

100g Turkish Coffee Beef Rub (page 247)

BROAD BEANS
400g frozen or fresh broad beans, podded

50ml extra virgin olive oil

grated zest and juice of 1 lemon

2 tbsp chopped mint

flaked sea salt (such as Maldon) and coarse ground black pepper

BURNT BUTTER YOGHURT
100g unsalted butter

250g full-fat natural yoghurt

2 tbsp lemon juice

FOR THE SMOKED BEEF BRISKET
Set a barbecue up for two-zone indirect grilling (page 17) or smoking with an internal barbecue temperature of around 115–120°C. It's important that you maintain the temperature within this range throughout the entire cook because brisket has a tendency to dry out if the temperature gets too high.

Rub the brisket all over with the Turkish coffee rub, place it, point-side up, on the grill rack, offset from the coals, and smoke for between 10–14 hours (each brisket will yield a different cook time with quite a wide spread in variability), until the internal temperature of the meat when probed with a thermometer at its thickest point is 87–88°C. Keep probing the meat throughout. There's nothing worse than shooting over the desired temperature, then lamenting a dried-out piece of beef and the wasted hours to boot.

When the beef is nearing the end of its cook time, start to prepare the remaining elements of the dish.

FOR THE BROAD BEANS
In a large bowl, dress the broad beans in extra virgin olive oil, lemon zest and juice and chopped mint, and season to taste with flaked salt and coarse black pepper. It should be quite sharp and fresh.

Don't make this too far in advance. The lemon will strip the broad beans and mint of their vibrant green – an important aesthetic to the finished dish.

FOR THE BURNT BUTTER YOGHURT

Melt the butter in a medium-sized heavy-based saucepan over a medium heat. Whisk or swirl the butter gently as it cooks, skimming any foam, until it caramelises and darkens to a nut-brown, about 5–6 minutes.

Transfer the burnt butter to a bowl and stir through the yoghurt and lemon juice. Season to taste.

TO FINISH THE BEEF BRISKET

Once the beef brisket has hit the optimum internal temperature, pull it out from your barbecue, wrap it in several layers of clingfilm and leave to rest on a wire rack set over a tray for a minimum of 30 minutes, preferably somewhere warm, loosely covered in tin foil. Turn the brisket halfway through its rest.

TO GARNISH AND SERVE

I like to serve all the elements together as a single, glorious platter of goodness, but this is entirely up to you – if you prefer, you can plate it up individually.

Slice the beef brisket against the grain (although the two muscles that make up the brisket, the flat and point, run in different directions, so you will have some beef running with the grain as you slice it) and layer it on top. I serve the brisket with cardamom and currant basmati rice (page 200), piled on a suitably sized serving platter, spread to its edges. I then top with the brisket and garnish the whole platter with broad beans, pomegranate seeds, chopped herbs, pine nuts and crispy shallots, and serve accompanied by the burnt butter yoghurt.

BARBECUE-ROASTED QUAIL
WITH LEMON THYME & LAVENDER HONEY, BLACK GRAPES & ZA'ATAR

SERVES 4

4 whole quail

BRINE
1 tbsp fennel seeds
2 tbsp coriander seeds
2 cinnamon sticks
60g soft light brown sugar
160g table salt
250ml just-boiled water,
  plus 2 litres cold water
3 dried bay leaves
2 garlic cloves, crushed

QUAIL MARINADE
2 garlic clove, grated
grated zest of ½ lemon
1½ tbsp ground cumin
80ml olive oil
1 tbsp za'atar

LEMON THYME AND LAVENDER
  HONEY
2 tbsp runny honey, loosened with
  ½ tbsp of warm water
1 tbsp chopped lemon thyme
  leaves
1 tbsp dried or fresh lavender
  flowers
grated zest of ½ a lemon

BLACK GRAPES
4 small bunches of black seedless
  (preferably) grapes
4–5 tsp water
2 tbsp soft light brown sugar

SERVE
1 lemon, quartered

FOR THE BRINE
Lightly toast the fennel and coriander seeds and cinnamon sticks in a frying pan until smoking and fragrant. In a container large enough to hold the quail (a saucepan works well), combine the sugar and salt with 250ml of just-boiled water, and stir to dissolve. Add the toasted spices, bay leaves, garlic and 2 litres of cold water, and stir. Immerse the quail and leave to brine for 2–4 hours.

FOR THE QUAIL MARINADE
Put all the marinade ingredients in a small bowl, and stir until well combined.

Remove the quail from the brine and pat dry with kitchen paper.

Rub the quail with the marinade, making sure they're well coated all over, and set aside, refrigerated, for 2–4 hours.

FOR THE LEMON THYME AND LAVENDER HONEY
Combine the honey, lemon thyme, lavender and lemon zest in a small bowl.

FOR THE THE QUAIL
Set a barbecue up for two-zone indirect grilling (page 17) with an internal barbecue temperature of 180°C.

Grill the quail, breast-side down, turning once halfway through, at 180°C for 15–20 minutes or until the internal temperature once probed reaches 65°C.

Alternatively, roast the quail in the oven. Preheat the oven to 200°C/180°C Fan/Gas mark 6 and cook for 10–15 minutes until the internal temperature when probed with a thermometer reaches 65°C and the juices all but run clear when pierced to the thigh. Let rest for 5–7 minutes before serving.

FOR THE BLACK GRAPES
Place the grapes in a cast-iron pan or roasting tray suitable for your barbecue, and sprinkle them with water followed by the sugar. Roast on the vine, indirectly with the barbecue lid on, alongside the quail. Alternatively, roast them in an oven preheated to 220°C/200°C Fan/Gas mark 7 for 10–12 minutes or until shrivelled but still juicy.

TO FINISH THE QUAIL
Finish the quail by reverse-searing them directly over the burning coals to colour the skin, about 1–2 minutes on each side.

TO SERVE
Serve the quail, seasoned with some flaked salt and coarse ground black pepper, drizzled with the honey and alongside the roasted black grapes. Add a lemon quarter to be squeezed over the top for good measure.

BUTTERMILK CHICKEN SHISH KEBAB
WITH QUICK LEMON PICKLE & OREGANO

Shish (or cis) kebab – skewered pieces of cubed meat – is commonplace to all the cuisines across the Levant and Middle East. Most chicken shish kebabs will use breast meat, which is lean but lacks the juiciness and flavour of thigh meat. I use thigh meat, but feel free to use whichever you prefer.

SERVES 2–4

BUTTERMILK CHICKEN SHISH

100ml buttermilk

½ tsp ground cumin

¼ tsp cayenne pepper

1 tsp sweet paprika

¼ tsp ground cinnamon

2 garlic cloves, minced

2 tbsp Garlic Oil (page 260) or olive oil

1 tbsp hot red pepper paste (biber salcasi)

grated zest and juice of 1 lemon

1 tsp salt

¼ tsp coarse ground black pepper

½ onion, sliced

8 chicken thighs, deboned, skinned and quartered

2 green pepper, deseeded and cut into chunks

2 red pepper, deseeded and cut into chunks

1 red onion, peeled and quartered

4 thin metal skewers, approximately 40–45cm long

GARNISH AND SERVE

pitas or flatbread

2 tbsp olive oil or Garlic Oil (page 260), plus extra to brush

1 tbsp thinly sliced spring onion

1 tbsp picked oregano leaves

12 Confit Garlic Cloves (page 260)

1 tbsp Quick-preserved Lemon Pickle (page 251)

Toum (Garlic Sauce) (page 261)

Middle Eastern Slaw (page 180)

FOR THE BUTTERMILK CHICKEN SHISH

Put the buttermilk, spices, garlic, garlic oil, hot red pepper paste, lemon zest and juice, salt, pepper and onion in a bowl and stir together to combine.

Add the chicken pieces to the marinade and massage the mixture into the chicken to ensure it's evenly distributed and well coated. Cover the bowl and leave in the fridge for 4–6 hours or preferably overnight.

TO FINISH THE CHICKEN

Skewer the chicken pieces intermittently with the red and green pepper and the red onion.

Set a barbecue up for single-zone, direct grilling (page 17) – ensuring that you are cooking on medium-hot embers. Grill the skewers directly over the burning coals, turning frequently to ensure both sides are well coloured and the chicken is cooked all the way through when checked with a knife (or to an internal temperature of 70°C or above when probed with a thermometer).

Brush the pitas or flatbreads with a little olive oil mixed with a few drops of water, and warm through briefly on the grill. They can be placed directly on top of the skewers if there isn't sufficient room in the barbecue.

TO GARNISH AND SERVE

Remove the pitas and transfer to a serving platter. Place the skewered chicken thighs atop, brushed with olive oil. Scatter the spring onion and oregano leaves liberally over the skewers, along with the confit garlic cloves and lemon pickle.

This kebab is great served with garlic sauce, Middle Eastern Slaw (page 180) and pickles of choice (see chapter 8).

PULLED SHAWARMA-SPICED LAMB
WITH GARLIC SAUCE, PICKLES & THE REST

I think this dish is the truest representation of what we at Berber & Q try to be about. A large pile of meat served to the whole table with bread to rip with your hands and sauces and salads and pickles, for everyone to share, with friends, family, loved ones, to enjoy, to laugh and to love. This is a philosophy of how we want to live, through our food and how we eat it.

Shawarma refers to the technique of carving slow-cooked meat from a rotating spit. Realistically, this is not something most people (or anybody) will be able to do at home. So we spice our lamb instead with sweet shawarma spices, and carve or pull it apart to create the same effect.

SERVES 4

LAMB SHOULDER
100g Shawarma Rub (page 243)
1 lamb shoulder, weighing
    2–2.5kg, on the bone
olive oil
80g unsalted butter, softened at
    room temperature

HERB SALAD
handful each of picked mint, dill
    and flat-leaf parsley leaves
bunch of chives, cut into 2.5cm
    batons
olive oil

SUMAC ONIONS
1 onion, thinly sliced
½ tbsp ground sumac
½ tsp salt

SERVE (OPTIONAL)
pita bread or flatbread
House Pickles (page 255)
Toum (garlic sauce) (page 261)
Tahina Sauce (page 262)
Yemenite Dynamite (S'chug) (page
    256)

FOR THE LAMB SHOULDER

Cover the lamb all over with the shawarma rub, making sure to get into all the folds in the meat. Season generously on both sides with salt and pepper. Leave to stand at room temperature for up to an hour whilst you ready the barbecue.

Set a barbecue up for two-zone indirect grilling (page 17) with an internal barbecue temperature ranging between 130°C and 150°C for slow roasting.

Rub the lamb shoulder on both sides with olive oil and then place it on the grill rack, offset from the coals, and cook with the lid on. Slow roast the lamb for 4–5 hours, or until the internal temperature reaches 88°C when probed with a thermometer. Brush the shoulder intermittently with the softened butter throughout the cooking process.

Once cooked, remove the lamb from the barbecue and wrap it in clingfilm and tin foil for up to 30 minutes to let it rest, turning halfway through.

Alternatively, you can slow-roast the lamb in the oven. Preheat the oven to 170°C/150°C Fan/Gas mark 3 and cook for 4–5 hours, until the lamb pulls from the bone easily and can be torn apart easily by hand or using two forks. Allow to rest for 20–30 minutes before serving.

Whilst the meat is resting, get on with the herb salad and sumac onions.

FOR THE HERB SALAD

Combine the herbs in a bowl and, just prior to serving, drizzle with olive oil.

FOR THE SUMAC ONIONS

Dress the sliced onions with sumac and salt just prior to serving the lamb. Make sure not to do this too far in advance, since the salt will wilt the onions, and the sumac will stain them an unappetising shade of grey.

TO FINISH THE LAMB SHOULDER

Pull the lamb into large chunks with your hands or two forks and season to taste with salt and black pepper, as well as adding any leftover rub.

TO SERVE

Serve with pita bread, herb salad, sumac onions, house pickles and kebab sauces. I like to use toum, tahina and Yemenite dynamite, but it is up to you.

SKILLET-ROASTED MECHOUI CHICKEN
WITH CONFIT GARLIC & PAN JUICE GRAVY

Cast-iron pans are integral to this recipe and an important barbecuing tool to own; I have many in all different shapes and sizes. Iron absorbs heat beautifully, distributing it evenly across the whole pan and retaining it long after it's taken off the heat. The pans never bend or warp, no matter how hot they might get, which makes them perfect for cooking over fire. What you pay in price for cast-iron cookware you easily get back in durability and lifespan, not to mention quality of your barbecued food.

SERVES 4

MECHOUI BUTTER

2 large spring onions, white parts only, cut in half lengthways

4 tbsp olive oil

½ tsp salt

80g unsalted butter (approximately 2 tbsp), softened to room temperature

4 tbsp cumin seeds, toasted and finely ground

2 tbsp hot smoked paprika

2 garlic cloves, finely grated

juice of 1 lemon

CHICKEN

4 chicken legs with thighs still attached

2 tbsp salt

2 tsp coarse ground black pepper

2 bay leaves

4 sprigs of lemon thyme

2 rosemary sprigs

PAN-JUICE GRAVY

100ml white wine

1 tbsp plain flour

200ml chicken stock (use the best quality you can afford or homemade)

grated zest and juice of 1 lemon

16 Confit Garlic Cloves (page 260)

2 tsp ground cumin

handful of picked basil leaves

FOR THE MECHOUI BUTTER

Preheat the grill to medium-high. Brush the spring onion halves with 1 tablespoon of the olive oil, season with salt and lay them on a wire rack. Blacken the spring onions under the grill until charred and softened, about 4–6 minutes. Remove from the grill and leave to cool before chopping them as finely as possible. Combine the remaining olive oil with butter, cumin, paprika, garlic and lemon in a bowl and add the chopped blackened spring onion. Whisk together until well incorporated or alternatively use a stand mixer if you have one.

FOR THE CHICKEN

Rub the butter all over the chicken, being sure to get under the skin of each piece. Season with salt and pepper, and set aside to marinate for 2–3 hours or preferably overnight. Preheat the oven to 200°C/180°C Fan/Gas mark 6. When ready to cook, heat a large heavy-based cast-iron pan over high heat until smoking hot. (You may need to use a couple of pans to accommodate all 4 pieces of chicken at the same time.) Wipe any excess marinade ingredients off the chicken and then place in the pan, skin-side down. Place a heavy-based pan on top to press the chicken pieces down. Cook for 5–7 minutes until the skin has turned a deep golden colour, before turning over to seal the underside for a few minutes. Add the bay leaves, lemon thyme and rosemary to the pan and transfer to the oven to continue to cook until the chicken has an internal temperature of 70°C when probed with a thermometer to the bone. Remove the chicken and sit it on a wire rack to rest while you make the gravy.

FOR THE PAN-JUICE GRAVY

Place the pan used for the chicken over high heat and pour in the wine, stirring to deglaze and making sure to scrape the meat juices that have caramelised and stuck to the bottom of the pan. Reduce until the wine has almost evaporated, then add the flour and whisk to incorporate. The sauce will thicken, forming a roux. Stir in the stock and lower the heat to medium, allowing the sauce to bubble and thicken as it reduces – it should be the consistency of thick double cream. Strain the sauce into a shallow, wide non-stick frying pan and place over low heat. Add the lemon zest and juice, the confit garlic cloves (with any residual oil that clings to them), the cumin and the basil leaves, then stir. Season the pan juices with salt and black pepper to taste, then return the chicken pieces to the pan to warm through and coat in the sauce.

GARNISH

2 tbsp finely chopped coriander

1 spring onion, green part only
(see above), thinly sliced

4 tbsp Chilli Pangratatto (optional)
(page 241)

TO GARNISH

Transfer the chicken pieces to a platter and serve immediately with the pan juices poured all over the top, garnished with the coriander, spring onion and chilli pangratatto.

PORK RIB ROAST
WITH CORN PURÉE, GRILLED SPRING ONION & ROSE HARISSA GRAVY

A standing pork-rib roast is an elegant joint of meat to serve over a Sunday lunch. Bring it to the table whole and slice it as you serve – which will bring a sense of theatre to the whole production.

Be mindful of the internal temperature of the meat. Pork dries out quite noticeably when pushed over its edge. It should be just blushing with a hint of pink hue. I take it out at 55°C with the knowledge that the temperature will increase during the resting time. If it gets to 60°C before you take it off, it's gone too far. Take a deep breath. Relax. There are worse things that can happen. (Pictured overleaf).

SERVES 4–6

MASTER BRINE
300g table salt
250ml just-boiled water, plus
   4 litres water
200g caster sugar

CORN PURÉE
4 corn-on-the-cobs, husks removed,
   kernels cut from cobs
160ml water
60g unsalted butter
1 tbsp sugar
40g soft goat's cheese (eg.
   Chavroux), crumbled
1 red chilli, deseeded and finely
   chopped
1 tsp Chinese chilli oil (optional)

PORK RIB ROAST
50g Pork Rub (page 247)
½ pork loin back rib roast, 6-bone,
   weighing 1.5–2kg, chine
   removed (ask your butcher)

ROSE HARISSA GRAVY
1 tsp coriander seeds, crushed
1 garlic clove, minced
200ml cider
100ml apple juice
250ml chicken stock or water
2 tbsp Rose Harissa or Harissa
   (page 259) or shop-bought

FOR THE MASTER BRINE

Add the salt to the hot water and stir to dissolve, forming a sludge-like consistency. Top up with the remaining 4 litres of water. Add the sugar and stir to combine.

Submerge the loin of pork in the brine and set aside, refrigerated, for 8–12 hours or overnight.

FOR THE CORN PURÉE

Heat the corn kernels in a saucepan with the water, butter and sugar, and season liberally with salt and pepper.

Bring to the boil over a high heat and then reduce the heat to low and simmer for 20 minutes, or until the corn is tender.

Drain the corn, reserving the liquor to help blend the purée. Transfer the corn to a food processor and blend until smooth, gradually adding some of the cooking liquor until the desired consistency is achieved. It should not be too loose, nor too dry, but maintain a steady balance between the two, with a consistency not too dissimilar to wet polenta or grits.

Transfer the purée to a small saucepan, and stir in the goats' cheese, chilli and, if using, Chinese chilli oil. Check the seasoning and adjust if necessary. Set aside until required.

FOR THE PORK RIB ROAST

Remove the pork from the brine and pat dry with some kitchen paper. Rub the pork all over with the pork rub, ensuring that it's coated thoroughly on all sides.

A pork loin roast benefits from slowly bringing the internal temperature up to the desired target, before being reverse-seared to colour it on the outside.

Set a barbecue up for two-zone indirect grilling (page 17) at a target temperature of 130–150°C. Roast the pork in a heavy-based cast-iron pan, bone-side down with the barbecue lid on, for 2–3 hours or until the internal temperature of the meat when probed with a thermometer reaches 55°C.

GARNISH AND SERVE
6 spring onions, halved and
blackened on the grill
picked purple basil leaves

Top up the fire with some fresh, hot coals and transfer the pork roast so that it's grilling directly over the burning hot embers to sear on all sides.

Pull the pork from the barbecue and leave to rest, loosely covered with foil, for 20 minutes, turning halfway through. Meanwhile, make the gravy.

FOR THE ROSE HARISSA GRAVY

Transfer the cast-iron pan that cooked the pork to the stovetop and place over medium heat. Add the coriander seeds and garlic, and cook gently whilst scraping off the residual meat juices that have collected around the edges of the pan with a wooden spoon.

Pour in the cider, apple juice and stock, and bring to a gentle simmer for 15 minutes or until the sauce has reduced to a thickened gravy consistency.

Stir in the rose harissa, season with salt and pepper to taste and keep warm until required.

TO GARNISH AND SERVE

You can serve the roast whole or sliced into individual chops, with the rose harissa gravy, corn purée and grilled spring onions alongside and some picked purple basil leaves (if using) strewn across each plate.

● ●

NOTE

The pork rib roast can also be slow-roasted in the oven. Preheat the oven to 120°C/100°C Fan/Gas mark ½ and roast for approximately 2.5 hours, until the internal temperature when probed with a thermometer reaches 55°C. Turn the temperature of the oven up to 250°C/230°C Fan/Gas mark 9 and cook for a further 15–20 minutes to let colour and crisp on the outside. Let rest for 15–20 minutes before serving.

SMOKED WHOLE CHICKEN MUSAKHAN

I guarantee that once you've smoked a chicken offset and indirect in the barbecue it will always be your preferred cooking method. There's something about its smoky juiciness and blackened skin that elevates it above and beyond your standard oven roast. Not that I'm knocking a good oven-roasted chicken, which has a dear place in all of our hearts. But give it a go and see for yourself.

Musakhan is a Palestinian dish in which taboon bread is used to soak up the juices from sweet caramelised onions and roasted chicken heavy in sumac. Whoever came up with it is a genius.

SERVES 4

SHAWARMA-SPICED GLAZE
100g runny honey
75ml olive oil
½ tbsp Shawarma Rub (page 243)
juice of ½ lemon

SMOKED WHOLE CHICKEN
MUSAKHAN
1 chicken, weighing 1.5–1.8kg
50g Shawarma Rub (page 243)
flaked sea salt (such as Maldon)
   and coarse ground black pepper
½ lemon
3–4 sprigs of thyme
½ head of garlic
3 red onions
80ml extra virgin olive oil
1½ tbsp date molasses
1½ tbsp ground sumac
4 small taboon breads, roughly
   15.5cm in diameter, or 2 large
   taboon breads roughly 25cm in
   diameter
2 tbsp pine nuts, toasted
1 tbsp flaked almonds, toasted

FOR THE SHAWARMA-SPICED GLAZE

Combine all the ingredients for the glaze in a saucepan and place over medium heat, whisking to incorporate. Set aside until required. Over time, the glaze will split out, but it's nothing a good old whisk with a firm hand won't bring back together.

FOR THE SMOKED WHOLE CHICKEN MUSAKHAN

Set a barbecue up for two-zone indirect grilling (page 17) with an internal barbecue temperature of around 180°C.

Rub the chicken all over with the shawarma rub and season generously inside the cavity with salt and pepper. Stuff the chicken with the lemon half, thyme sprigs and garlic, and set on the grill rack, offset from the coals. Add a few chunks of wood to the fire to impart some smokiness, and cook indirectly, breast-side up, with the barbecue lid on, for 1¼–1½ hours until the juices run clear when probed at the thigh joint and the internal temperature reads 70°C. Baste the chicken intermittently throughout with the shawarma-spiced glaze.

Whilst the chicken is cooking, place the onions in the white coals of your barbecue or fire pit, and leave them to char and soften all the way through, ideally so they still have a bit of bite in them.

Once the onions are cooked, leave them to cool slightly and then peel off the outer layers of charred skin, preferably using gloves. Transfer the peeled onions to a chopping board and hack them up into rough, bite-size pieces. Dress with extra virgin olive oil, date molasses and 1 tablespoon of sumac, and season generously with salt and pepper.

Once the chicken has cooked all the way through, finish by quickly grilling it directly over the coals for 1–2 minutes on all sides, just to colour up the skin nicely. Remove it from the barbecue and leave it to rest somewhere warm for 10 minutes, loosely covered with tin foil.

Preheat a grill to 220°C. Spread the onion mix onto the base of the taboon bread. Hack the chicken into 8 pieces and divide evenly amongst them. Drizzle some olive oil over the top of the chicken and sprinkle the pine nuts and toasted flaked almonds over the whole thing.

Grill the musakhan for 3–4 minutes – just enough time to nicely char the chicken and warm the bread through without burning any of the elements. Keep your eye on it as it grills.

TO GARNISH AND SERVE
(OPTIONAL)

½ tbsp za'atar

small handful of picked flat-leaf
   parsley leaves

Jerusalem Chopped Salad
   (page 192)

Garlic Yoghurt (page 59)

1 lemon, halved and blackened
   on the grill

TO GARNISH AND SERVE

Transfer the musakhan to serving plates, sprinkle liberally with za'atar and the remaining sumac, and throw some picked parsley leaves on top.

I like to serve this dish accompanied by a fresh, sharp salad such the Jerusalem chopped salad, with some yoghurt and a blackened lemon half to squeeze over the top. Don't ever be afraid to finish with a final drizzle of extra virgin olive oil – it almost always makes food, and life, taste even better.

BARBECUED CUMIN LAMB CHOPS
WITH ANCHOVY BUTTER & LEMON YOGHURT

Ansel Mullins manages Istanbul Eats, a company running the most brilliant food tours in Istanbul. If you're ever in the city, I implore any food lover to look up his services. His knowledge and passion for the food of Turkey and Istanbul is unparalleled. It was he who took me to Al Zubeyir, in the Beyoglu. It's easily one of my favourite places to eat. Make a booking in advance and ask to sit at the grill face. To watch the usta ('master' in Turkish) prepare your food is like watching a theatrical performance unfold before your very eyes, full of grace, energy, elegance, endurance (and sweat).

The lamb chops are the best I've eaten anywhere, cooked with little more than some salt and black pepper. The recipe here is a little more elaborate, but still tastes awesome.

SERVES 4

LAMB CHOPS

½ onion, finely grated

2 tbsp full-fat natural yoghurt

2 tbsp ground cumin

1 tbsp olive oil

2 tbsp lemon juice

12 whole lamb chops, best end

CUMIN SPICE RUB

2 tbsp cumin seeds

½ tsp caraway seeds

½ tsp coarse ground black pepper

1 tbsp caster sugar

1 tbsp salt

1 tbsp smoked paprika

ANCHOVY BUTTER

80g unsalted butter

2 garlic cloves, minced

2 tbsp lemon juice

10 anchovies in olive oil, finely chopped

1 tbsp picked lemon thyme leaves

GARNISH AND SERVE

2 tbsp chopped flat-leaf parsley

4 tbsp Lemon Yoghurt (page 261)

M'sabaha (page 52) (optional)

Anchovy and Lemon Pangratatto (page 241)

FOR THE LAMB CHOPS

Mix the onion, yoghurt, cumin, olive oil and lemon juice in a large bowl. Add the lamb chops and use your hands to massage the marinade into the meat, ensuring that each chop is well coated. Leave to marinate covered in the fridge for a minimum of 2 hours, or preferably overnight.

FOR THE CUMIN SPICE RUB

Place the cumin and caraway seeds in a heavy-based pan. Toast over medium-high heat until smoking and fragrant but not burnt. Remove from the heat and transfer to a bowl, adding the pepper, sugar, salt and paprika. Stir to combine, then blend the spice mix to a powder using a spice or coffee grinder, or mortar and pestle. Set aside or store in an airtight container for up to 10 days.

FOR THE ANCHOVY BUTTER

Melt the butter in a small frying pan over medium-low heat, then add the garlic and fry to soften for a few minutes (being careful not to burn it). Whisk the butter gently as it cooks, until it darkens to a nut-brown, about 4–5 minutes, then add the lemon juice, anchovies and lemon thyme. Continue to cook for a few minutes before turning off the heat. Set aside, reheating when ready to serve.

TO FINISH THE LAMB CHOPS

Set a barbecue up for single-zone, direct grilling (page 17) – ensuring that you are cooking on hot embers.

Scrape off the excess marinade, dredge the chops in the rub and place on the grill rack directly above the coals. Cook for 2–3 minutes on each side, until nicely charred around the edges, the fat crisped and golden, but still soft to the touch and pink on the inside.

TO GARNISH AND SERVE

Remove from the grill and transfer to a bowl. Toss with any remaining rub and the parsley. Pile the chops on a plate and serve piping hot, with lemon yoghurt spooned over, anchovy butter and more parsley. These are great served with m'sabaha and strewn with anchovy and lemon pangratatto.

SWEET TEA-BRINED QUAIL
WITH ROMESCO

You have to work quite hard with quail for what amounts to a small yield of meat. But it's packed with flavour and worth every bit of effort.

I like to brine quail because I think it keeps the bird moist and juicy and prevents it from drying out on the grill. Some might disagree and deem this step unnecessary. As with most debates in cookery, this is entirely subjective. The sweet tea brine used in this recipe adds some sweetness (unsurprisingly) and aids the caramelisation of the skin, which should be well charred and oozing with smokiness. It was inspired by a dish I had at St Anselm in Brooklyn, New York City, one of my favourite restaurants in a city packed full of amazing places to eat.

SERVES 2

SWEET TEA BRINE
1 litre water
2 English Breakfast tea bags
200g soft light brown sugar
100g salt
10 sprigs of lemon thyme
1 head of garlic, cut in half crossways
1 lemon, thinly sliced
ice cubes

QUAIL
4 quail, butterflied

ROMESCO
2 tbsp pine nuts
1 large garlic clove, peeled
1 heaped tbsp Confit Chilli Salsa (page 260)
1½ tbsp red pepper paste (biber salcasi)
2 tbsp sherry vinegar or red wine vinegar
1½ tbsp fresh breadcrumbs
1 egg yolk
80ml extra virgin olive oil

FOR THE SWEET TEA BRINE
Bring the water to the boil using a kettle or on the stovetop and steep the tea bags for 10–15 minutes.

Remove and discard the tea bags, add the remaining ingredients and stir to dissolve the sugar and salt. Cool the brine down with some ice cubes.

FOR THE QUAIL
Place the quail in the cooled brine and transfer to resealable freezer bags, or submerge in a deep storage container, covered. Refrigerate for no less than 2 hours, but no more than 4 hours.

FOR THE ROMESCO
Blitz the pine nuts and garlic in a food processor to a fine crumb-like consistency. Add the confit chilli salsa, red pepper paste and vinegar, and continue to blitz until combined.

Add the breadcrumbs and egg yolk, then pulse to combine.

With the motor running, gradually pour in the extra virgin olive oil, very slowly, until the mixture is emulsified. Season with salt and black pepper to taste and leave aside until required.

The romesco sauce will keep well in the fridge for up to 5 days.

TO FINISH THE QUAIL
Set a barbecue up for single-zone, direct grilling (page 17) – ensuring that you are cooking over hot embers.

Grill the quail for 4–5 minutes on each side until well browned and crisped.

Remove from the barbecue and serve, hacked into quarters, with the romesco sauce alongside.

ROASTED LEG OF LAMB MECHOUI
WITH HARISSA & CUMIN SALT

I stumbled across Mechoui alley in Marrakech's medina by accident and fell in love. Admittedly it's not the most hygienic-looking display of food in the world: large joints of slow-cooked lamb strewn across a butcher's block like missing body parts, a head here, a shoulder there, warming in the midday sun. But risk and reward are often closely aligned.

The entire lamb carcass is rubbed with cumin and paprika, skewered whole, and lowered into a smouldering pit dug out directly underneath the storefront, to be slow cooked for 4–6 hours, basted periodically with smen (a Moroccan version of clarified butter). They serve the lamb in large chunks on brown paper, unctuous melt-in-the-mouth fat and all, with cumin salt, harissa, some local bread and nothing else. I knew I needed to have a version of it on our menu. Unfortunately the local council wasn't open-minded enough when it came to the proposal of digging a pit underneath our restaurant, so we smoke our lamb instead.

In the absence of a large fire pit, you can replicate this easily at home by using lamb leg, or the whole front forequarter. Cook the meat indirectly, offset from the coals, with the barbecue lid on, at between 130°C and 150°C, until the meat pulls from the bone with ease (5–6 hours). Alternatively tie the lamb with butcher's twine and hang over a smoldering fire. Keep the fire burning, the meat turning, and raise or lower the leg as necessary.

SERVES 8–10

MECHOUI LAMB

1 leg of lamb (approximately 3–3.5kg), trimmed of fat and sinew

1 lemon, halved

30ml extra virgin olive oil

60g Mechoui Rub (page 247)

80g unsalted butter, softened to room temperature

1 tbsp finely chopped rosemary

2–3 garlic cloves, finely chopped

1 tbsp honey

SERVE

50g smoked paprika

50g coarse sea salt mixed with 50g ground cumin

400g Harissa (page 259)

flatbread or crusty bread

FOR THE MECHOUI LAMB

Cover a large surface or table with clingfilm upon which to lay your lamb leg. Make several slashes at random intervals across the leg and rub the lamb all over with the cut side of the halved lemon, exerting gentle pressure as you do so as to release the lemon juice.

Brush or drizzle the olive oil over the lamb on both sides. Season the leg generously with salt and coarse ground pepper and liberally dust the leg with half the mechoui rub, making sure it's completely covered.

Blend the butter with the rosemary, garlic, honey and the remaining half of the rub in a food processor to form a rough paste. Set aside until required.

Set a barbecue up for two-zone indirect grilling (page 17) with an internal barbecue temperature ranging between 130°C and 150°C for slow roasting. Place the lamb on the grill rack, offset from the coals, with a drip pan stationed directly underneath it, and cook with the lid on. Slow roast the lamb for 5–6 hours, brushing the leg regularly with the softened butter throughout the cooking process, until the juices run clear and the meat easily pulls away from the bone.

Alternatively, roast the lamb in the oven. Preheat the oven to 250°C/230°C Fan/Gas mark 9 for 20 minutes to colour on the outside before turning the temperature down to 160°C/140°C/Gas mark 3. Basting every 15–20 minutes or so with the collected butter and pan juices, cook for approximately 2.5 hours, until the lamb is completely tender and falling from the bone.

TO SERVE

Once cooked, set aside to rest for 20 minutes before carving into large chunks. Serve the lamb with a small pile of smoked paprika, salt mixed with cumin and some harissa for dipping, and flatbread or a crusty loaf of bread.

CALF'S LIVER
WITH POMEGRANATE-GLAZED ONIONS, SAGE & TAHINA YOGHURT

I have a love for all things liver-related. I eat, and enjoy it, any-which-way it comes.

Grilled lamb's liver chopped up into small pieces and served with harissa and bread is a streetfood speciality sold in the medina of Marrakech. In Turkey, there are restaurants dedicated to selling only skewered cow and lamb liver kebabs, where it is revered as a delicacy. The Lebanese and Israelis prefer to use chicken, which is often served as a mezze, or as part of a Jerusalem grill.

This recipe uses calf's liver, drawing on inspiration from one of my favourite Italian dishes, in which it's seared and served with sweet, slow-cooked caramelised onions and balanced with the sharpness of some balsamic vinegar glaze.

All liver, no matter the animal, should be cooked in the same way; seared hard and fast over a medium-high heat so that it caramelises quickly on its outside but stays pink on the inside. Check the heat of your fire with the back of your hand at the distance you intend to cook from. Three seconds is all you should be able to manage.

SERVES 2
AS A LIGHT MEAL

POMEGRANATE-GLAZED
   ONIONS
50ml olive oil
3 red onions, thinly sliced
3 garlic cloves, left whole
4 sprigs of lemon thyme
1 tbsp unsalted butter
2½ tbsp pomegranate molasses

TAHINA YOGHURT
2 tbsp Tahina Sauce (page 262)
1 tbsp full-fat natural yoghurt
½ tbsp lemon juice

CRISP SAGE LEAVES
vegetable oil, for frying
6–8 picked sage leaves

CALF'S LIVER
250–300g calf's liver, outer
   membrane removed, cut into
   4 pieces
olive oil, for brushing and drizzling
small handful of pomegranate
   seeds (optional), to garnish

FOR THE POMEGRANATE-GLAZED ONIONS
Heat the olive oil in a heavy-based frying pan over medium heat and add the onions, garlic and lemon thyme. Sauté for 7–10 minutes to soften and caramelise the onions.

Season to taste with salt and black pepper, then add the butter to the pan and allow it to melt, before finishing by adding the pomegranate molasses. Allow the molasses to bubble and simmer to reduce it to a thickened, glaze-like consistency before taking the pan off the heat and setting aside until required.

FOR THE TAHINA YOGHURT
Combine the tahina sauce, yoghurt and lemon juice in a bowl and whisk to incorporate. Check for seasoning and add more salt or lemon juice if necessary.

FOR THE CRISP SAGE LEAVES
Heat the vegetable oil in a cast-iron pan or shallow frying pan over medium-high heat, until bubbling hot. Fry the sage leaves until crisp and transfer to kitchen paper to absorb any excess oil. Season generously with salt.

FOR THE CALF'S LIVER
Calf's liver is best served pink and requires quick searing on both sides over a high heat, as opposed to gentle cooking over a low one.

Set a barbecue up for single-zone, direct grilling (page 17) – ensuring that you are cooking on hot embers, adjusting the distance between the coals and grill rack if practical and possible, in order to minimise the distance between the meat and the heat.

Season the liver with salt and pepper on both sides and brush with olive oil. Warm the onions up in a cast-iron pan on the grill next to where you plan to cook your liver. Alternatively, bring the onions back to temperature on the stovetop.

Flash-grill the liver on the grill rack directly over the burning embers for approximately 2 minutes on both sides, turning only once to ensure the meat is well scored. Transfer the liver to the pan containing the onions and cook for a further minute, glazing the meat with the sauce. Remove the pan from the heat and allow the liver to rest in the pan for a couple of minutes.

TO SERVE
Spread the tahina yoghurt on a serving plate, then place the onions on top, as a bed for the incoming liver. Transfer the liver to the plate and garnish with the crisp sage leaves and pomegranate seeds. You could finish with a drizzle of oil, but you know that already.

SAFFRON & TURMERIC CHICKEN THIGHS (JOOJEH KEBAB)
WITH SAFFRON YOGHURT, BURNT LEMON & ZA'ATAR

Jujeh, meaning chicken or grilled chicken in Persian, is a kebab of Iranian origin and a staple of any self-respecting Persian grill house. We've had this on our menu since we first opened. Marinate for as long as possible, since the turmeric stains it a beautiful yellow, that intensifies over time.

SERVES 2–4

CHICKEN THIGHS

2 garlic cloves, peeled and chopped

1 onion, coarsely grated

juice of 2 lemons

1 tbsp ground turmeric

1 tsp ground cumin

1 tsp salt

½ tsp coarse ground black pepper

120ml saffron water (a pinch of saffron soaked in 120ml boiling water, infused for 15 minutes)

2 tbsp full-fat natural yoghurt

1½ tbsp vegetable oil

8 chicken thighs, deboned, cleaned, skinned and cut in half

1 red onion, sliced into 1cm rounds

1 lemon, sliced into 0.5cm rounds

4 flat metal skewers, approximately 2cm wide and 40–45cm long

SAFFRON YOGHURT

50ml saffron water (see above)

1 garlic clove, grated

160g Greek yoghurt

1½ tbsp lemon juice

1 tbsp extra virgin olive oil

GARNISH AND SERVE

pita or flatbread

2 tbsp olive oil

1 tbsp pomegranate seeds

1 tbsp finely chopped parsley

pinch of za'atar

Blackened Chilli Kebab Sauce (page 256)

FOR THE CHICKEN THIGHS
Put the garlic, onion, lemon juice, spices, salt and pepper in a bowl and stir to combine. In a separate bowl, combine the saffron water with the yoghurt and vegetable oil, and stir together until well mixed. Add the garlic and onion mixture to this bowl. Pat the chicken thighs dry and add them to the marinade. Massage the mixture into the chicken to ensure it's evenly distributed and well coated in the marinade. Cover the bowl and leave in the fridge for 4–6 hours or preferably overnight. The flavours will intensify the more time it is given.

FOR THE SAFFRON YOGHURT
Combine all the ingredients in a bowl and stir well. Set aside in the fridge until required. The flavours will improve and the colour of the yoghurt will intensify with time, so it's best prepared at the same time as marinating the chicken. Whisk or stir the yoghurt one last time just before serving.

TO FINISH THE CHICKEN
Set a barbecue up for single-zone, direct grilling (page 17) ensuring you are cooking on medium-hot embers. Weave the marinated chicken pieces on to the metal skewers, making sure the chicken is well affixed. Grill directly over the burning coals, turning frequently to ensure both sides are well coloured and the chicken is cooked all the way through when checked with a knife (or to an internal temperature of 70°C or above when probed with a thermometer). Meanwhile, blacken the onion and lemon slices on both sides.

TO GARNISH AND SERVE
Brush the pitas or flatbreads with a little garlic oil mixed with a drop of water, and warm through briefly on the grill. They can be placed directly on top of the skewers if there isn't sufficient room on the barbecue grill.

Remove the pitas and transfer to a serving platter. Place the skewered chicken thighs atop, brushed with garlic oil, and drizzle the saffron yoghurt over everything. Top with the red onion and lemon slices, pomegranate seeds, parsley and za'atar. Serve with kebab sauce.

● ●
TIP
If the chicken is burning on the outside without cooking internally, shuffle the coals to one side of the barbecue and transfer the skewers to the other side. Put a lid on and cook the thighs indirectly until cooked all the way through.

CHAPTER 03

FISH & SHELLFISH

SKEWERED MONKFISH KEBABS
WITH GREEN CHARMOULA DRESSING & CAPER MAYONNAISE

My dear mother Evelyn, to who I owe not just my life but also my love of food, insisted I find a way of mentioning her in this book. She used to make a version of this dish for my brothers and me when we were kids. This is a riff on her dish, which I always used to love.

Monkfish has an almost meat-like quality to it, great for the barbecue and perfect for sandwiching between bits of bread. Play around with the fillings. Go crazy.

SERVES 4

MONKFISH

800g monkfish tail, skinned and
   filleted (ask your fishmonger)

3 garlic cloves

zest of 1 lemon

100ml olive oil

2 cardamom pods, seeds ground

1 small bunch of spring onions,
   thinly sliced, white parts only,
   green parts reserved (see below)

4 thin metal skewers, 30–35cm
   long

GREEN CHARMOULA

green parts of spring onion (see
   above), sliced thinly

2 tbsp finely chopped coriander

1 tbsp chopped flat-leaf parsley

70ml olive oil

2 garlic cloves, grated

3 green chilli, finely chopped

1 tsp ground cumin

2 tbsp lemon juice

CAPER MAYONNAISE

100g mayonnaise

1 tbsp soured cream

1 tbsp capers, drained and rinsed

GARNISH AND SERVE

1 large baguette, cut into 4 pieces,
   sliced open

sliced green parts of spring onion

picked coriander leaves

Herb Salad (optional) (page 263)

FOR THE MONKFISH

Portion the monkfish into rough 5cm pieces and transfer to a bowl. Grate the garlic and lemon zest over the top. Add the olive oil, ground cardamom seeds, the white part of the sliced spring onion and some seasoning. Work the marinade into the fish using your hands.

Set aside, covered and refrigerated, for at least 1 hour, preferably 4–6 hours.

FOR THE GREEN CHARMOULA

In a bowl, combine half the sliced spring onion greens with the remaining ingredients for the charmoula, except the lemon juice and seasoning, and set aside until required. You can make this mix in advance and keep it refrigerated until required. Reserve the remaining half of the spring onion greens for garnish.

Fold the lemon juice through the chermoula just prior to using. Taste for seasoning and adjust accordingly. Add more lemon juice if necessary.

FOR THE CAPER MAYONNAISE

Combine the mayonnaise, soured cream and capers in a small bowl and mix well. Season to taste with salt and black pepper.

TO FINISH THE MONKFISH

Set a barbecue up for single-zone, direct grilling (page 17) – ensuring that you are cooking over medium-hot embers.

Thread the monkfish onto metal skewers and grill directly over the coals for 4–5 minutes on each side, basting with the marinade juices. (If the fish is sticking to the grill, leave for a few minutes, until it releases naturally; don't force it.)

The kebabs should be nicely coloured on the surface and be firm to the touch, with just the slightest give when pressed. Ideally, the flesh should still be blushing and moist, not dry. For this, there is no substitute for practice.

TO GARNISH AND SERVE

Brush the bottom half of each baguette with the caper mayonnaise. Remove the fish from the skewers, using the individual baguette pieces as a glove to safely handle and de-skewer the kebab. Liberally drizzle the green charmoula over the entire sandwich, so that it soaks into the bread as well as coating the fish.

Garnish with spring onions and coriander leaves and serve with the herb salad.

GRILLED OCTOPUS SABICH

Sabich is a traditional Jewish sandwich of Iraqi origin usually consisting of fried aubergine, hard-boiled egg, amba sauce and tahini (of course), though, as with most things food-related in Israel, the precise components are fiercely contested. I subbed out the egg and replaced it with octopus. And I took away the bread, so it's not actually a sandwich at all. Plunging the tentacles into boiling water several times will tenderise the meat. Ensure the fire is searing hot when you grill the octopus.

SERVES 4–6

AMBA YOGHURT

50g Amba Dressing (page 157), or shop-bought

100g full-fat natural yoghurt

½ tbsp extra virgin olive oil

OCTOPUS

1 onion, quartered

2 large carrots, peeled and quartered

2 celery stalks, cut into large pieces

6–8 garlic cloves, peeled and smashed

8–10 peppercorns

1 tbsp coriander seeds

2–3 bay leaves

parsley stalks

500ml white wine

250ml white wine vinegar

1 octopus, about 1.8kg, cleaned

30ml olive oil

2 tsp sweet paprika

GARNISH AND SERVE

1 large aubergine

1 garlic clove, grated

grated zest of 1 lemon and the juice of ½

1½ tbsp olive oil, plus extra

120g Tahina Aioli (page 264)

2 tbsp Yemenite Dynamite (S'chug) (page 256)

160g Saffron Potato Salad (page 182)

handful of picked coriander leaves

FOR THE AMBA YOGHURT

Combine the amba, yoghurt and extra virgin olive oil in a bowl. Season to taste with salt and black pepper.

FOR THE OCTOPUS

Fill a large, deep stockpot with water and add the onion, carrots, celery, garlic, peppercorns, coriander seeds, bay leaves, parsley stalks, white wine and vinegar. Season with salt and bring to the boil over high heat. Plunge the octopus into the boiling water for 3–5 seconds and pull out. Bring the water back to the boil and repeat this step a further two times.

Gently lower the octopus into the pot, reduce the heat to a gentle rolling simmer and cook for 1–1½ hours until tender to a toothpick or sharp knife. The tentacles should all but pull away from the connected head. Turn off the heat and let the octopus cool completely in the water.

Once cool enough to handle, separate the tentacles from the head with a knife and peel away the gelatinous skin, which should easily rub off in your hands. Toss the octopus in a large bowl with the olive oil and paprika, and season generously with salt and black pepper. Set aside until required.

TO FINISH THE OCTOPUS

Set a barbecue up for single-zone, direct grilling (page 17) – ensuring that you are cooking over hot embers.

Pierce the aubergine all over with a skewer and blacken on the grill until soft. Cut the aubergine open in half lengthways through the root. Scoop out the flesh onto a chopping board, add the garlic to the aubergine flesh, and chop together until a coarse and chunky purée has formed. Transfer to a large bowl and add the lemon zest and juice, and a drizzle of olive oil, then mix. Season with salt and black pepper. Add more lemon juice or seasoning as required.

Place the tentacles directly on the grill rack and sear for 2–3 minutes on both sides, turning once. Resist the urge to flip the tentacles too early or too often; you want to char them so they develop a crunchy, slightly blackened crust that will counter the tenderness of the flesh. Season each with salt and pepper.

TO GARNISH AND SERVE

Spoon some aubergine purée on each plate and dot with the amba yoghurt, tahina aioli and Yemenite dynamite (s'chug). Add some potato salad and top with the octopus. Garnish with the coriander and a drizzle of olive oil.

SEARED TUNA FISH
WITH OLIVE, PRESERVED LEMON & SLOW-ROASTED TOMATO SALSA

Of all the meaty fish out there, tuna fish is the meatiest. I treat it in much the same way you would a good piece of steak, only the cooking time is shorter. Bring it up to room temperature before grilling, and give it a brief rest once it comes off.

I have a huge aversion to tuna that's overcooked; it becomes almost inedible for me. Tuna fish should always be served rare, medium-rare at most. I think it's so important.

SERVES 4

BLACK OLIVE AND SLOW-ROASTED TOMATO SALSA

200g plum cherry tomatoes

1 tbsp caster sugar

50ml extra virgin olive oil or garlic oil (page 260)

1 tbsp finely chopped lemon thyme leaves

2 tbsp red wine vinegar

1 preserved lemon, skin only, finely chopped

1½ tbsp capers, drained and rinsed

12–15 Kalamata olives, pitted and ripped in half

2 tbsp Confit Chilli (page 260) or use 1 red chilli, finely chopped

2 tbsp roughly chopped coriander

WHITE BEAN AND ONION SALAD

1 medium white onion, very finely sliced

400g tin white beans, drained

2 tbsp chopped flat-leaf parsley

50ml extra virgin olive oil

2 tbsp white wine vinegar

TUNA

4 x 150g tuna loin steaks, ideally sashimi grade (ask your fishmonger), cut into 2.5cm thick slices

olive oil, for coating

FOR THE BLACK OLIVE AND SLOW-ROASTED TOMATO SALSA
Preheat the oven to 100°C/80°C Fan/Gas mark ¼.

Spread the tomatoes on a baking tray lined with parchment paper. Season scantly with salt and black pepper, and sprinkle the caster sugar over the entire tray. Drizzle the tomatoes with half the olive oil and throw the chopped lemon thyme on top.

Slow roast the tomatoes for 1½ hours, until shrivelled and sweetened whilst still retaining a plump moistness.

Transfer the tomatoes to a bowl. Add the rest of the oil and the remaining ingredients. Toss the salsa together gently and check for seasoning. Adjust according to taste. Try not to break the tomatoes too much whilst tossing the salsa together.

FOR THE WHITE BEAN AND ONION SALAD
Combine the onion, white beans and parsley together in a small bowl and dress with the oil and vinegar. Season with salt to taste.

FOR THE TUNA
Set a barbecue up for single-zone, direct grilling (page 17) – ensuring that you are cooking over burning hot embers.

Brush the tuna with olive oil on both sides and season liberally with salt and black pepper. Place the steaks on the hottest part of the grill rack and sear for no more than 2 minutes on each side, turning them 90 degrees halfway through, so as to score the tuna with criss-crossed grill marks. The tuna should be taken to just past rare, and certainly no more than medium.

Remove from the grill, cut in half immediately and transfer to individual plates. Douse each steak in the salsa and serve with the white bean and onion salad.

CIDER-BRAISED MUSSELS & COCKLES
WITH CHORIZO XO

Chorizo XO is dangerously delicious. It works brilliantly with fish, but is also good with grilled vegetables such as hispi cabbage. You can make it ahead of time and store it in your fridge. It will keep for at least five days. The problem is being disciplined enough to keep your hands off it until such time as it's needed.

This is a wonderful dish, full of body and soul. It will warm the cockles of your heart (pun intended).

SERVES 4

CHORIZO XO

50g dried shrimp

30g dried squid (optional)

12 garlic cloves, peeled

200g cooking chorizo (about 3 sausages)

80ml rapeseed oil

2 tbsp Confit Chilli Salsa (page 260)

1 tsp dried chilli flakes

1 tbsp demerara sugar

MUSSELS AND COCKLES

1kg live mussels, cleaned of dirt, grit and any beard

1kg cockles, cleaned of dirt and grit

50g unsalted butter

2 shallots, thinly sliced

450ml good apple cider

2 tbsp roughly chopped coriander

crusty bread

FOR THE CHORIZO XO

Soak the dried shrimp and squid (if using) overnight in tepid water to rehydrate them. Drain, transfer to a food processor and blitz to a coarse crumb-like consistency. Set aside until required.

Pulse the garlic cloves in the food processor until finely chopped.

Slice the chorizo sausage lengthways just to break the surface of the casing, and peel it away to expose the chorizo meat. Remove the meat and process it in the blender, with the garlic, until coarsely chopped.

Heat the oil in a saucepan over medium-high heat and, when shimmering, add the chorizo meat and, breaking it up with a wooden spoon as you go, fry until crisp and browned, about 4–5 minutes. Add the confit chilli salsa and chilli flakes, and continue to cook for a further 2–3 minutes.

Turn the heat down to low and fold the rehydrated shrimp and squid into the chorizo mix. Sprinkle the sugar on top, and cook for 30–35 minutes, until the sauce is all but dry and the seafood has taken on a lovely orange hue from the chorizo. Set aside until required.

FOR THE MUSSELS AND COCKLES

Tap any open mussels and cockles to make sure that they close (and are therefore still alive), and discard those that don't.

Heat a large cast-iron pan or heavy-based frying pan over the fire or on the stovetop over medium-high, and melt the butter. Sweat the shallots until translucent, but not coloured, and pour in the cider followed by the mussels, cockles and chorizo XO.

Cook for 4–5 minutes until the mussels and cockles have opened.

Serve, straight from the pan, with some chopped coriander strewn all over and some crusty bread to go to town with.

GRILLED WHOLE SEA BASS CHREIME
WITH GINGER & CORIANDER RELISH

Chreime, a Tunisian fish stew heavy on paprika and garlic, is a not too distant cousin of the bouillabaisse, brought to Southern France by the North African communities that settled there.

I like to make my chreime sauce separately and add the grilled fish fresh off the barbecue (as opposed to stewing the fish in the stock as traditional methods would have you do), since I find it imparts that heady aroma of smoke into the finished dish, which makes such a difference.

SERVES 2

GINGER AND CORIANDER
  RELISH

thumb-sized piece of ginger, peeled
  and grated

grated zest and juice of 1 lemon

1 tbsp finely chopped coriander

1 spring onion, thinly sliced

1½ tbsp extra virgin olive oil

1 tsp runny honey

CHREIME

8 garlic cloves, peeled and roughly
  chopped

1 tbsp salt

1½ tsp caraway seeds, toasted and
  ground in a spice blender

1 tsp cumin seeds, toasted and
  ground in a spice blender

120ml olive oil, plus 2 tsp olive oil
  for brushing

2 tbsp smoked paprika

1 tsp cayenne pepper

50g tomato paste

1 tbsp Red Chilli Vinegar (page
  263) or use red wine vinegar

1 tsp caster sugar

1 sea bass (preferably wild),
  600–800g, scaled and gutted

SERVE

4 slices of sourdough

FOR THE GINGER AND CORIANDER RELISH
Combine all the ingredients together in a small bowl. Season with salt and black pepper to taste and set to one side until required.

FOR THE CHREIME
Crush the garlic with the salt, caraway and cumin seeds in a mortar and pestle to a rough paste. Add a tablespoon of olive oil, as well as the paprika and cayenne pepper, and stir to combine.

Heat the rest of the olive oil in a heavy-based wide pan over medium heat. Add the garlic and spice mix to the pan and fry, stirring frequently, to infuse the oil without burning. Add the tomato paste and stir to incorporate with the oil, followed by 180ml of water.

Bring to a gentle simmer before adding the vinegar and sugar. The chreime should be rich and well spiced, balanced with a hint of sweet and sour. Taste for seasoning and adjust accordingly. Keep the sauce warm and covered whilst you sear the sea bass.

Score the sea bass 3 or 4 times with a very sharp knife, at parallel 45-degree angles on both sides. Drizzle the fish with oil and season both sides with salt and black pepper.

Set a barbecue up for single-zone, direct grilling (page 17) – ensuring that you are cooking over hot embers.

Place the sea bass horizontally in a fish barbecue basket and grill for 3–4 minutes on each side until almost cooked through. The flesh should be just opaque, slightly firm and flake when pressure is gently applied.

Transfer the sea bass carefully to the pan of sauce and bring back to a gentle simmer, spooning the sauce over the fish several times as it finishes cooking.

TO SERVE
Brush the sourdough slices with some olive oil and char over the grill until crisp at the edges and well scored. Remove the sea bass from the heat source. Strew the ginger and spring onion relish over the fish and serve straight from the pan with the grilled bread.

BARBECUED WHOLE LOBSTER & CRAWFISH BOIL

WITH TURMERIC BUTTER, BURNT BREAD, POTATOES & MERGUEZ

Of all our theatrical displays of food, our lobster and crawfish boil is probably the most immense and jaw dropping. We run it as a Sunday special as and when we feel like it and it always sells out. I've always loved what a good old-fashioned 'boil' represents. Sitting around with close family or friends, sinking beer, eating with your hands, making a mess: enjoying life. These are the virtues and aspects we wanted our restaurant to be about, captured succinctly in a single dish.

There's a lot going on in this recipe and it can be a challenge to get your head around it but I guarantee it's worth giving it a go. It helps to have a few extra pairs of hands, preferably those of people you like, cooking concurrently. The fun is as much in its preparation as it is in eating it.

And it really helps to have a big ole cool box to dump all the ingredients in as they come off the grill. It will take the pressure off having everything ready at precisely the same time by keeping everything steaming hot in the interim. (Pictured overleaf).

SERVES 12–15

TURMERIC BUTTER
1.5kg unsalted butter
4 tbsp ground turmeric
grated zest and juice of 2 lemons
12 garlic cloves, thinly sliced

LOBSTER AND CRAWFISH BOIL
6 corn-on-the-cobs, husks removed
1.5kg fingerling potatoes (or else use new potatoes if fingerlings aren't available), scrubbed
2kg live American native crawfish
1 head of celery, coarsely chopped
1 white onion, roughly chopped
2 lemons, halved
160g Pork Rub (optional) (page 247)
4–5 bay leaves
handful of flat-leaf parsley stalks with leaves
12 pink peppercorns

FOR TURMERIC BUTTER

Melt the butter in a heavy-based saucepan; add the turmeric, lemon zest and juice and garlic cloves. Tick over on medium-low heat to infuse but not to caramelise. Set aside, kept warm, until required.

FOR THE CORN AND POTATOES

Bring a large saucepan of salted water to the boil over high heat, and blanch the corn for 4–5 minutes until slightly softened and vibrant yellow in colour. Lift from the water, retaining for later use, and transfer to a chopping board. Divide each piece of corn into 3 or 4 pieces and set to one side, ideally in a sealed insulated cool box to keep warm until required.

Return the water to the boil and cook the potatoes for 12–15 minutes until tender to a knife all the way through. Lift the potatoes from the water and add them to the corn.

FOR THE CRAWFISH

Set a deep stockpot of water over high heat and bring to the boil.

Whilst you wait for the water to come up to temperature, wash the crawfish in a sink filled with cold water and salt to remove any dirt and grit. Drain and rinse the crawfish under running water and then repeat the process at least a further two times.

Add the celery, onion, lemon halves, pork rub, bay leaves, parsley and pink peppercorns to the pot and season liberally with salt.

Boil the crawfish over a rolling simmer for 4–5 minutes, until the tails curl up and they turn a lovely dark red hue. Transfer the crawfish to an insulated cool box and seal shut whilst you prepare the remaining elements of the dish.

3 live whole lobster, approximately 1–1.2kg

500g samphire

1kg merguez sausages

2kg mussels or clams, or a mixture of both, cleaned of dirt and any beard

100ml beer or apple cider

1 large ciabatta loaf

½ garlic clove (optional)

80ml olive oil

TO SERVE

12 lemons, halved and blackened on the grill

3 bunches of spring onion, blackened on the grill

bunch of coriander

450g Harissa Aioli (page 264)

FOR THE LOBSTER

While the crawfish are cooking, split the lobster in half lengthways, plunging the tip of a sharp knife into the cross shape located just beneath its head and pushing through all the way to the board, before splitting it down the middle. Remove and discard the sac and liver, and detach the claws to cook separately.

Crack the claws open slightly with the back of a heavy knife or small kitchen hammer. This will make it easier to remove the flesh once cooked.

Set a barbecue up for single-zone, direct grilling (page 17) – ensuring that you are cooking over medium hot embers.

Grill the lobster, flesh-side down, for 3–4 minutes, and then flip them over, season the flesh and brush each one liberally with some turmeric butter. Finish cooking for a further 3–5 minutes until the lobster is cooked through but tender. Transfer, as they are, to the insulated cool box with the crawfish.

FOR THE REST

Whilst the lobsters are cooking, blanch the samphire in boiling salted water for no more than 3–4 minutes. Refresh in iced water until cool, drain and set aside until required.

Grill the sausages for 5–6 minutes until cooked all the way through and transfer to the insulated cool box used for storing the rest of the boil elements.

Concurrently, heat a wide cast-iron pan or roasting tray over a hot part of the fire, and add the mussels and some beer to steam them open. Lift the bivalves from the pan using a slotted spoon, and transfer them also to the insulated cool box.

Cut the loaf of ciabatta in half lengthways, brush with the cut side of half a garlic clove (if you have one to hand) and drizzle with olive oil. Grill the bread over searing heat on the barbecue, or over a ridged grill pan heated over high to smoking hot, until charred. Remove once evenly blackened all over, and, once cool enough to handle, rip into bite-size pieces. Transfer to a bowl, drizzle generously with olive oil and season with salt and black pepper.

TO FINISH

Hack the lobster shells in half using a meat cleaver (or very big knife) and crack the claws open slightly so that your guests can easily get to the meat. Toss the lobster into the cool box, along with all the remaining turmeric butter and the blackened ciabatta bread. With the lid sealed, give the entire cool box a generous shake, stir with a suitable piece of equipment, and dump the contents out onto a large picnic table lined with several layers of newspaper.

Squeeze the blackened lemon halves over the top and throw them randomly on to the pile. Garnish with the blanched samphire, grilled spring onions and coriander liberally strewn all over the place. Serve with harissa aioli, for dipping everything into.

Serve with finger bowls filled with water and a slice of lemon, and napkins.

GRILLED RED MULLET
WITH CHARMOULA & SWEET ONIONS

I use red mullet here, one of the most underrated and underutilised fish at the market. It punches above its weight when it comes to taste, is quick to cook and great off the grill. So it ticks a lot of boxes. But charmoula works with just about any white fish, so opt for whatever is your preference.

This is a dish that requires you to lift the flesh from the bone as you eat. This used to be something I would hate doing. But now I find pleasure in the almost ritualistic nature of it. Plus I think it makes the end product more flavoursome. Give it a go and see how you feel. If you still don't like it, I can't blame you – ask your fishmongers for fillets the next time.

SERVES 4

RED CHARMOULA

4 red bird's eye chillies, deseeded and finely chopped

1 tbsp cumin seeds, toasted and ground

1½ tbsp sweet paprika

1 shallot, finely chopped

2 garlic cloves, grated

2 tbsp finely chopped coriander

1 tbsp finely chopped flat-leaf parsley

80ml extra virgin olive oil

1 tsp salt

1 tbsp runny honey

juice of 1 lemon

SWEET ONIONS

25g unsalted butter

2 tbsp olive oil

2 medium white onions, sliced

1 tsp finely chopped lemon thyme leaves

RED MULLET

4 whole red mullet, descaled and gutted

30ml olive oil

12 Kalamata olives, pitted and halved

small handful of picked coriander leaves

FOR THE RED CHARMOULA

Combine all the ingredients except the lemon juice and honey together in a small bowl and mix well. You can make this mix in advance and keep it refrigerated until required.

Just prior to using, whisk the lemon juice and honey together and add to the charmoula mix. Season to taste and add more lemon juice if necessary. The charmoula should be quite sharp.

FOR THE SWEET ONIONS

Heat the butter and olive oil in a heavy-based saucepan over medium-low heat. Add the onions and lemon thyme and caramelise until deep, golden brown in colour. Taste them – they should be rich and sweet. Season with salt according to taste and set aside until needed.

FOR THE RED MULLET

Score each mullet 3 or 4 times with a very sharp knife, at parallel 45-degree angles on both sides. Drizzle the fish with olive oil and season both sides with salt and black pepper.

Set a barbecue up for single-zone, direct grilling (page 17) – ensuring that you are cooking over burning hot embers.

Bring the onions back to temperature on the top and keep warm over low heat.

Place the mullet in a fish barbecue basket and grill for 4–5 minutes on each side until cooked through. The flesh should be firm and flake when pressure is gently applied.

Alternatively, in the absence of a fish basket you can cook the fish directly on the grill rack. Make sure it's been brushed with oil before adding the fish.

Spoon the onions on to individual serving plates or a large serving platter, and make a bed upon which to sit the mullet. Place the fish on top of the onions and liberally dress with the red charmoula. Garnish with the olives and coriander leaves strewn all over the plate.

GRILLED SARDINES
WITH CHILLI & LEMON THYME DRESSING

The sardines (and seafood) of Essaouira and Safi are legendary, served fresh out of the sea, grilled simply with little more than some seasoning and a good squeeze of lemon.

I marinate my sardines before they go on the grill and serve them in a pool of chilli and lemon thyme dressing. It's a touch more work but I think it's worth it. Serve with cold beer and wet wipes. (Pictured overleaf).

SERVES 4
AS A LIGHT SNACK,
OR 2 AS A MAIN

SARDINES

3–4 sprigs of lemon thyme, leaves picked and finely chopped

2 garlic cloves, grated

60ml extra virgin olive oil

grated zest of 1 lemon

1 tbsp cumin seeds, crushed

1 tsp sweet paprika

16 sardines, butterflied

2 tbsp roughly chopped coriander

CHILLI AND LEMON THYME DRESSING

4 red chillies, finely chopped

4 green chillies, finely chopped

1 shallot, finely chopped

4 garlic clove, finely chopped

2 tbsp finely chopped picked lemon thyme leaves

180ml olive oil or Garlic Oil (page 260)

1 tsp salt

2 tsp honey

juice of 1 lemon

GARNISH AND SERVE

small handful of picked dill leaves

1 lemon, quartered into wedges

4 soft, sweet rolls such as a brioche bun or a challah roll

Pickled Red Onion (page 252)

FOR THE SARDINES

Put the picked thyme leaves, garlic, olive oil, lemon zest, cumin seeds and sweet paprika in a small bowl and mix well to combine.

Lay the sardines flat in a suitable storage vessel, skin-side down, ideally single-layered, and pour the marinade over the top. Cover with clingfilm and refrigerate for 1–2 hours.

FOR THE CHILLI AND LEMON THYME DRESSING

Combine all the ingredients except the salt, honey and lemon juice together in a small bowl. Make this mix in advance and keep it refrigerated until required.

Just prior to using, whisk the salt, honey and lemon juice together and add to the chopped dressing. Check for seasoning and add more salt and/or lemon juice if necessary.

TO FINISH THE SARDINES

Set a barbecue up for single-zone, direct grilling (page 17) – ensuring that you are cooking over burning hot embers.

I like to use a fish barbecue basket for these sardines, as they can be quite delicate and disintegrate quite easily on the grill rack.

Season the sardines generously with salt and black pepper. Grill on both sides until lightly charred.

TO GARNISH AND SERVE

Transfer the sardines to a serving platter and pile high. Spoon the chilli and lemon thyme dressing lavishly over the top, trying to ensure that all the sardines are well dressed. Garnish with picked dill leaves and some lemon wedges and serve immediately, piping hot, alongside some bread. I like to use a sweet roll, such as a brioche or challah, but a sourdough or some pita bread, charred on the grill, would also work.

Some pickled red onion makes a welcome accompaniment to cut through the oiliness of the sardines.

PLANK-SMOKED GILTHEAD BREAM
WITH SPICY TOMATO & BLACK OLIVE SAUCE

I like to use cedar planks when barbecuing fish; it's incredibly easy and circumvents any of the stress often associated with delicate fish sticking to the grill grate. You don't have to worry yourself with the flip, a common source of angst amongst most grown men pretending they know how to barbecue. Most importantly, it imparts a depth of woody smokiness into the fish that's difficult to achieve otherwise.

Cedar planks are available from online timber merchants and certain hardware stores and can be cut to size as per requirements. You need the wood to be untreated, about 2.5cm thick and long enough to fit in your barbecue whilst accommodating whatever fish it is you're cooking.

SERVES 4
AS A LIGHT SNACK
OR 2 AS A MAIN

**SPICY TOMATO SAUCE
(YIELDS ABOUT 400ML)**

4 tbsp olive oil, plus another 4 tbsp olive oil

2 garlic cloves, thinly sliced

1 tbsp dried chilli flakes

½ tsp smoked paprika

1 tbsp tomato paste

800g over-ripe tomatoes, roughly chopped

1 tsp honey (optional)

10–12 pitted Moroccan olives, cut in half and flattened with the back of a large, heavy knife

GILTHEAD BREAM

2 gilthead bream, scaled and gutted, backbone cut out, pin bones removed, fins removed and left whole with head on (ask your fishmonger)

4 tbsp cardamom curing salt (page 32)

1 lemon, thinly sliced

6 sprigs of lemon thyme

4 tbsp Garlic Oil (page 260),or olive oil

2 cedar planks, approximately 20cm x 30cm

FOR THE SPICY TOMATO SAUCE

Warm 2 tablespoons of olive oil in a heavy-based frying pan over medium heat and sauté the garlic with the chilli flakes and paprika until softened and caramelised, about 3–4 minutes. Add the tomato paste and cook for a further 1–2 minutes, then fold in the tomatoes and bring to a simmer.

Turn the heat down to low and continue to cook for 30–45 minutes, stirring occasionally, until the tomatoes have reduced and sweetened, losing some of their acidity in the process. You want the sauce to be quite dry, almost paste-like in its consistency.

Check the sauce for seasoning and adjust accordingly with salt and black pepper. If the sauce requires any sweetening, stir through some honey, but it's possible the tomatoes might be sweet enough without. Remove the sauce from the heat and fold in the olives. Set aside until required.

FOR THE GILTHEAD BREAM

Lay each fish on a baking tray and sprinkle liberally with the curing salt, both inside the cavity and out. Refrigerate, covered, for 45 minutes to an hour.

Whilst the fish is curing, set a barbecue up ready for single-zone direct grilling (page 17).

Remove the fish from the fridge, rinse off the cure and pat dry with kitchen paper. Make three large cuts diagonally across the bream, using a very sharp knife. Stuff each cut with a slice of lemon and fill each fish with the lemon thyme sprigs. Brush both sides of the fish with garlic oil and transfer to the soaked wooden planks.

Place the planks on the grill rack, directly above the burning embers. Put the lid on the barbecue and cook the fish for 20–30 minutes, checking on them every so often to see when they're done. The bream should be flaking and opaque as opposed to rigid and translucent. Five minutes before the end of cooking, place the flatbreads on top of the fish just to warm through, and heat up the spicy tomato sauce if it's gone cold.

flatbreads, warmed in the oven or
on the grill

1 preserved lemon, rind only, thinly
sliced

2 tbsp roughly chopped flat-leaf
parsley

2 tbsp Crispy Shallots (page 240)

TO GARNISH AND SERVE

Remove the planks from the barbecue, smother each fish with the sauce and
garnish with the sliced preserved lemon rind, chopped parsley and shallots.

Serve the bream with the warmed flatbreads for ripping and making little wraps
with. A fresh salad works well as an accompaniment – I like to use the Turkish
'Shepherds' salad for this dish (page 174).

TIP

No less than an hour before you plan to cook your fish, soak the wooden
planks in water. This will keep them moist and prevent them from burning when
on the barbecue.

MARINATED MONSTER PRAWNS
WITH PIL-PIL SAUCE

Gambas pil-pil is a dish that originates from the Basque region in Spain, consisting of prawns cooked with lots of garlic, chilli and olive oil, usually prepared in an earthenware dish and brought to the table still sizzling. There's not a lot wrong with any of the words in that sentence.

Ask your fishmonger for the biggest prawns he can find. Make a statement. Avoid the tiny ones often used. And bread is obligatory. I say that a lot, but this time I really mean it.

SERVES 2

MONSTER PRAWNS

8 giant black tiger prawns, or any large prawns you can find, the bigger the better

2 tbsp extra virgin olive oil

1 garlic clove, minced or grated

1 tbsp chopped dill

1 tsp dried chilli flakes

PIL-PIL SAUCE

100ml olive oil

3 garlic cloves, thinly sliced

½ tsp salt

1 tsp cumin seeds, lightly toasted

1 tsp ground coriander

pinch of cayenne

3 tbsp Confit Chilli Salsa (page 260)

8–10 cherry tomatoes, quartered and deseeded

GARNISH AND SERVE

2 tbsp lemon juice

2 basil leaves, finely sliced

2 slices of sourdough or ciabatta, lightly grilled on both sides (optional)

FOR THE MONSTER PRAWNS

Start by deshelling the prawns, leaving the heads and tails on for aesthetic appeal. Use a small knife to create a slit and cut out the vein that runs down the back of each prawn.

Season the prawns with salt and pepper, toss them in olive oil, garlic, dill and chilli flakes, and put in the refrigerator to marinate for 2–4 hours.

FOR THE PIL-PIL SAUCE

Heat the olive oil in a heavy-based (preferably cast-iron) frying pan and gently sauté the garlic for 2–3 minutes, until softened and translucent but not coloured.

Remove the garlic from the oil with a slotted spoon (be sure to take out all of it and don't leave any stragglers behind) and transfer to a mortar and pestle, leaving the cooking oil in the pan. Add the salt, cumin seeds, ground coriander and cayenne to the garlic and work the mix until it forms a paste.

Return the pan and oil to the stovetop and warm over medium heat. Add the confit chilli salsa, cherry tomatoes and garlic mix, and cook for few minutes to heat through. Turn the heat down as low as it can go and let the sauce gently bubble away and intensify in flavour whilst you finish the prawns.

TO FINISH THE MONSTER PRAWNS

Set a barbecue up for single-zone, direct grilling (page 17) – ensuring that you are cooking on hot embers. Set the prawns on the grill rack directly over the burning coals, turning once or twice to colour both sides well, until the prawns are cooked all the way through, about 2–3 minutes on each side depending on the strength of your fire. Alternatively, heat a cast-iron pan over high heat until smoking hot and grill the prawns until done.

Whilst the prawns are grilling, have the pan with the pil-pil sauce set on the outer edges of the barbecue or grill to warm through.

TO GARNISH AND SERVE

Once cooked, transfer the prawns to the pan of pil-pil sauce and finish with the lemon juice. Garnish with the basil leaves and serve immediately. Some lightly grilled bread of any sort will be needed to mop up the pan juices.

MOROCCAN FISH KEFTA
WITH TAKTOUKA & YOGHURT

Margaret Tayar runs an eponymous North African restaurant in the old Arab quarter (Jaffa) in Tel Aviv serving delicious, homely food. If you're lucky enough to find it open, her fish kefta will blow your mind. This is my attempt to recreate them.

SERVES 4

TAKTOUKA

80ml olive oil

2 red peppers, blackened on
   a grill, peeled and diced

2 green peppers, blackened on
   a grill, peeled and diced

2 bird's eye chillies, deseeded
   and finely chopped

800g plum tomatoes, peeled,
   chopped, seeds and flesh

2 garlic cloves, finely chopped

1 tsp cumin seeds

1 tsp flaked sea salt

2 tbsp finely chopped coriander

1 tbsp paprika

1 tsp honey

juice of ½ lemon

½ tsp coarse ground black pepper

FISH KEFTA

50g white bread, crusts removed

600g hake, skinless and boneless

2 tbsp finely chopped coriander

2 tsp finely chopped dill

2 tsp ground cumin

½ tsp ground turmeric

grated zest of 1 lemon

½ red onion, finely chopped

2 tsp salt

1 tsp coarse ground black pepper

2 large eggs, lightly beaten

2 tbsp olive oil

GARNISH AND SERVE

4 tbsp full-fat natural yoghurt

1 lemon

2 tbsp roughly chopped mint

Extra virgin olive oil

THE TAKTOUKA

Warm 30ml of olive oil in a large frying pan over medium-low heat and gently cook the peppers, chillies and tomatoes for a few minutes.

With a sharp knife, chop the grated garlic, cumin seeds, salt and coriander until puréed to a smooth paste. You can also use a mortar and pestle for this if you'd prefer.

Add the coriander purée to the pepper mix, stir in the paprika and the rest of the olive oil and continue to cook over low heat, gently simmering until all the excess moisture has evaporated and stirring regularly to ensure the taktouka does not catch on the bottom. Once the sauce is almost completely dry, add the honey and lemon juice, season with black pepper and additional salt (if required), and remove from the heat (or keep warm) until needed. The taktouka can keep, refrigerated and covered, for up to 5 days, during which time it will intensify and improve in flavour.

FOR THE FISH KEFTA

Place the bread in a food processor and blend to a rough crumb. Remove and set to one side. Cut the hake into several large pieces, then place in a food processor and pulse to a coarse mince. You want the fish to retain some texture; so don't over-blitz it.

In a large bowl, mix the minced hake with the breadcrumbs, chopped herbs, spices, lemon zest and red onion, and season with salt and pepper. Add the eggs and use your hands to mix everything together well. Shape the mixture into patties, 2cm thick by 10cm wide. Refrigerate for 30 minutes to an hour, just to firm up whilst you prepare a fire.

Set a barbecue up for single-zone, direct grilling (page 17) – ensuring that you are cooking on medium-hot embers. Brush the kefta with olive oil and place on the grill rack directly over the coals. Grill on both sides until lightly charred and cooked all the way through, turning intermittently as they cook. Use a small knife to break the kefta – the fish should be just opaque but not translucent.

TO GARNISH AND SERVE

Place the grilled kefta on a serving platter alongside the warm taktouka and yoghurt. Squeeze some lemon juice over the top and finish with a sprinkling of chopped mint and a final drizzle of extra virgin olive oil. Serve immediately, or at room temperature – it's up to you. I like to serve these alongside a grain, such as Cardamom and currant basmati rice (page 200).

CHAPTER 04

VEGETABLES & SIDES

CAULIFLOWER SHAWARMA
WITH POMEGRANATE, PINE NUTS & ROSE

If there were a single dish – the dish – that has come to symbolise Berber & Q, a 'signature' so to speak, it would be our cauliflower shawarma.

SERVES 4–8

SHAWARMA-SPICED BUTTER

40g unsalted butter, softened to room temperature

juice of 1 lemon

1 garlic clove, minced

1½ tbsp finely chopped coriander

1 tbsp ground cinnamon

1 tbsp ground sumac

1½ tsp ground cumin

½ tsp ground allspice

pinch of ground nutmeg

pinch of ground cardamom

CAULIFLOWER

1 whole cauliflower

GARNISH

4 tbsp Tahina Sauce (page 262)

1 tbsp pomegranate molasses

1½ tbsp pine nuts, toasted

1 small green chilli, finely chopped

2 tbsp pomegranate seeds

1 tsp dried rose petals

1 tbsp roughly chopped flat-leaf parsley

extra virgin olive oil (optional)

FOR THE SHAWARMA-SPICED BUTTER

Combine all the ingredients in a stand mixer and mix using the paddle attachment. In the absence of a mixer, whisk in a large bowl until thoroughly incorporated. The butter should be aerated, slightly stiff and one colour (as opposed to streaked). Set aside until needed. It can be kept in the fridge for several weeks, but must be brought to room temperature before being used.

FOR THE CAULIFLOWER

Trim some of the outer cauliflower leaves, but leave some stragglers left behind – they taste delicious and look great when burnt and crisped.

Set a large saucepan of salted water on high heat and cover with a lid so as to bring the water up to the boil. Once the water is boiling, gently lower the cauliflower into the pan, being careful not to let it drop from a height and thereby avoiding the potential of burning yourself with the splash-back of boiling water, which nobody wants, least of all you.

Bring the water back to the boil, then turn the heat down to medium so the water has a gentle roll. The intention is to par-cook the cauliflower before finishing it in the oven or on the barbecue. It should be removed from the water when tender to a knife, yet retain some resistance – 'al dente', as they say. It's important not to overcook the cauliflower. Much like pasta or a lovely piece of steak, cauliflower doesn't like being cooked for too long. We've found it to take 7 minutes from when the water comes back to the boil.

Set the cauliflower on a cooling rack over a roasting tray and allow to drip-dry. Brush liberally all over with the spiced butter, and where possible, try and get beneath the floret canopy to reach the inner sections. Retain some of the butter for brushing at a later stage. Season generously with salt and pepper.

TO FINISH THE CAULIFLOWER

Preheat the oven to its highest setting (240°C/220°C Fan/Gas mark 9) and blast the cauliflower for 5–7 minutes, until blackened all over. (You want it to lightly char, not to form an acrid burnt crust.) Once sufficiently oven-roasted, transfer it to finish on the barbecue for a few minutes (if you have one going) for a final hit of smokiness, basting it periodically with any leftover butter.

TO GARNISH AND SERVE

Transfer to a serving plate. Spoon over the tahina sauce and pomegranate molasses, and finish by sprinkling over the pine nuts, green chilli, pomegranate seeds, rose petals and parsley. A drizzle of olive oil adds a nice glossy finish. Serve immediately – the cauliflower tastes so much better when hot.

GRILLED NECTARINE
WITH AMBA DRESSING & HARISSA-GLAZED PEANUTS

This is another one of Shaun's recipes and he's rightly very proud of it. It's a brilliant balance of sweet and spicy, sharp but bitter, soft and crunchy.

Nectarine season runs late summer, from August to the end of September. Blink and you might miss it, which would be a shame. This is a particularly great accompaniment to pork.

SERVES 4

AMBA DRESSING
5g fenugreek seeds
5g yellow mustard seeds
50ml cider vinegar
50ml water
25g caster sugar
10g salt
10g ground turmeric

HARISSA-GLAZED PEANUTS
20g fennel seeds
20g coriander seeds
150g caster sugar
150g Harissa (page 259) or shop-bought
500g toasted peanuts (or any nut of your choice)

GRILLED NECTARINES
4 firm nectarines, destoned and quartered
extra virgin olive oil
flaked sea salt (such as Maldon) and coarse ground black pepper
handful of Harissa-glazed Peanuts (see above)
small handful of mixed herbs such as flat-leaf parsley, mint and chives, coarsely chopped

FOR THE AMBA DRESSING
Heat a heavy-based pan over medium heat and toast the fenugreek and mustard seeds until golden and fragrant.

Add the rest of the dressing ingredients to the pan and warm through, whisking until the sugar and salt have dissolved. Remove from the heat and leave to settle back to room temperature and for the flavours to infuse properly. The dressing is better left to settle overnight, but a couple of hours will suffice if time is short.

FOR THE HARISSA-GLAZED PEANUTS
Heat a heavy-based pan over medium heat and toast the fennel and coriander seeds until golden and fragrant. Add the sugar and leave to caramelise gently, then stir in the harissa and peanuts. Cook until the mixture goes sticky but don't allow it to become brittle. Spoon the nuts onto a parchment-lined baking tray and leave to cool.

Smash the nuts up with a rolling pin or roughly chop them using a knife. Store in an airtight container, where they will keep for several weeks. These nuts are great by themselves as a late-night snack or as a garnish for meats and salads.

FOR THE GRILLED NECTARINES
Set a barbecue up for direct grilling (page 17), ensuring that you're cooking over searing hot embers. Alternatively, heat a cast-iron ridged pan over high heat until smoking hot.

Lightly brush the nectarines with oil and char them on the hottest part of your grill until well scored and caramelised but not overcooked. The nectarines must retain some firmness to them and not be too soft.

Once cooked, toss the nectarines in a bowl with the amba dressing and some extra virgin olive oil. Season with flaked salt and coarse black pepper.

Spoon the grilled nectarines onto a plate and drizzle over any leftover dressing that collected in the bowl. Top with some of the chopped harissa-glazed peanuts and throw some mixed herbs over the plate. Finish with a final drizzle of extra virgin olive oil for good measure.

BLACKENED AUBERGINE
WITH TAHINA YOGHURT & BURNT CHILLI

Blackened aubergine is one of our most popular dishes in the restaurant and always on the menu in one form or another. There's seemingly something about the words 'blackened' and 'aubergine' which, when put together, make for compulsive ordering – and rightly so. An aubergine blistered over charcoal until charred and smoky is one of life's simplest but greatest pleasures.

Aubergines are sponge-like in their capacity to absorb oils (or dressings and sauces for that matter), and their flavour and texture are enhanced by it, so don't scrimp or save on oil here – drizzle more than you would probably anticipate needing to. You won't regret it.

SERVES 2–4

AUBERGINE

2 aubergines

2 red chillies

80ml olive oil or Garlic Oil
(page 260)

GARNISH AND SERVE

Tahina Yoghurt (page 124)

1 tsp pine nuts

1 tsp tomato seeds

pinch of ground sumac

6–8 picked flat-leaf parsley fronds

1–2 basil leaves, finely chopped

1 lemon, halved and blackened
on the grill

pita bread or flatbread, warmed
on the grill

FOR THE AUBERGINE

Set a barbecue up for two-zone indirect grilling (page 17). Pierce each aubergine several times with a sharp knife or skewer and place on the grill rack with no burning coals underneath. Add some wood chips to the burning coals, close the vents off at the bottom but allow the lid's vents to remain partially open. Put the lid on the barbecue and smoke for 20–25 minutes until the aubergines are soft when pierced with a knife, but retain their shape. Remove from the grill and set aside until cool enough to handle. Whilst the aubergines are cooking, blacken the red chillies directly over the coals until softened and charred.

Peel the aubergines carefully, doing the best you can to retain the integrity of its original shape, whilst leaving the stem attached. Season the aubergines generously with salt and pepper, and drizzle generously with olive oil.

TO GRANISH AND SERVE

Spread the tahini yoghurt generously around a serving platter and place the aubergines on top. Lay the blackened chillies alongside, sprinkle the pine nuts, tomato seeds and sumac all over and garnish with parsley, basil and the lemon halves. A generous final drizzle of olive oil is obligatory. Encourage your friends or guests to squeeze the lemon halves over the dish. Don't worry about the seeds; they're of no harm to anyone.

Serve as is, or with warmed pita bread (naturally).

KALE, ASPARAGUS & BROAD BEAN TABBOULEH

Tabbouleh, in its traditional form, is a fresh salad made from lots of parsley, fine bulgur wheat and tomato. Don't scrimp on the parsley if you're making that version. It's the main event and should be the most prominent ingredient. Too often I find the tabbouleh I'm served is too heavy on bulgur.

This particular tabbouleh appears on our menu around springtime, when asparagus and broad beans are at their bountiful best. There's no parsley in it. It's a variation on a theme and our interpretation. As with all tabbouleh however, it must be well oiled and sharp. Check for seasoning and add more lemon juice or extra virgin olive oil as necessary.

SERVES 6

60g fine bulgur wheat

8–10 asparagus spears, blackened on the grill and roughly chopped

200g broad beans, podded

1 shallot, finely chopped

2 bunches of finely shredded mint

2 large handfuls of kale leaves, stems removed, shredded

80g walnuts, toasted and roughly chopped

75ml extra virgin olive oil

3 tbsp lemon juice

grated zest of 1 lemon

small handful of pomegranate seeds

1½ tbsp flaked sea salt (such as Maldon)

coarse ground black pepper

In a small bowl, cover the bulgur wheat with boiling water and soak it for roughly 5 minutes. Drain. Lightly run a fork through the grain to fluff it, so that it doesn't coagulate and become clumpy, and set to one side until cool.

Combine all the ingredients together in a large bowl, mixing well with your hands or a large spoon. Check for seasoning and adjust accordingly. It might need some more olive oil, or lemon juice, or possibly both.

Serve immediately, piled high on a serving plate.

HASSELBACK POTATOES
WITH RED TAHINA & SOUR CREAM

Unsurprisingly, 'hasselback' potatoes are neither Middle Eastern nor North African in origin, but rather Swedish. But they're so good I had to have a version in this book. Doused in red tahini and studded with confit garlic, this is one of my favourite ways to eat a potato. They'd be almost as enjoyable with nothing more than some soured cream and chopped chives. In fact, these are amazing by themselves.

SERVES 4

RED TAHINA
100g Tahina Sauce (page 262)
1 tbsp Harissa (page 259) or shop-bought

HASSELBACK POTATOES
800g medium-sized waxy potatoes, such as Cara or Charlotte
100g unsalted butter
60ml olive oil
3–4 sprigs of rosemary, finely chopped
20 Confit Garlic Cloves (optional) (page 260)

SERVE
2 tbsp soured cream
2 tbsp finely chopped chives

FOR THE RED TAHINA
Combine the tahina sauce and harissa in a small bowl and stir well.

FOR THE HASSELBACK POTATOES
Preheat the oven to 200°C/180°C Fan/Gas mark 6.

Make 6 or 7 deep incisions into each potato, at intervals of roughly 2mm, about two-thirds of the way into the flesh.

Melt the butter in a saucepan over medium heat, add the olive oil and rosemary and cook for a few minutes to infuse.

Dip and roll each potato in the butter so that they're generously coated. Lay the potatoes in a cast-iron pan or roasting tray, season generously with salt and black pepper, and roast in the oven for 45 minutes to an hour, basting regularly with the excess butter mix. The potatoes should turn golden and crisp. Ten minutes before the end of cooking time, insert 2 or 3 confit garlic cloves into the slits of each potato.

TO SERVE
Drizzle the potatoes with soured cream and the red tahina and finish with a sprinkling of chopped chives.

HERITAGE TOMATO BREAD SALAD
WITH PICKLED RED ONION & ALEPPO CHILLI LABNEH

This salad is best in summer, when tomatoes are most vibrant. We use heritage tomatoes, as they bring variety of colour, taste and shape, which makes for a more interesting salad. That said, if you can't get hold of them, a selection of more readily available varieties such as plum and beef would work. And if you have confit cherry tomatoes kicking about, now's their moment to shine.

Don't make the burnt bread croutons too far in advance. They'll lose their charred crispness with time and taste best when fresh off the grill. Yellow pea shoots aren't that easy to find, so don't lose any sleep over it if you can't find them.

> **SERVES 2**
> AS A MAIN OR 4 AS A
> GENEROUS SIDE SALAD

ALEPPO CHILLI LABNEH
olive oil
2–3 tbsp Aleppo chilli flakes or
  1–2 tsp dried chilli flakes
80g Labneh (page 261)

SHERRY VINEGAR DRESSING
1 tsp honey
2 tbsp aged sherry vinegar
2 tbsp lemon juice
100ml extra virgin olive oil
2 garlic cloves, minced

HERITAGE TOMATO
  PANZANELLA
200g ciabatta or sourdough
½ garlic clove
extra virgin olive oil, for drizzling
500g heritage tomatoes, cut into
  random sizes
handful of cherry tomatoes
12–16 pitted kalamata olives,
  halved
small handful of picked oregano,
  dill and basil leaves
2 tbsp Pickled Red Onion (page
  252)
small bunch of yellow pea shoots
  (optional, if available)
2 tbsp pumpkin seeds, toasted

FOR THE ALEPPO CHILLI LABNEH
Set a small bowl with some olive oil to one side, for rubbing through your hands to keep them well lubricated. You won't need more than 3–4 tablespoons. Place the Aleppo chilli flakes on a baking tray and spread to a thin layer.

Keeping your hands well oiled at all times, roll the labneh into balls, about the size of a marble, and transfer them to the baking tray to be rolled and coated in the Aleppo chilli flakes. Once all of the labneh has been rolled and coated, transfer to a small container, cover with oil and refrigerate until required.

Kept in this way these labneh balls will keep refrigerated for several weeks, and can be used as a component for all sorts of salads, as well as a great garnish for some fish and meat.

FOR THE SHERRY VINEGAR DRESSING
Whisk the honey, vinegar and lemon juice together in a small bowl, and gradually add the extra virgin olive oil, whisking to emulsify. Add the garlic and season with salt and pepper to taste.

FOR THE HERITAGE TOMATO PANZANELLA
Cut the loaf of ciabatta in half lengthways, brush with the cut side of a halved garlic clove, and drizzle generously with olive oil. Grill the bread over searing heat on the barbecue, or over a ridged grill pan heated over high to smoking hot, until well charred. Remove once evenly blackened all over, and, once cool enough to handle, rip into bite-size pieces. Transfer to a bowl, drizzle generously with olive oil and season with salt and black pepper.

Place the tomatoes in a bowl with the ciabatta chunks, olives and half the picked herb leaves. Toss the salad with the sherry vinegar dressing until mixed through, check for seasoning and add some more salt and pepper if required, then transfer to a serving platter. Dot the labneh balls around the plate, and garnish with the pickled red onion, reserved herbs and yellow pea shoots (if using). Throw the toasted pumpkin seeds on top and finish with a generous glug of olive oil. Serve immediately – you want the bread to soak up the juices without becoming soggy.

HONEY-ROASTED SQUASH
WITH CINNAMON BUTTER & ALMONDS

Squash, much like pumpkin, is such a great autumnal ingredient and can be used in an endless number of ways. It's fantastic in a salad with spring onion, pomegranate seeds, lime yoghurt dressing and walnuts. I like to roast it, coated in olive oil and brown sugar, seasoned well and serve it garnished with feta, za'atar and crispy shallots. It's also excellent as a soup, or in stews and tagines, for when the nights draw in and winter grips.

In this recipe, we steam it until just softened and then finish it in the pan to colour the flesh side, drenched in cinnamon butter so that it soaks all the way through until rich and moreish.

I use acorn or butternut squash for this recipe, but you can experiment with any of the gourd family that you can get your hands on.

SERVES 4

80g unsalted butter

1 tbsp olive oil

2 onions, finely sliced

25g green sultanas (or normal sultanas)

1 acorn or butternut squash

2 tbsp honey

80ml chicken stock

1 tsp finely chopped lemon thyme

1 tsp ground cinnamon

1 tsp lemon juice

2 tbsp flaked almonds, toasted

2 tbsp pumpkin seeds, toasted

Heat 30g of butter and the olive oil over medium-high heat in a wide heavy-based frying pan and cook the onions until caramelised, about 10–12 minutes. Add the sultanas for the final few minutes to warm through and soften. Season with salt and black pepper and set aside until required.

Top and tail the squash, cut in half widthways, then quarter, deseed and remove any membrane.

Set a steamer over boiling water and steam the squash, covered, until tender but still holding shape, about 45 minutes. Set aside to cool. Remember to check on your water throughout and top it up if necessary.

Whilst the squash is steaming, heat the remaining 50g of butter in a small saucepan over medium-low heat and whisk it as it melts. Cook for 2–3 minutes, until caramelised and nutty brown in colour. Add the honey and chicken stock and warm through to dissolve. Stir in the lemon thyme and cinnamon. Remove from the heat and whisk in the lemon juice.

Put a very large, wide, cast-iron pan or heavy-based frying pan over the highest heat or else set the pan directly over burning embers on the fire.

Place the squash, cut-side down, in the pan and baste with the cinnamon butter. Cook for 5–7 minutes until crisped and charred along its edges. Watch the heat and reduce it slightly if the squash starts to catch. Continue basting with the butter throughout. Flip the squash and cook its other side in the same manner. Resist the urge to break the first point of contact by flipping too early. The squash will tell you when it's ready by releasing from the pan once charred.

Return the onions to the pan and serve the squash, cut-side up, drenched in more butter and topped with toasted flaked almonds and pumpkin seeds.

WATERMELON & GRILLED MANOURI
WITH GREEN OLIVE & MINT SALSA VERDE

I especially like the way the sweet and crunchy watermelon balances with the crumbly saltiness of the manouri cheese in this salad, whilst the sharpness of the salsa verde really ties the whole dish together. This is a great summer salad that is both light and fresh.

MINT SALSA VERDE

2 tbsp lemon juice

½ tsp Dijon mustard

½ shallot, finely chopped

6–8 pitted green olives, finely chopped

1 anchovy fillet, minced

1 tbsp capers, drained, rinsed and finely chopped

1 garlic clove, minced

4 tbsp Herb Oil (page 264) or olive oil

2 tbsp finely shredded mint

WATERMELON AND GRILLED MANOURI

150g manouri cheese, cut into 1cm thick wedges

500g watermelon, cut into chunks

handful of picked mint leaves

2 tbsp whole almonds, toasted and roughly chopped

2 green chillies, thinly sliced

2 tbsp Herb Oil (page 264) or olive oil

FOR THE MINT SALSA VERDE

Whisk the lemon juice and mustard together in a bowl, and add the shallot, olives, anchovy, capers and garlic.

Whisk the oil into the sauce. I like to use herb oil (page 264) for my salsa verde, as it gives the dressing a lovely vibrant green colour, but this recipe works just as well with normal olive oil.

Set to one side until required. The salsa verde can be made several hours ahead of time, just be sure not to add the mint until just before serving.

FOR THE WATERMELON AND GRILLED MANOURI

I wouldn't suggest firing up a barbecue just for the purpose of grilling some manouri cheese, but if you happen to have a fire going for other culinary purposes (or otherwise), then use it to grill your cheese. As with any ingredient cooked on an open fire, the manouri will only taste better for it. In the absence of a barbecue, heat a cast-iron ridged skillet pan on the stovetop over high heat until smoking hot, and griddle-score the manouri on both sides in a cross formation, as you might a piece of steak.

Remove the manouri from the grill and transfer to a serving platter alongside the watermelon chunks. Drizzle the salsa verde over the top and garnish the salad with some picked mint leaves, the almonds, chillies and a final drizzle of herb oil for good measure.

BLACKENED HISPI CABBAGE
WITH LEMON CRÈME FRAÎCHE, URFA CHILLI & PISTACHIO BUTTER

Hispi cabbage is one of my favourite vegetables to barbecue. It absorbs the flavour of the fire so well, and looks so sexy when blackened along its edges.

I like to blanch Hispi in boiling water before it goes on the grill, just to soften her up in preparation for her hot date, and to penetrate deeper into the cabbage to reach its core. You can put it straight on the grill if you can't be bothered with the blanching stage, but the heart might retain some crunch. I'm fine with that if you are.

SERVES 4

LEMON CRÈME FRAÎCHE
100g crème fraîche
1 tbsp lemon juice
grated zest of ½ lemon
1 tbsp finely chopped chives
1 tbsp extra virgin olive oil

HISPI CABBAGE
1 green Hispi cabbage, outer leaves removed and quartered
2 tbsp olive oil
small handful of basil, to garnish

URFA CHILLI BUTTER
60g unsalted butter
1 tbsp urfa chilli flakes
1 tsp dried chilli flakes
40g pistachios, toasted and roughly chopped

FOR THE LEMON CRÈME FRAÎCHE
Put all the ingredients together in a bowl and stir to combine. Season to taste. Set aside, refrigerated and covered, until required.

FOR THE HISPI CABBAGE
Prepare a bowl of iced water large enough to accommodate the cabbage. Bring a saucepan of water to the boil over high heat. Blanch the cabbage in the water for roughly 2 minutes, until softened but still al dente, refreshing it in the ice bath immediately to stop the cooking process. Drain once cool and pat dry with kitchen paper.

FOR THE URFA CHILLI BUTTER
Melt the butter in a saucepan over medium heat until it starts to froth and darken to brown with a nutty, caramelised aroma. Turn the heat to as low as it will go and fold through both chilli flakes and the pistachios. Fry for a further 1–2 minutes to infuse, then remove the pan from the heat source until required.

TO FINISH THE HISPI CABBAGE
Brush the cabbage liberally with olive oil and season with salt and black pepper. Prepare a barbecue for single-zone direct grilling (page 17) – ensuring you are cooking over burning hot embers. Grill the cabbage on all sides until evenly charred.

TO GARNISH AND SERVE
Spread the lemon crème fraîche across a serving platter as a base. Transfer the cabbage on top of the crème fraîche and drizzle the urfa chilli butter on top. Garnish with ripped basil leaves.

GRILLED BROCCOLI SALAD

SERVES 4–6

2 heads of broccoli, ends trimmed

30ml lemon juice

70ml extra virgin olive oil

2 garlic cloves, grated

2 tsp Aleppo chilli flakes (also known as pul biber or red pepper flakes) or ½ tsp dried chilli flakes

Cut the broccoli through the stem to make 6–8 large 'trees' per broccoli.

Set a pan of salted water over high heat and bring to a rolling boil. Prepare a bowl filled with iced water and blanch the broccoli trees for no more than 2 minutes. Transfer with a slotted spoon or lifter to the ice bath as soon as the broccoli is al dente. It's important not to overcook the broccoli at this stage.

Set a barbecue up for single-zone direct grilling (page 17), ensuring that you are cooking over hot embers.

Whilst waiting for the fire, prepare the dressing by whisking all the remaining ingredients together in a small bowl. Taste for seasoning and adjust accordingly.

Grill the broccoli over high heat on both sides until charred and crisped in parts, no more than a couple of minutes. Transfer to a bowl and toss with the dressing. Check for seasoning. Serve warm or at room temperature.

• •

MIXED GRILLED VEGETABLES

These grilled vegetables are a standard accompaniment to any type of meat served in a Turkish grill restaurant.

The onions take the longest to cook, followed by the tomatoes and lastly the Turkish chilli peppers (which should cook the quickest), but you can whack them on the grill at the same time, just keep each component warm once it comes off. The stragglers won't be far behind in any case.

SERVES 4–6

6 Turkish chilli peppers

6 white onions or shallots, quartered

6 tomatoes, halved

extra virgin olive oil

2 narrow metal skewers, about 45cm long

2 thick metal skewers, about 38–45cm long

Skewer the vegetables separately, using two narrow metal skewers to hold the chilli peppers in place, and a single thicker skewer for both the onions and tomato halves.

Grill the vegetables directly over burning hot coals, until nicely blackened or charred on the outside but softened on the inside. Brush each skewer with the olive oil intermittently as the vegetables cook, and season with salt and pepper.

Remove from the skewers, transfer to a plate and serve immediately.

SLOW-BRAISED PIT BEANS
WITH OXTAIL & CRISPY SHALLOTS

Slow-cooked beans with cheap cuts of meat are a staple of many cuisines around the world, usually born out of a need for inexpensive sustenance to serve the working classes.

I like to use oxtail for my beans. The downside is it requires patience. Oxtail tells you when it's ready, not the other way around. And it can make you wait and wait and then wait some more. Stick with it. Top the pan up with water or stock periodically to make sure the meat is kept covered, and when she's quite ready she'll reward you with the most flavourful braise.

SERVES 10–12

CANNELLINI BEANS

400g dried cannellini beans, soaked overnight

1 onion, peeled and cut in half

2–3 sprigs of rosemary

2 sprigs of sage

4–5 garlic cloves

1 tsp cumin seeds

120ml olive oil

BRAISED OXTAIL

800g oxtail

100ml olive oil

knob of unsalted butter

1 onion, finely chopped

1 large carrot, peeled and cut into 1cm dice

3 celery stalks, finely chopped

4 garlic cloves, finely chopped

2 sprigs of thyme

2 bay leaves

2 cinnamon sticks

2 star anise

120g tomato paste

100ml red wine

1kg tomato passata

2 tbsp date syrup

SERVE

Crispy Shallots (page 240)

handful of picked dill fronds

Chilli Oil (page 260)

FOR THE CANNELINI BEANS

Drain the soaked beans and rinse them under cold water for 30 seconds or so. Transfer to a large saucepan, cover with water, add the onion, rosemary, sage, garlic and cumin seeds and bring to the boil over high heat. Once boiling, reduce the heat to medium-low and gently simmer the beans for 1–1½ hours until tender. Be sure to periodically skim off any impurities or scum that rise to the surface as the beans cook. Once cooked, drain the beans in a colander and set to one side until needed.

FOR THE BRAISED OXTAIL

Season the oxtail liberally with salt and black pepper. Heat the olive oil over medium-high heat and, working in batches, seal the meat so that it's browned on all sides. Don't overcrowd the pan – you want the meat to sear and colour quickly rather than stew laboriously. Remove the meat to a wire rack using tongs and set aside until required.

Heat the butter in a large heavy-based saucepan (preferably a cast-iron pan) over medium heat and sweat the onion, carrot and celery until softened and translucent but not coloured. Season with salt and black pepper, add the garlic, thyme, bay leaves, cinnamon and star anise, and continue to cook for a few more minutes. Stir in the tomato paste and fry for a further 5 minutes, before pouring in the red wine and stirring to deglaze the pan. Fold through the passata and date syrup, lower the oxtail into the pan carefully, and add enough water to cover. Bring to a gentle simmer, turn the heat down to the lowest setting and cook, covered, for 3–4 hours, until the sauce has reduced and thickened, darkening in colour. The oxtail should all but fall from the bone with the lightest of pressure. Don't be afraid to add some water – the oxtail should be submerged at all times, and may need topping up before it's cooked through.

Add the beans back to the pan. Set a barbecue up for smoking (page 19), and try and reach (and maintain) a steady temperature of 120°C. Smoke the beans, uncovered, for a further 2–3 hours, checking on them periodically to stir and ensure they haven't dried out. You can always add some water to the pan should this happen. (As an alternative, bake the beans in an oven preheated to 160°C/140°C Fan/Gas mark 3 for a further 1–1½ hours.)

Serve topped with crispy shallots, picked dill and a drizzle of chilli oil.

TURKISH 'SHEPHERDS' SALAD

SERVES 4

6 tomatoes, deseeded

½ cucumber, deseeded

small handful of picked flat-leaf parsley leaves

1 tbsp roughly chopped mint

1 spring onion, green parts only, thinly sliced

2 long green peppers, thinly sliced

75ml extra virgin olive oil

45ml lemon juice

1 tsp ground sumac

1 tsp Aleppo chilli flakes (also known as pul biber or red pepper flakes) or ½ tsp dried chilli flakes

Cut the tomatoes and cucumber into small batons, about 0.5cm by 2cm, but don't be too precise or get hung about it – life's too short. Combine in a bowl with the herbs, spring onion greens and peppers.

Dress the salad with the olive oil and lemon juice. Season with the spices and salt, and toss well to combine.

Serve immediately. This salad will lose its vibrancy and freshness with time, so it's important to dress it at the table.

• •

GRILLED ROMAINE
WITH ANCHOVY, CHILLI & LEMON DRESSING

SERVES 2

60ml olive oil

2 garlic cloves, roughly chopped

3–4 anchovies (best quality you can afford), chopped

1 red chilli, thinly sliced

2 tbsp lemon juice

1 tbsp roughly chopped flat-leaf parsley

1 red pepper

1 romaine lettuce, cut in half

flaked sea salt (such as Maldon) and coarse ground black pepper

Heat 30ml of olive oil in a small saucepan over medium heat and caramelise the garlic, being careful not to burn it, which will make it taste bitter. Remove from the heat, and add the anchovies, red chilli, lemon juice and parsley.

Blacken the red pepper on a barbecue grill, or directly on the gas flame on the stovetop, until charred and softened, and transfer to a bowl. Cover with clingfilm and set aside to cool. Peel, quarter and deseed the peppers, removing any inner membrane as you do. Cut into 1cm dice and toss through the dressing.

Brush the romaine lettuce halves with the remaining 30ml of olive oil and season with flaked salt and black pepper.

Prepare a barbecue for single-zone direct grilling (page 17) and once the embers are burning hot, char the romaine halves on each side until blackened and slightly softened.

Spoon the warm dressing over the grilled romaine and serve immediately.

CHARRED CARROTS
WITH SPICED NUTS & LIME YOGHURT

Carrots are available throughout the year but they're at their sweetest and most intense over late summer into autumn. I like to use heritage carrots for this dish, small ones, with leaves trimmed but not removed. Ask your greengrocer if he can source them. If he can't, find another greengrocer. The carrots must be well charred. It will enhance the final taste of the dish. (Pictured overleaf).

SERVES 4–6

LIME YOGHURT

100g full-fat natural yoghurt

grated zest of 1 lime, plus the juice of ½

1½ tbsp extra virgin olive oil

SPICED NUTS

½ tbsp coriander seeds

¼ tbsp fennel seeds

1 star anise

¼ tbsp ground cinnamon

pinch of ground nutmeg

20g walnuts, toasted

20g almonds, toasted

5g pumpkin seeds, toasted

¼ tsp salt

olive oil

CHARRED CARROTS

3 bunches of small heritage carrots or 6 medium carrots, peeled and halved lengthways

2 tbsp olive oil

1 tbsp finely chopped thyme leaves

2 tbsp golden raisins

1½ tbsp runny honey

GARNISH

picked dill fronds and coriander leaves

2 spring onions, green parts only, thinly sliced

1 tsp Aleppo chilli flakes or ½ tsp dried chilli flakes

extra virgin olive oil

FOR THE LIME YOGHURT

Mix all the ingredients together in a bowl, whisking to incorporate. Check for seasoning and adjust according to taste.

FOR THE SPICED NUTS

Toast the coriander seeds, fennel seeds and star anise in a small frying pan over low heat until smoking and fragrant. Transfer to a spice grinder, add the cinnamon and nutmeg, and grind to a fine powder.

Combine the spice mix, nuts and pumpkin seeds together in a food processor and pulse to a coarse and chunky paste. Season with salt and a drizzle of olive oil and set aside until required.

FOR THE CHARRED CARROTS

Toss the carrots in a bowl with the olive oil and season liberally with salt and black pepper.

Set a barbecue up for single-zone indirect grilling (page 17). Heat a large cast-iron pan directly on the fire and, when smoking hot, add the carrots, cut-side down. Don't overcrowd the pan; cook only in a single layer so that each carrot has a generous contact point with the pan.

Char the carrots until blackened but not burnt, then turn once to char the reverse side. The carrots should be tender to a knife, with a lovely blackened crust on the outside. Finish by adding the thyme, raisins and honey to glaze the pan for 1–2 minutes until the raisins have softened, coating all the carrots.

TO GARNISH AND SERVE

Transfer the carrots to a large serving platter. Spoon the yoghurt on top and finish with the spiced nuts. Garnish with dill fronds, coriander leaves and spring onions, along with a sprinkle of chilli flakes. Finish with a final drizzle of extra virgin olive oil. Serve piping hot, warmed or at room temperature. They'll taste good regardless of their temperature.

SWEET POTATO, FIG & BLUE CHEESE SALAD

WITH CHAMOMILE DRESSING

My parents have a small house up in the mountains in the south of France. They have two fig trees, and every August for about two weeks we're treated to a deluge of the most intensely ripe and beautiful figs that would convert even the most militant of fig haters. The local sweet potatoes are also phenomenal, bursting with a deep orange flesh quite unlike anything we can get in the UK.

This recipe was born out of having some left-over barbecued sweet potatoes from the night before that needed to be used up, and figs of such abundance we didn't know what to do with them.

At the time I used Roquefort, but upon returning to home shores I found a Dorset Blue or Stilton worked just as well. You just need something crumbly and quite dry with the punchy force of a strong blue cheese to counter the overwhelming sweetness of the softer sweet potatoes and fig.

SERVES 2–4
AS A SIDE SALAD

HONEY AND CHAMOMILE DRESSING

1 tbsp runny honey

2 tbsp lemon juice

3 tbsp extra virgin olive oil

1 tsp dried chamomile

½ tsp chilli flakes

SWEET POTATO AND FIGS

1 sweet potato

3 figs, quartered

50g lamb's lettuce

2–3 tbsp hard, crumbly blue cheese (such as Dorset Blue or Stilton)

picked dill fronds

1 spring onion, green part only, thinly sliced

1½ tbsp chopped toasted walnuts

½ tsp dried chamomile, to serve

extra virgin olive oil, to serve

FOR THE HONEY AND CHAMOMILE DRESSING
Put the honey and lemon juice in a bowl and stir to combine. Whisk in the olive oil until emulsified; add the dried chamomile and chilli flakes, and season to taste with salt and black pepper.

This dressing will benefit from being allowed to marinate at room temperature, so that the flavours can infuse and intensify. Ideally, you would make this dressing up several hours in advance, whisking it all back to an emulsified state as and when it's needed. In the absence of available time, it still tastes great, so don't fret and proceed regardless.

FOR THE SWEET POTATO AND FIGS
Preheat the oven to 180°C/160°C Fan/Gas mark 4 and bake the sweet potato for 1–1½ hours, until soft and tender all the way through when pierced with a knife. Remove from the oven and cool.

When cool enough to handle, peel the sweet potato and crumble into chunks, then scatter across a large serving platter. Place the quartered figs randomly around in the gaps, and fill up any further gaps with the lamb's lettuce. Crumble the blue cheese over the top, and spoon over the dressing liberally.

Finish by garnishing with dill fronds, spring onion greens and the walnuts strewn all over. A final dusting of dried chamomile and a drizzle of olive oil and away you go. Serve immediately.

MIDDLE EASTERN SLAW

Everybody loves a good slaw, and we're no different. We often have one on our menu, and it will change according to season. Our summer slaw uses kohlrabi, runner beans, mangetout and fennel. This recipe is my favourite of all our variations. It comes on towards the end of autumn as the nights are drawing in, and when red cabbage and beetroot are at their sweetest.

SERVES 4–6
AS A SIDE

SLAW DRESSING

1 tbsp maple syrup

1½ tbsp date syrup

1 tbsp pomegranate molasses

2 tbsp red wine vinegar

100ml extra virgin olive oil

MIDDLE EASTERN SLAW

½ head of red cabbage

1 tbsp salt

½ red onion, thinly sliced

1 red chilli, deseeded and finely sliced

1 beetroot, peeled and ends trimmed

1 large carrot, peeled and ends trimmed

grated zest of 1 lemon

small handful of picked dill leaves, plus extra to garnish

2 tbsp finely chopped flat-leaf parsley

2 tbsp finely chopped coriander

3 tbsp toasted and chopped pecans

small handful of pomegranate seeds

FOR THE SLAW DRESSING

Whisk the maple syrup, date syrup, pomegranate molasses and vinegar together in a bowl.

Gradually whisk in the olive oil until the mixture is emulsified, and season with salt and black pepper to taste.

FOR THE MIDDLE EASTERN SLAW

Cut the halved red cabbage in half again, peel off the outer layers, and cut out the core. Slice the cabbage as thinly as you can, preferably using a mandoline, but in the absence of one, a sharp knife and some handy knife skills will suffice.

Toss the shredded cabbage in the salt, ensuring it's well mixed through. Set the cabbage in a colander over a sink, and place a heavy weight atop to act as a press – I like to use a small bowl filled with water for this – enabling the cabbage to release some of its juices and soften whilst retaining crunch.

Allow the cabbage to press for an hour, before transferring it to a large bowl with the onion and chilli. Thinly slice the beetroot and carrot into flat strips, using a mandoline (if available), or with a sharp knife, and cut each strip into matchsticks, about 10cm in length. Mix all the ingredients together in the bowl, along with the lemon zest, herbs and half the pecans and set aside, refrigerated, until ready to serve.

Dress the slaw just prior to serving, and toss well with your hands to ensure the salad is evenly coated. Garnish the salad with the reserved pecans, some picked dill fronds and a sprinkling of pomegranate seeds.

This salad is excellent accompanied by some labneh (page 261) or yoghurt if you happen to have either lying around in your fridge.

VEGETABLES & SIDES

SAFFRON POTATO SALAD
WITH GARLIC & TURMERIC DRESSING

SERVES 4
AS A SIDE SALAD

POTATOES

500g Charlotte potatoes, peeled

100ml saffron water (a generous pinch of saffron soaked in 100ml boiling water and left to infuse for 15 minutes)

1 tbsp salt

2 pickled jalapeños, thinly sliced, to garnish

1 tbsp finely chopped flat-leaf parsley, to garnish

GARLIC AND TURMERIC DRESSING

200ml Garlic Oil (page 260) or extra virgin olive oil

2 shallots, finely chopped

2 Confit Garlic Cloves (page 260), ground or chopped to a paste

2 tsp ground turmeric

2 tsp ground cumin

2 tsp flaked sea salt (such as Maldon)

3 tbsp lemon juice

2 tbsp chopped coriander

2 pickled jalapeños, thinly sliced

coarse ground black pepper

FOR THE POTATOES

Place the potatoes in a heavy-based saucepan with the saffron water, and top up with water to cover. Add the salt and bring to the boil over a high heat. Reduce to a gentle simmer and cook the potatoes for 15–20 minutes, until tender to a knife, but still al dente. Remove from the heat and leave in the water until cool enough to handle but still warm.

FOR THE GARLIC AND TURMERIC DRESSING

Put all the ingredients in a bowl and stir to combine.

TO FINISH THE POTATOES

Drain the potatoes from the water and slice into 5mm rounds. Dress whilst still warm and leave to marinate for an hour or preferably longer. Season with salt and pepper to taste. Garnish the salad with the sliced pickled jalapeños and chopped parsley.

This can keep in the fridge for up to 3 days; the flavours will intensify with time.

PATLICAN SOSLU
AUBERGINE IN TOMATO SAUCE

A favourite of mine, this Turkish starter varies from restaurant to restaurant. I slice the aubergine lengthways into steaks, roughly a centimetre thick, as opposed to the more common preparation of cutting them into very thin rounds or triangles. I feel it makes for a more interesting aesthetic. I don't salt my aubergine before frying. There's good flavour in there that you want to retain.

This dish can work as a mezze, starter, side (perhaps with lamb chops), or vegetarian main with some Mejaderah (page 186) or rice. As with most recipes in this book, you'll be grateful for some accompanying bread.

SERVES 2–4

TOMATO SAUCE

2 tbsp olive oil

1 onion, finely sliced

2 garlic cloves, thinly sliced

100g cherry tomatoes, cut in half

1 tbsp tomato paste

2 tbsp roughly chopped flat-leaf parsley

AUBERGINE

1 aubergine, cut lengthways into 1cm thick slices

60ml olive oil or Garlic Oil (page 260)

flaked sea salt (such as Maldon)

150g cherry tomatoes, halved

handful of basil leaves, ripped

FOR THE TOMATO SAUCE
Warm the olive oil in a wide heavy-based frying pan over medium-high heat and sweat the onion until softened and translucent, about 7–10 minutes. Add the garlic and fry for a few more minutes, before throwing in the cherry tomatoes to soften and break down as they cook. Stir in the tomato paste, turn the heat down to medium-low and continue to fry for a further 2–3 minutes. Throw in the parsley, season to taste and remove from the heat. Throw some more oil at the sauce if it seems too dry. It should be well oiled.

FOR THE AUBERGINE
Brush the aubergine slices generously with the olive oil and season with flaked salt and black pepper.

Heat a cast-iron pan, wide enough to accommodate the aubergine, over medium-high heat, on the stovetop or over a fire and brush generously with olive oil.

Add the aubergine slices to the pan and cook for 5–7 minutes until well browned. Continue to baste the top half with more oil as the aubergine cooks. Turn the aubergine over and continue to cook for a further 5–6 minutes until the aubergine has crisped and browned all over.

Heat a separate cast-iron pan (if there isn't sufficient room in the initial one you are using), over medium-high heat and brush generously with more oil. Blacken the cherry tomato halves, flesh-side down, for 3–4 minutes, until well charred and slightly softened. The tomatoes should release themselves from the surface of the pan once sufficiently blackened, so resist the urge to meddle with them until such time as they tell you to.

TO FINISH THE PATLICAN SOSLU
Warm the tomato sauce through on the stovetop. Arrange the aubergine slices on a serving platter and smother in the sauce. Scatter the blackened tomatoes around the platter and garnish with ripped basil leaves and a further drizzle of olive oil if necessary. Serve hot or just slightly warmed.

PANEER SABZI – FRESH HERB & SOFT CHEESE SALAD
WITH HONEYED WALNUTS & RADISH

Paneer sabzi (pronounced 'shab-shee') is a Persian herb salad – citrus sharp with herby bitterness – that is brilliant for cutting through rich and fatty meats such as pork belly or rib-eye. It also works as a garnish to barbecued whole fish.

I like to use ricotta salata in this salad, a dried and crumbly version of the more readily available creamy version more familiar and accessible to all. If you can't find it, you can use the original, or a soft goat's cheese instead.

SERVES 2
AS A SIDE SALAD

HONEYED WALNUTS

50g toasted walnuts, roughly
   chopped

1½ tsp runny honey

pinch of cayenne pepper

LEMON DRESSING

1½ tbsp lemon juice

3 tbsp extra virgin olive oil

½ tsp ground sumac

PANEER SABZI

small handful of Chilli Pangratatto
   (page 241)

6–7 radishes, thinly sliced

small handful each of picked mint,
   parsley and dill leaves

small bunch of chives, cut to
   2.5cm batons

1 shallot, sliced as finely as
   possible

1 spring onion, finely sliced on
   an angle

40g ricotta cheese, crumbled

2 tbsp pomegranate seeds

FOR THE HONEYED WALNUTS
Combine the walnuts in a bowl with the honey (let down with a drop of warm water if particularly thick). Add the cayenne pepper and season with salt to taste. Set aside whilst you prepare the other components of the salad.

FOR THE LEMON DRESSING:
Whisk the lemon juice and olive oil together in a small bowl to emulsify, and stir the sumac through. Season with salt and black pepper to taste.

FOR THE PANEER SABZI
Crush the pangratatto into coarse crumbs, either by using your hands, as I like to do, or else by placing them on a work surface and using a rolling pin.

In a large bowl, toss the radishes, herbs, chives, shallot and spring onion with the lemon dressing, mixing well with your hands.

Transfer the dressed salad to a serving plate, place a mound of the crushed pangratatto alongside, and do the same with the ricotta cheese and honeyed walnuts. Garnish with the pomegranate seeds and a final drizzle of olive oil to add a lovely gloss. Serve immediately.

MEJADERAH

@thegirlwhoatelondon is a (lovely) regular of ours who fell deeply in love with our mejaderah, to the point where she hounded us incessantly when we took it off the menu until it came back on. It became quite terrifying. We now keep it on the menu almost all of the time, if only to keep her happy. We're all scared of the consequences of what might happen to us in our sleep if we take it off again.

This is my ultimate comfort food, perfect for a cold night in by the fire, or any other night for that matter.

SERVES 6–8

2 tbsp olive oil

1 tbsp unsalted butter

200g white onions, thinly sliced

5g cumin seeds

5g coriander seeds

2 star anise

2 cinnamon sticks

500g basmati rice

250g brown lentils, cooked in water to al dente

½ tsp ground turmeric

1 tbsp ground allspice

2 bay leaves

GARNISH AND SERVE

generous handful of Crispy Shallots (page 240)

3 tbsp roughly chopped flat-leaf parsley

150g Tahina Sauce (page 262)

Heat the olive oil and butter in a heavy-based pan over medium-low heat and cook the onions, covered, until caramelised and deep golden brown. This should take between 30 and 45 minutes. Remember to keep checking back and stirring occasionally.

In a separate pan, dry-toast the cumin and coriander seeds, star anise and cinnamon sticks for a couple of minutes over medium-high heat, until fragrant and just starting to smoke.

Add the caramelised onions, rice, lentils, turmeric, allspice and bay leaves, and fry for a further 1–2 minutes.

Add water to the rice, just enough to cover, and seal the pan as tightly as possible with clingfilm. Try to avoid leaving any openings for steam to escape.

Reduce the heat to low and cook the rice for 20 minutes. Turn off the heat, allowing the clingfilm to be sucked in by the vacuum created. Set aside for a few minutes, before removing the clingfilm carefully. Be wary of escaping steam – it will leave a nasty burn – so approach and treat with caution. Fluff the rice and lentils with a fork and serve immediately, garnished with crispy shallots, the parsley and the tahina sauce alongside. Add a fresh chopped Jerusalem salad (page 192) or salad of choice to convert this side dish into a meal in its own right.

BRAISED COLLARD GREENS
WITH LAMB SHANK

Braised 'collards' (or spring greens as they're known in the UK) are a feature of American barbecue, often stewed with ham hock to yield a porky broth full or warmth and soul. We use lamb shank for our braised greens, sweetened with some date molasses. It creates an interesting, North African version. Swiss chard would be a good substitute for the greens if you want to go crazy and mix things up a little bit.

SERVES 4–6

100ml olive oil

1.2kg lamb or veal shanks, on the bone

2 red onions, thinly sliced

2 garlic cloves, peeled and sliced

1 tsp sweet paprika

200ml red wine vinegar

150g Harissa (page 259) or shop-bought

4 large bunches of spring greens, washed, stemmed and ripped into pieces

2 litres water

½ bunch of thyme, tied into a bundle with twine

1 preserved lemon, rind only, quartered

120ml date syrup

Heat the olive oil in a large, deep stockpot over medium-high heat and brown the lamb shanks on all sides until golden brown. Turn the heat down to medium, shift the lamb to one side of the pan, and add the onions to the opposite side. Fry the onions in the oil for 4–5 minutes, then add the garlic and paprika. Continue to cook for 5 minutes, until the onions are softened and translucent.

Pour in the vinegar and stir to deglaze the pot, then add the harissa, followed by the spring greens and water. Add the thyme bundle and preserved lemon, cover the pot and reduce the heat to medium-low.

Cover the greens and lamb with a cartouche (a small circle of parchment paper with a hole in the middle) so as to ensure the ingredients stay submerged, and braise for 1½–2 hours, undisturbed, until such time as the meat falls from the bone with ease.

Lift the shanks from the pot and pull the meat from the bone using some forks, discarding the bones once finished. Remove the fat that has risen to the surface of the pot with a ladle, and return the pulled lamb meat to the braised greens. Stir through the date syrup and season to taste with salt and black pepper. Serve immediately, whilst piping hot.

ROASTED BEETROOT SALAD
WITH WHIPPED FETA, HAZELNUT & SAFFRON CANDIED ORANGE

This salad was on our starting menu when we first opened and rarely comes off. It's the perfect balance of earthy sweetness from the beetroot, drawn out by being roasted on a bed of salt, sharp acidity from the sherry vinegar, and saltiness from the feta.

Date syrup can be found in most Arabic or Turkish grocery stores, but if you can't find any you could substitute with half the quantity of maple syrup and adjust according to taste. Try and buy good-quality sherry vinegar. It will make a worthwhile difference that I think justifies the expense.

SERVES 4–6

BEETROOT
800g beetroot
coarse sea salt or rock salt

SAFFRON CANDIED ORANGE PEEL
1 orange, peeled in strips using a canele zester, or peeled into strips and very finely sliced
100g caster sugar
120ml water
30ml saffron water (a scant pinch of saffron soaked in 30ml boiling water and infused for 15 minutes)

DATE SYRUP DRESSING
2 tbsp date syrup
2 tsp pomegranate molasses
75ml sherry vinegar
50ml olive oil
large pinch of ground cinnamon
2 tbsp finely shredded mint

GARNISH AND SERVE
120g Whipped Feta (page 261)
3 tbsp roasted hazelnuts, roughly chopped or crushed
picked dill fronds
10–12 pieces of Candied Saffron Orange Peel (see above)
2 tbsp dill oil (1 tbsp extra virgin olive oil mixed with 1 tbsp chopped dill)

Preheat the oven to 180°C/160°C Fan/Gas mark 4.

FOR THE BEETROOT
Rinse and scrub the beetroot to remove excess dirt and pat dry with kitchen paper. Make a bed of coarse sea (or rock) salt in a shallow roasting tin, on which to place the beetroot, and roast uncovered for approximately 1½ hours. The salt will draw out the moisture, intensifying the beetroot's flavour as it cooks.

The beetroot is cooked when a knife reaches the centre easily but still retains just the slightest of resistance. Once cooked, remove from the oven and cool. Whilst the beetroot is cooking prepare the remaining components of the dish.

FOR THE SAFFRON CANDIED ORANGE PEEL
Blanch the orange peel in a saucepan of boiling water for 20–30 seconds and drain. Repeat the process two more times to remove any bitterness.

Combine the sugar with the water and saffron water, and bring to the boil. Cook the blanched orange peel in this syrup for 15–20 minutes until candied. It should be sticky and sweet.

Stored in a sterilised jar, unrefrigerated but in a cool place, the saffron candied orange peel can be kept for up to 6 months and beyond.

FOR THE DATE SYRUP DRESSING
Put the date syrup, pomegranate molasses and vinegar together in a bowl and whisk to combine. Place the bowl on a damp cloth or tea towel, and, whilst pouring in the olive oil slowly with one hand, whisk with the other to emulsify the dressing. Add the cinnamon and stir through the chopped mint.

TO FINISH THE BEETROOT
Once the beetroot is cool enough to handle, peel and cut into (roughly) 2.5cm chunks. Transfer to a large bowl and stir in the dressing using a spoon or preferably your hands to combine. Season the beetroot to taste with salt and black pepper and leave to marinate for at least 1 hour at room temperature.

TO GARNISH AND SERVE
Serve the beetroot atop the whipped feta and garnish with the hazelnuts, picked dill fronds and candied saffron orange peel. Drizzle dill oil all over.

SKILLET GARLIC POTATOES
WITH LEMON, GARLIC & HERBS

My dad makes a dish he calls 'Greek potatoes' that he serves alongside some of his legendary roasts and stews. I don't know where he got the recipe from, or what makes them Greek for that matter, but that's neither here nor there. They're delicious and always greatly appreciated. This is my version. I call them 'skillet garlic potatoes', which doesn't roll off the tongue quite so easily but at least it makes sense.

SERVES 4

1kg small starchy potatoes, such as Russet or Yukon Gold, scrubbed

80ml olive oil

40g unsalted butter

8 sprigs of lemon thyme

2 garlic cloves, finely chopped

grated zest and juice of 1 lemon

2 tbsp roughly chopped flat-leaf parsley, to serve

Fill a deep pan with salted water, add the potatoes whole, with the skin on, and bring to a boil over high heat. Turn the heat down to medium so that the water has a gentle roll and boil the potatoes for 20–25 minutes, or until al dente. Drain, cool and quarter the potatoes into wedges. Set the wedges on a wire rack or some kitchen paper and leave to air-dry whilst you get on with the rest of the recipe.

Heat the olive oil and butter in a heavy-based frying pan or cast-iron skillet pan over medium heat until melted. Add the lemon thyme sprigs to infuse.

Lay the potatoes in a single layer in the hot oil and season with salt and pepper. Cook on both sides until deeply coloured a dark golden brown and crispy on the outside, about 3–5 minutes on each side.

A few minutes before finishing the potatoes, mix the garlic cloves, lemon zest and lemon juice together in a small bowl and pour over the top of the potatoes. Continue to cook until the lemon juice has all but been absorbed and the potatoes are dry.

Transfer the potatoes to a serving platter and serve immediately, with some parsley strewn over the top.

BERBER & Q FATTOUSH

My favourite fattoush in London was served at the iconic Beirut Express on the Edgware Road, where I lived for six years. Commendable and honest, it was nothing fancy. I would often go after my shift had finished at work and always order the same thing, a kebab wrap, some hummus Beiruty (spicy hummus) and a fattoush salad. Tragically, the restaurant recently closed down.

Essentially a fattoush salad is, at its most basic, just a chopped salad with baby gem and pita croutons. I actually get a little 'cheffy' in this recipe with the addition of some whipped feta and olive tapenade, but, as with most 'cheffy' touches, these are not essential.

SERVES 4
AS A MEZZE,
OR AS A SIDE SALAD

ZA'ATAR PITA CROUTES

2 tbsp Garlic Oil (page 260), or olive oil

1 pita, ripped into bite-size pieces

1 tsp za'atar

GREEN CHILLI AND LEMON DRESSING

1 tbsp za'atar

3 tbsp lemon juice

1 garlic clove, minced

2 green bird's eye chillies, finely chopped

½ tsp salt

pinch of ground black pepper

60ml extra virgin olive oil

FATTOUSH

1 baby gem lettuce

2 tomatoes, cut into eighths

½ cucumber, deseeded and cut into large chunks

1 tbsp chopped flat-leaf parsley

1 tbsp finely shredded mint

GARNISH

4 tbsp Whipped Feta (page 261)

2 tbsp olive tapenade, shop-bought

2 tbsp pomegranate seeds

4 radishes, thinly sliced

2 tsp za'atar

1 tsp dried mint

Herb Oil (page 264) or olive oil (optional)

FOR THE ZA'ATAR PITA CROUTES

Heat the garlic oil in a frying pan over medium heat until warm. Add the pita bread and toss in the oil. Don't overcrowd the pan – you want each piece of pita to absorb as much oil as possible. Don't be afraid to add more oil to the pan if necessary. Cook the pita pieces until golden brown and crisp, tossing in the pan from time to time to ensure they don't burn. Remove from the pan and drain on kitchen paper to soak up any excess oil. Season with the za'atar sprinkled all over and salt and pepper to taste.

These croutes can be made well in advance and set aside until required. They can be kept in an airtight container for a couple of days before losing their crispness. They're good with almost any salad, so make a double batch whilst you're at it and bask in the glory of your efficiency when you get to use them the next day.

FOR THE GREEN CHILLI AND LEMON DRESSING

Put all the ingredients together in a small bowl and whisk to combine. Leave the dressing to infuse for up to an hour at room temperature before use.

FOR THE FATTOUSH

Separate the baby gem lettuce into individual leaves, wash in cold water and rinse dry using a salad spinner. Cut each leaf into three and combine with the tomatoes and cucumber in a large bowl. Add the parsley and mint as well as the za'atar pita croutes, pour in the dressing and mix well, preferably using your hands so you can be gentle and not break up the tomatoes too much. Check for seasoning at this point, and add more salt or pepper as required.

TO GARNISH AND SERVE

Drag the whipped feta around the outside edges of a serving bowl using the back of a spoon. Place the fattoush on top, studded intermittently with some drops of olive tapenade (if using), the pomegranate seeds sprinkled on top and the radish slices delicately positioned at random intervals around the bowl. Garnish with a sprinkling of za'atar and dried mint and finish with a drizzle of herb oil (if you have any) over the top.

JERUSALEM 'CHOPPED' SALAD

I've had this salad countless times in Israel. They seem to serve it with everything. It's always a medley of freshly chopped seasonal vegetables. Since I'm rarely there any time other than summer, this always tends to be some combination of cucumber, tomato, peppers and onion.

I like to serve this salad with a big dollop of tahini and some pine nuts, which provide a buttery and rich foil to the salad's sharpness, but you can serve it without if you'd prefer. No one's judging.

SERVES 4
AS A MEZZE,
OR 2 AS A SIDE SALAD

---

4 plum tomatoes, cut into rough dice

1 red pepper, deseeded and roughly diced

1 cucumber, cut into rough chunks

¼ red onion, very finely chopped

1 spring onion, green parts only, finely sliced

1 green chilli, deseeded and finely chopped

80ml olive oil

50ml lemon juice, plus extra to taste

1 tsp za'atar

½ tsp dried mint

2 tbsp roughly chopped picked flat-leaf parsley

2 tbsp finely chopped picked mint

SERVE
80g Tahina Sauce (page 262)
1 tbsp pine nuts, toasted
pinch of ground sumac

Put the tomatoes, red pepper, cucumber, red onion, spring onion greens and chilli in a bowl and stir to combine.

Pour in the olive oil and lemon juice, season with salt and pepper to taste, add the za'atar and dried mint and mix well.

Just before serving, fold through the parsley and mint and check for seasoning. The salad needs to be quite sharp, so add more lemon juice if required.

Serve the salad piled high with the tahina sauce spooned over the top, a sprinkling of pine nuts and a pinch of sumac for the garnish.

EMBER-BURNT LEEKS
WITH CORIANDER DRESSING & SAFFRON AIOLI

Try and find younger, smaller leeks for this dish. They're more intense in flavour and better suited to being the star of the show than their larger counterparts, which I mainly use for stocks or as an ingredient in some other dish.

Steak knives also help. Leeks can be quite stringy when served whole and difficult to cut through. Or else go primitive and eat them with your hands, ripped apart using your teeth. If you're unfortunate enough not to have any teeth, revert to steak knives.

SERVES 6–8

LEMON CORIANDER DRESSING
½ bunch coriander
2 tbsp water
grated zest and juice of 1 lemon
1 tbsp runny honey
1 garlic clove, minced
80ml extra virgin olive oil
1 tsp salt
½ tbsp coriander seeds, toasted
¼ tsp ground cardamom

SAFFRON AIOLI
2 garlic cloves, minced
1 tsp salt
1 tsp Dijon mustard
1 egg yolk
120ml vegetable oil
2 tbsp olive oil
1 tbsp lemon juice
2 tbsp saffron water (a scant pinch of saffron soaked in 2 tbsp boiling water and left to infuse for 15 minutes)

LEEKS
8 leeks, green tops trimmed
Garlic Oil (page 260) or olive oil
2 tbsp Pickled Pomegranate Seeds (page 251)

FOR THE LEMON CORIANDER DRESSING

Blitz the coriander, stalks and all, in a food processor with the water until a coarse purée has formed.

In a bowl, combine the lemon juice, honey and garlic and whisk in the extra virgin olive oil gradually to emulsify.

Add the blended coriander to the dressing base, season with salt, and add the lemon zest, coriander seeds and ground cardamom. Set aside until required. The dressing is best made fresh but can be kept in the fridge for up to 2 days.

FOR THE SAFFRON AIOLI

Blitz the garlic, salt, mustard and egg yolk in a food processor.

Gradually pour in the vegetable oil, very slowly at first, but more steadily as the aioli emulsifies and thickens. Once the vegetable oil has been fully incorporated, continue to blend as you pour in the olive oil. Add the lemon juice and pulse to combine. Gradually add the saffron water, ½ tablespoon at a time, until the aioli has the desired consistency. For this dish I like the aioli to be quite loose so that it can serve as a sauce for the leeks and generously coat them. Check for seasoning and stir in more salt or lemon juice as required.

FOR THE LEEKS

Wash the leeks in cold running water and drip-dry on a cooling rack.

Prepare a fire for grilling (page 17) and once the embers are burning hot spread them across the base of the barbecue to form a bed for the leeks. (Alternatively, heat a griddle pan on the stove until smoking hot.) Grill the leeks directly on the embers for 8–10 minutes, turning frequently, until tender when pierced with a knife. The outer layers will blacken and burn, but don't be concerned by this. They can be peeled off at the end, and provide a protective coat within which the inner layers of the leek will steam.

TO SERVE

Remove from the fire and transfer to a serving platter. Peel off the outer, burnt layer but don't be too obsessive about removing it all – some blackened skin left behind will add flavour. Brush the leeks with garlic oil, season with salt and pepper and douse in the lemon coriander dressing. Serve with the saffron aioli over the top or in a bowl for dipping, with the pickled pomegranate seeds.

GRILLED BROCCOLINI
WITH ROSE HARISSA & ANCHOVY SAMBAL

I have a deep affinity with many cuisines of the world, but especially Malaysian. It has such depth and heart, influenced and shaped by the coming together of so many different cultures, which makes it so interesting and varied.

The sambal, known as sambal ikan teri, is used to garnish many of my favourite Malaysian dishes, made from fried peanuts, dried anchovy and chilli flakes bound together by a sweet caramel. It's the perfect balance of sweet and salt, spice and crunch. I can eat it by itself as a bar snack.

I use rose harissa (page 259) to make my own sambal. It elevates the broccolini to new heights.

SERVES 4–6

ROSE HARISSA AND
  ANCHOVY SAMBAL

50g dried anchovies, gutted
  and split

vegetable oil, for frying

40g peanuts

30g caster sugar

75g (about 5 tbsp) Rose Harissa
  (page 259)

BROCCOLINI

400g broccolini or tenderstem
  broccoli

2 tbsp olive oil

small handful of picked basil leaves

2 tbsp thinly sliced spring onion

2 tbsp lemon juice

FOR THE ROSE HARISSA AND ANCHOVY SAMBAL

Wash the anchovies in a sieve under running water briefly to remove any impurities, and pat dry with kitchen paper. Warm some vegetable oil in a shallow frying pan or wok until nearly smoking and deep-fry the anchovies until golden. Don't overcrowd the pan; work in batches if necessary. Transfer the anchovies to some kitchen paper to soak up any excess oil.

Heat some more vegetable oil in a pan over medium heat and deep-fry the peanuts for 3–4 minutes, until coloured and crunchy. Remove from the oil using a slotted spoon, set to one side and season with salt.

Melt the sugar in a small saucepan over medium-high heat, until it just starts to caramelise. Turn the heat down to low, add the anchovies and peanuts and toss to coat. Fold through the rose harissa and stir to combine thoroughly. Continue to fry for a further 1–2 minutes, then remove from the heat to cool down completely.

The sambal will keep in an airtight container for several weeks.

FOR THE BROCCOLINI

Set a saucepan of salted water on high heat and bring to the boil. Prepare a bowl of iced water large enough to accommodate the broccoli. Blanch the broccoli in the boiling water for no more than a couple of minutes, then drain and refresh in iced water immediately to stop the cooking process. Drain once cool and pat dry with kitchen paper.

Set a barbecue up for single-zone direct grilling (page 17), ensuring you are cooking over hot embers. Alternatively, heat a ridged griddle pan on the stove until smoking hot.

Roll the broccoli in 1 tablespoon of olive oil and season with salt and pepper. Flash-grill for 1–2 minutes on each side. The fire needs to be hot enough to char the broccoli quickly otherwise they will overcook and lose their vibrancy. (You can always use a cast-iron pan on the stove, set over high heat until smoking hot, as a substitute for using a barbecue.)

TO GARNISH AND SERVE

Remove the broccoli from the grill and transfer to a large bowl. Throw in the basil leaves, spring onion, lemon juice and rose harissa sambal, and toss together well. Transfer to a serving bowl and eat whilst still warm.

BLACKENED CORN-ON-THE-COB
WITH HARISSA AIOLI, KEFALOTYRI & PERSIAN LIME

Café Habana in New York City has been serving grilled corn with grated lime zest and crumbled Cotija cheese to I-don't-know-how-many punters a day, every day, for the best part of 20 years. In fact, it became so popular that they opened up a takeaway hatch next door to funnel all the corn orders through a separate service point. I make my pilgrimage every time I'm in the city and it's always as good as I remember it – a dish truly worthy of its 'signature' status. This is our version of it. I'm sure we can't be the only ones who've used it for inspiration.

Persian lime can be found in most Arabic or Turkish corner stores. It has a distinctive taste that makes it worth seeking out. If your search ultimately proves fruitless (no pun intended), you can always use the grated zest of a fresh lime instead. (Pictured overleaf).

SERVES 2

2 corn-on-the-cob, husks retained

50g unsalted butter, melted

2 tbsp Harissa Aioli (page 264)

ground zest of 1 dried Persian lime (or fresh lime if unavailable)

1 tbsp Aleppo chilli flakes (also known as pul biber or red pepper flakes) or 1 tsp dried chilli flakes

20g grated Kefalotyri cheese or Parmigiano Reggiano

Prepare a barbecue for single-zone direct grilling (page 17) over medium-hot embers, and place the corn on the grill rack, with the husks on and all.

Grill the corn for 15–20 minutes, turning regularly, until charred and completely blackened. The outer husk will burn, providing protection to the corn kernels within, which will steam and cook from the heat generated.

Remove the corn from the grill. Pull off and discard the outer burnt husks, leaving some inner husk attached but peeled back.

Ensure the fire is searing hot, and transfer the corn to the grill rack directly on top of the coals. Blacken the corn quickly on all sides, keeping the retained and gnarled husks away from the fire so that they don't catch. If they do, it's not the end of the world; they're only there to make the dish look pretty. Alternatively, blacken the corn on a cast-iron pan heated on the stovetop to smoking hot.

Transfer the corn to a serving plate and brush with the melted butter. Season generously with salt and black pepper, then smear half the harissa aioli on the exposed top side of each corn, followed by a sprinkled line of Persian lime zest and chilli flakes along the length of the corn. Cover the entire plate with grated Kefalotyri cheese. Serve immediately whilst piping hot.

CARDAMOM & CURRANT BASMATI RICE

Rice, in one form or another, is an integral part of North African and Middle Eastern cuisine, always served as a side to grilled or braised meats. I use sweet spices in this recipe as aromatics to infuse and perfume the rice, and currants to stud the rice with little pearls of sweetness. Have the confidence to play around with these and come up with your own combination of spices, dried fruit, herbs and nuts. The joy of rice is that it can be quite forgiving and partners well with most dried goods.

SERVES 8-10
AS A SIDE DISH

100ml olive oil

2 tbsp unsalted butter

3 large white onions, thinly sliced

20 cardamom pods

4 cinnamon sticks

5 whole cloves

1½ tbsp ground allspice

pinch of ground nutmeg

750g basmati rice

120g currants

1.5 litres boiling water

2½ tsp salt, plus extra to taste

Heat the olive oil and butter in a heavy-based pan or casserole dish over medium-low heat and cook the onions, covered, until caramelised and deep golden brown. This should take between 30 and 45 minutes. Remember to keep checking and stirring occasionally, and to season with salt and black pepper.

In a separate pan, dry-toast the cardamom pods, cinnamon sticks and cloves until fragrant. Toss these into the caramelised onions, along with the allspice and nutmeg, and give everything a good stir.

Add the rice to the onions and spices, and stir through, making sure the rice is well coated in the flavoured oil. Throw the currants into the pan and top up with the boiling water. Season with the salt and a generous amount of coarse black pepper. Cover the pan and cook over very low heat for 30 minutes. Remove the pan from the heat, take off the lid, cover the rice with a clean tea towel and return the lid to the pan. Allow the rice to stand for a further 10–15 minutes to fluff in its own steam.

We serve this with smoked brisket (page 102), but it also works particularly well with smoked whole chicken musakhan (page 116), as well as a leg of lamb (page 122).

BARBECUE-ROASTED SWEET POTATO
WITH PECAN & ROSE DUKKAH, HABANERO HOT SAUCE, CRÈME FRAÎCHE & FENNEL SALT

At Berber & Q we serve this as a side dish to accompany our barbecued meats. I'd happily have it as a meal all by itself, however, sometimes with a boiled egg and a fresh, sharp salad served alongside.

If you plan on eating it in this way, don't bother building a fire or setting your barbecue up for the purposes of cooking a single potato. I love a fire as much as the next guy, but that would be plain ludicrous. Just roast them in a preheated oven at 180°C/160°C Fan/Gas mark 4 for up to one hour, until softened. Job done.

SERVES 4

HABANERO HOT SAUCE
80ml olive oil

6 garlic cloves, finely grated

250g fresh habanero chillies, finely chopped

6 dried habanero chillies, rehydrated in boiling water for 15 minutes, drained and then finely chopped

1 tbsp ground cumin

1 tsp chilli powder

1 tsp caster sugar

1 tsp salt

2 tbsp Red Chilli Vinegar (page 263) or red wine vinegar

SWEET POTATO
4 sweet potatoes

2 tbsp runny honey

100g Pecan and Rose Dukkah (page 242)

120g crème fraîche

olive oil, to drizzle

fennel salt (1 tbsp toasted fennel seeds, lightly crushed and mixed with 2 tbsp flaked sea salt) (optional)

FOR THE HABANERO HOT SAUCE
Heat some olive oil in a saucepan over medium-low heat and fry the garlic and chillies until softened but not coloured. Stir in the spices, sugar and salt, and cook for a few minutes. Add the vinegar, reduce by two-thirds, then remove from the heat and cool.

Once cooled, blend in a food processor and then pass through a fine sieve.

FOR THE SWEET POTATO
Set a barbecue up for two-zone indirect grilling (page 17), ensuring you're cooking over a medium-high heat with an internal barbecue temperature of around 180–200°C. Barbecue-roast the sweet potatoes indirectly, offset from the coals, for approximately 1½ hours, until softened all the way through.

Alternatively, you can preheat an oven to 180°C/160°C Fan/Gas mark 4 and roast the sweet potatoes for 45 minutes to an hour.

Once cooked, transfer the sweet potatoes to a serving plate and squeeze each one gently with the tips of your fingers from its base, so that the flesh is forced upwards and erupts through the skin. Season the potatoes with black pepper, and drizzle each one with some honey (let down with warm water if it's particularly thick).

Sprinkle the dukkah liberally over the top of each one and place a generous dollop of crème fraîche either directly on top, or alongside. Finish with a generous drizzle of the habanero hot sauce and some olive oil, and garnish with a small pile of fennel salt.

GRILLED COURGETTES & LABNEH

Andrew Clarke, legendary chef of Brunswick House fame, hairy biker, friend of the restaurant (and of ours) and all-round rock star, took over our mangal grill one Monday night in June 2017 as part of a collaborative series we ran for London Food Month. He served this dish on his menu and I've subsequently stolen it from him, unashamedly. It's a winner, and very easy to recreate.

There are several varieties of courgettes, and this recipe utilises a few of them. But if you can't get hold of anything other than the more generic and widespread everyday courgettes sold in all supermarkets, that's fine as well. Don't be put off, just substitute one type for the other.

SERVES 2–4
AS A SIDE DISH

1 trombetta courgette
1 romana courgette
1 yellow courgette
1 leek, outer leaves removed
80ml olive oil, plus extra to drizzle
50ml lemon juice
2 tbsp chopped mint
1 heaped tbsp urfa chilli flakes
100g Labneh (page 261)
60g flaked almonds, toasted

Prepare a barbecue for single-zone direct grilling (page 17) and once the embers are medium-hot, char the courgettes and leek whole, blackening them all over until softened.

Don't be concerned about burning the vegetables, that's the whole point of this, but if the fire is too hot, and the vegetables are burning too fiercely, pull them off the embers slightly and put a lid on the barbecue to finish barbecue roasting them indirectly, or wait until the fire has died down a bit, shovel the coals out to the perimeter of the barbecue and grill the vegetables at a lower heat.

Remove the vegetables from the grill once cooked all the way through and transfer to a chopping board.

Roughly hack the courgettes and leek up into thumb-sized pieces. Don't be too precious about it – it's supposed to be textured and imprecise.

Dress the courgette mix with olive oil and lemon juice, and fold the chopped mint and urfa chilli through the mix. Season generously with salt and black pepper to taste.

Serve whilst still warm, on top of the labneh, garnished with flaked almonds and a further drizzle of oil.

VEGETABLES & SIDES

GRILLED PUMPKIN
WITH GREEN APPLE HARISSA & RICOTTA

Pumpkin comes into its own towards the middle of September and hangs around through to December. But it's in autumn that they're at their peak and should be most sought after.

The important part is to get a good char on each wedge, which will caramelise the sugars and reveal the pumpkin's intense inner sweetness. Otherwise it can sometimes lack a bit of flavour.

An oiled chapa, or solid cast-iron plate, set over the fire works just as well, if not better, than a grill grate, but not everyone has one.

I like to use ricotta for this dish, but any soft and creamy goat's cheese could work as a substitute.

SERVES 8

GREEN APPLE HARISSA

½ tsp cumin seeds

½ tsp coriander seeds

¼ tsp fennel seeds

pinch of caraway seeds

6 green chilli (bird's eye if available), roughly chopped

2 garlic cloves, grated

100ml extra virgin olive oil

½ bunch of coriander, leaves and stalks

100g spinach, stalks removed

2 Granny Smith apples, cored and roughly chopped

½ tbsp runny honey

PUMPKIN

50g unsalted butter

2 tbsp olive oil

1 large white onion, thinly sliced

50g green sultanas (or normal sultanas)

1 pumpkin, cut into 12 wedges roughly 2.5cm thick

2 tbsp runny honey, thinned with 1 tbsp warm water

4 tbsp ricotta

4 tbsp Green Apple Harissa (see above)

handful of walnuts, toasted and roughly chopped

pea shoots (optional)

FOR THE GREEN APPLE HARISSA

Place the seeds in a heavy-based pan and roast over medium-high heat until smoking and fragrant. Transfer to a spice grinder and blend to a fine powder.

Put the chilli and garlic in a food processor with the olive oil and blitz to a purée. Add the coriander and spinach with the spice mix and continue to blitz until smooth. You might need to add a touch more oil to get the blender moving. Add the apples and honey and pulse until incorporated into the sauce. It should have a thick consistency, not too dissimilar to a pesto. Season with salt and pepper to taste, and set aside until required. The green harissa will keep refrigerated for up to 3 days, but is better when fresh as it will lose its green vibrancy with time.

FOR THE PUMPKIN

Warm the butter and olive oil over medium-high heat in a wide heavy-based frying pan and sear the onion until caramelised, about 5 minutes. Add the sultanas to the pan for the final few minutes to warm through and soften. Season with salt and black pepper and set aside until required.

Prepare a campfire or set your barbecue up for two-zone grilling (page 17) over medium-hot. Alternatively, or simultaneously, heat a cast-iron plancha or large griddle pan, either on the stove over high heat or over your fire. Place the pumpkin either straight on the grill rack, directly over the coals, or on the griddle pan, to blacken and char lightly for a couple of minutes on both sides. Lift the pumpkin onto the opposite side of the grill rack, brush with the rest of the olive oil, and continue to cook indirectly with the barbecue lid on, until softened and tender to a knife, about 30–35 minutes. You can also preheat your oven to 180°C/160°C Fan/Gas mark 4, and transfer the charred pumpkin wedges on a roasting tray (or straight in the pan) to be finished in the oven until softened and caramelised (approx 20–25 minutes).

Arrange the pumpkin on a serving plate and season to taste with salt and black pepper. Top with the onions and sultana mix, dress with a drizzle of honey and spoon the ricotta and green apple harissa all over the plate. Garnish with walnuts and, if using, pea shoots.

CHAPTER 05

LAZY SUNDAYS

STEAK & EGGS
WITH LABNEH, CHARRED TOMATOES & ZA'ATAR

A solid way to start any weekend, this is a great post-workout breakfast. Not that I work out, but if I ever did, I could imagine that this would be the kind of breakfast I'd like to have afterwards.

The tomatoes need to be the best you can find. Sub-standard tomatoes are only good for sauces, stews and throwing at those neighbours you don't like.

SERVES 2

2 onglet steaks, 120g
2 plum tomatoes, best you can find
olive oil
1 tbsp finely chopped oregano
2 slices of sourdough
½ garlic clove
60g Labneh (page 261)
2 medium, free-range eggs, fried
    sunny-side up
1 tsp za'atar
grated zest of ¼ lemon
2 tbsp Herb Oil (page 264)

Set a barbecue up for single-zone direct grilling, ensuring you're cooking over medium-high. Alternatively, heat a ridged skillet over high until smoking hot.

Season the steaks with Maldon flaked salt and coarse black pepper and grill for 4–5 minutes on both sides, until medium-rare to the touch, or 55°C when probed with a thermometer. Rotate the steaks once at a 45-degree angle on both sides to ensure a lovely crosshatch pattern. If using a ridged skillet, you may need to flip the steak several times to prevent it from burning.

Whilst the steak is grilling, prepare the other elements of the dish.

Brush the cut side of the tomato halves with olive oil and season with salt.

Heat a cast-iron pan or heavy-based frying pan over medium-high heat, add some oil and, once shimmering, place the tomatoes cut-side down in the pan and leave, untouched, for 5–7 minutes. Be patient; resist the urge to move them too soon. They will burn and loosen from the pan to tell you they're ready.

Lift the tomatoes from the pan using a spatula and transfer to a serving plate. Drizzle with more olive oil, season with black pepper and more salt if necessary, and sprinkle the oregano on top.

Meanwhile, rub the cut side of half a garlic clove liberally all over the slice of sourdough, brush with olive oil and blacken under the grill. Transfer to a serving plate.

Transfer the steak to a resting rack or chopping board and rest for 3–4 minutes.

Smear the labneh on the grilled sourdough, top with the onglet steak, a well-seasoned fried egg and garnish with za'atar and lemon zest. Drizzle over the herb oil to finish and serve the tomatoes alongside.

MERGUEZ PATTY MELT
WITH GOAT'S CHEESE, CONFIT SHALLOTS, ROSE HARISSA & WALNUTS

Al Bahia, an Algerian butchery in Finsbury Park, serves the most authentic merguez sausages I can find in London, packed full of rose harissa flavour. They'll serve them to you in an authentic manner as well. You don't have to ask.

I love this combo of hot oozing goat's cheese, spicy merguez and sweet confit shallots. Pure filth.

SERVES 4

CONFIT SHALLOTS

4 shallots, peeled and halved lengthways through the root

olive oil, to cover

1 bay leaf

2–3 sprigs of rosemary

½ head of garlic

MERGUEZ PATTY MELT

600g merguez sausages

100g butter, unsalted

8 slices of rye bread

2 tbsp Rose Harissa (page 259) or shop-bought

200g soft goat's cheese, such as Rosary

2 tbsp walnuts, toasted and roughly chopped

1 tbsp honey (loosened with a little warm water if too thick), to serve

few dried rose petals, to garnish

FOR THE CONFIT SHALLOTS

Preheat the oven to 160°C/140°C Fan/Gas mark 3.

Place the shallots in a small roasting tray or casserole dish. Cover with olive oil and add the bay leaf, rosemary and garlic.

Cover tightly with tin foil and roast for 1–1½ hours until the shallots are soft throughout. Season with salt and black pepper, and set aside until needed.

FOR THE MERGUEZ PATTY MELT

Remove the skin from the sausages and reconstitute the meat into 4 evenly shaped meat patties the size and shape of a hamburger, about 2cm thick.

Melt 2 tablespoons of butter in a heavy-based pan and sauté the patties, in batches, over medium heat until cooked all the way through. Lift the patties from the pan and set on a wirerack to assemble the sandwich.

Spread the slices of rye across a table and lather the bottom slice with rose harissa, followed by half the cheese and then the merguez patty. Top the patty with the remaining half of cheese, the confit shallots and the chopped walnuts, before returning the top slice to make a sandwich.

Melt the remaining butter over medium heat in a heavy-based pan, wide enough to accommodate all 4 sandwiches. Drop each sandwich into the pan and press down intermittently using a spatula, working your way around each sandwich as they cook. Fry the patty melt until golden brown and crisp, about 3 minutes, and then flip the sandwich and do the same for the reverse side. Remove from the heat and cut in half. The sandwich should be hot all the way through and the cheese should be oozing.

Transfer the sandwich halves to a plate, drizzle with some honey and garnish the plate with a few dried rose petals and any reserved chopped walnuts.

BISSLI PIE

Frito pie is popular across the southern states of the US and consists of Frito chips smothered in beef chilli topped with salsa, cheese and soured cream. I wondered what the Middle Eastern equivalent of this dish would look like, and I settled on Bissli. Bissli aren't that readily available in the UK, but they're sold in several kosher shops and sections of well stocked supermarkets.

SERVES 2
AS A LIGHT SNACK

HARISSA WHIPPED FETA
3 tbsp Whipped Feta (page 261)

1½ tbsp Harissa (page 259) or shop-bought

lemon juice, to taste

SPICED LAMB
25ml olive oil

½ onion, peeled and finely chopped

½ tsp salt

1 garlic clove, finely chopped

½ tsp ground cumin

½ tsp dried chilli flakes

¼ tsp ground cinnamon

¼ tsp ground allspice

pinch of ground nutmeg

scant pinch of ground cloves

250g minced lamb

½ tbsp tomato paste

60ml water

30g pine nuts, toasted

1½ tbsp chopped flat-leaf parsley

TOMATO SALSA
150g cherry tomatoes, quartered and deseeded to make petals

½ shallot, finely chopped

1 tbsp chopped flat-leaf parsley

1½ tbsp extra virgin olive oil

1 tbsp red wine vinegar

BISSLI PIE
1 large pack of Bissli, onion flavour

2 pickled Turkish chillies (page 255) or shop-bought, sliced

FOR THE HARISSA WHIPPED FETA
Combine the whipped feta and harissa together in a small bowl, whisking to incorporate. Check for seasoning and add more salt or lemon juice if necessary.

FOR THE SPICED LAMB
Heat the olive oil in a saucepan over medium heat and sweat the onion, seasoned with the salt, until softened and translucent but not coloured.

Add the garlic and spices to the onion, and fry for a further 1–2 minutes to infuse the flavours.

Turn the heat up to high and add the minced lamb to brown, breaking it up with the back of a fork or spoon as it cooks. Once the lamb starts to colour, stir in the tomato paste and add the water. Bring to a rolling simmer, reduce the heat to low and continue to cook for 10–15 minutes until almost dry. Add the pine nuts and parsley, and season to taste with salt and black pepper.

FOR THE TOMATO SALSA
Combine the cherry tomato petals, shallot and parsley in a small bowl and dress with the olive oil and vinegar. Season with salt and pepper to taste.

FOR THE BISSLI PIE
Open the pack of Bissli gently, being careful not to rip the packaging down its sides. Pour the harissa whipped feta directly on top of the crisps, as well as the spiced lamb. Roll the Bissli packet so that it's sealed, leaving some room at the top, and give it a good shake to distribute the toppings as best as you can.

Open the Blssli packet back out and serve with the tomato salsa and sliced pickled chillies strewn on top. Eat immediately, with your hands.

TURKISH EGGS (CILBIR)
WITH ALEPPO CHILLI BUTTER, SPRING ONION & SPINACH

I've loved Turkish eggs ever since I first had them in The Providores and Tapa Room way back when. A fusion restaurant way ahead of its time when it first opened its doors, it introduced us Brits to ingredients and dishes from Peter Gordon's travels that we'd never heard of before, like smashed avocado, kumquat and yuzu. It was, and still is, very Marylebone darling.

Turkish eggs (or cilbir) are still on The Providores' breakfast menu to this day. Despite having had them countless times in Turkey since, I still associate the dish with this restaurant. I think I always will.

This is such a simple dish to prepare, but one that is far greater than the sum of its parts. If you can't find pul biber (red pepper flakes), then substitute them with half each of both chilli flakes and paprika instead. The butter must glow red.

SERVES 1

100g full-fat natural yoghurt (or Greek yoghurt)

1 tsp finely chopped dill

1 tbsp extra virgin olive oil

½ garlic clove, finely grated

100g spinach, washed

2 large eggs

flaked sea salt (such as Maldon)

50g unsalted butter

1 tbsp Aleppo chilli flakes (also known as pul biber or red pepper flakes) or 1 tsp dried chilli flakes and a pinch of smoked paprika

1 spring onion, green parts only, thinly sliced

picked coriander leaves

pita bread or country bread

In a small bowl, mix together the yoghurt, dill, olive oil and garlic, and season with salt and black pepper to taste. Set aside until required.

Set a steamer over a pan of boiling water and steam the spinach until completely wilted. Season to taste and keep warm until required.

Fill a shallow, wide pan just over half full and bring to the boil over high heat. Turn the heat down to medium-low, so that the water is gently simmering. Add a drop of vinegar to the water, which should help the egg whites to coagulate. I like to crack the eggs into small ramekins or bowls before gently lowering them into the water. Use a spoon to shape the eggs, gently lifting the egg white and scooping it back over the yolk. Lightly poach the eggs for 3–4 minutes until the whites are cooked but the yolk remains runny. Lift from the water using a slotted spoon and transfer to some kitchen paper to drain. Season with flaked salt and coarse black pepper.

Melt the butter in a small saucepan over medium-low heat. At first it will froth, but as the froth subsides it will caramelise to nutty golden-brown, about 3–5 minutes. Add the chilli flakes, remove from the heat and give the butter a good swirl in the pan to infuse. It should take on a deep red colour. Keep warm until ready to use.

To serve, place the spinach at the base of a serving plate or shallow bowl, topped with the yoghurt and followed by the poached eggs. Drizzle the butter over the entire dish and garnish with the spring onion greens and coriander leaves. Eat immediately, with some pita or country bread on the side.

SAFFRON BUTTERMILK-FRIED CHICKEN
WITH TAHINA GRAVY

I love fried chicken as much as the next guy. Possibly even more. We make this for our staff dinner with boneless jujeh kabab thigh meat, but I've suggested using the whole bird here.

SERVES 4

SAFFRON BUTTERMILK
CHICKEN

600ml buttermilk

60ml saffron water (pinch of saffron
soaked in 60ml boiling water and
left to infuse for 15 minutes)

1 tsp coarse ground black pepper

1 tsp flaked sea salt, plus extra

1½ tsp ground turmeric

1 tsp ground cumin

½ tsp smoked hot paprika

¼ tsp cayenne pepper

1 onion, sliced

2 garlic cloves, finely chopped

1 whole chicken, weighing roughly
1.5kg, cut into 8 pieces (2 legs,
2 thighs, 2 wings and 2 breasts)

about 2 litres vegetable oil

TURMERIC DREDGE

200g plain flour

150g cornmeal

1½ tbsp cornflour

1 tsp salt

1 tsp ground turmeric

1 tsp ground coriander

½ tsp ground cumin

½ tsp cayenne pepper

½ tsp garlic granules or powder

½ tsp caster sugar

SERVE

Tahina Gravy (page 263)

Fermented Green Chilli Kebab
Sauce (page 258) (optional)

Bread and Butter Pickles (page
254) (optional)

FOR THE SAFFRON BUTTERMILK CHICKEN

Combine all the ingredients except the chicken and oil in a small bowl and mix to combine. Add the chicken pieces to the buttermilk mixture and leave to marinate, refrigerated, for a minimum of 6 hours, or better still overnight.

FOR THE TURMERIC DREDGE

Put all the ingredients together in a bowl and mix together well.

TO FINISH THE CHICKEN

Remove the chicken from the buttermilk marinade and dredge the chicken pieces in the flour mix, tossing to coat thoroughly. Leave the chicken to sit for 10–15 minutes before shaking off any excess and transferring to a wire rack to rest whilst you warm up the oil.

In a large, heavy-based deep stockpot or saucepan, heat enough oil to comfortably accommodate the chicken pieces so that they are almost submerged. Don't fill the pot more than halfway, for your own safety, nobody else's. Take the oil to 150°C when probed with a thermometer. Start by frying the thighs and breasts, which will take longer to cook, before adding the wings and legs 3 minutes afterwards. At this point, start making the gravy (see below).

Cook the chicken for a further 5–6 minutes, and then turn over to cook for an additional 10 minutes. Keep an eye on the chicken and the temperature of the oil throughout, and turn it if it starts to burn on either side. (If you do not have a pan big enough to accommodate all of the chicken in one go, you can work in batches, keeping the first half of the fried chicken warm in the oven at a low temperature of 50°C to prevent it drying out. Just make sure to return the oil to starting temperature before you fry the second batch.)

Once deep-golden brown all over and an internal temperature of 70°C has been reached when probed with a thermometer, carefully lift out the chicken using tongs and transfer to a wire rack. Leave to rest for just under half the cooking time, roughly 7–8 minutes. Season liberally with flaked salt.

Serve the chicken straight from the rack with the tahina gravy alongside and, if using, some fermented green chilli sauce and pickles.

SWEET POTATO & SPICED LAMB HASH

<table>
<tr><td>

SERVES 2
AS A LIGHT BREAKFAST

</td></tr>
</table>

2 tbsp olive oil

1 sweet potato, peeled and cut
into 2.5cm cubes

1 red onion, roughly chopped

½ green pepper, diced into chunks

½ red pepper, diced into chunks

1 jalapeño chilli, sliced into rings

200g Spiced Lamb (page 212)

2 large eggs

SERVE

pinch of paprika

2 tbsp roughly chopped flat-leaf
parsley

1–2 pickled Turkish chillies

60g Tahina Aioli (page 264)

Heat a deep, heavy-based cast-iron pan over high heat. Add the olive oil and sauté the sweet potato cubes for 5–6 minutes, giving them a toss or turn halfway through to ensure that they're evenly coloured.

Add the onion, peppers and jalapeño chilli to the pan and sear over a high heat, so that the vegetables caramelise quickly and char a lovely golden brown on the outside – no more than 3–4 minutes. Season with salt and black pepper, then toss the spiced lamb in to warm through for 4–5 minutes. Turn the heat down to low and keep the hash warm whilst, in a separate pan, you fry the eggs sunny-side up. Be sure to keep the yolks still runny and season with salt and black pepper.

Transfer the sweet potato hash to individual serving plates, topped with a fried egg, a pinch of paprika, some parsley and a pickled Turkish chilli or two. Serve piping hot with tahina aioli drizzled over the top.

TUNISIAN FRICASSEE SANDWICH
WITH PORK BELLY, PUMPKIN JAM & EGG

Tunisian fricassee are fried balls of dough, cut open to make a sandwich that consists of tinned tuna fish, harissa, egg and any number of different toppings depending on who's serving you.

I first encountered them in Haifa in the north of Israel, where they were being sold as street food at the weekend flea market. As I've already mentioned in this book, I have a particular aversion to cooked tuna fish, especially of the tinned kind, but I had to try one, because I could see such potential for the sandwich. With all the will in the world I wanted to enjoy it, but I couldn't. Tinned tuna obscures my enjoyment for life much like a Coldplay song at a good house party.

I've swapped out the tuna for pork belly, which elevates all that potential and turns it into godly-greatness. It's just so much better. But if you're one of those pro-tinned tuna freaks, as I find the vast majority of people are, you can substitute it back in and have it the way it's supposed to be.

SERVES 6–12

PORK BELLY
30g coarse sea salt
50g caster sugar
1 tbsp fennel seeds
½ tbsp coriander seeds
1.4kg pork belly, skinned

PUMPKIN JAM
800g pumpkin
2 tbsp salt
pinch of ground ginger
1 tsp ground cinnamon
¼ tsp ground turmeric
1 tbsp runny honey
25g unsalted butter

FRICASSEE DOUGH
250g plain flour
½ tsp caster sugar
1 tsp active dried yeast
200ml tepid water
1 medium egg
pinch of salt
1½ tbsp vegetable oil
sunflower oil, for deep-frying

FOR THE PORK BELLY

Combine the salt, sugar, fennel seeds and coriander seeds in a small bowl and rub it all over the pork belly. Transfer the pork belly to a suitable storage container and store it, covered and refrigerated, for no less than 6 hours but no more than 12 hours.

Once the pork has dry-brined for a sufficient amount of time, preheat the oven to 220°C/200°C Fan/Gas mark 7. Set the belly in a roasting tray, fat-side up, on a roasting rack, and roast it until deep golden brown (1–1½ hours), basting continually in the fat that renders and collects in the roasting tray.

Turn the oven down to 120°C/100°C Fan/Gas mark ½, and continue to cook the pork for a further 1½ hours, until tender to the touch, but not falling apart.

Remove from the oven, wrap it in clingfilm and place on a cooling rack, set over a shallow tray, pressed with a heavy weight such as a roasting tray filled with water or a couple of extra large tins, to be left overnight in the refrigerator.

FOR THE PUMPKIN JAM

Cut the pumpkin in half and scrape out the seeds and the inner membrane. Grate the pumpkin using the coarse side of a box grater, or a food processor, if your machine comes with the appropriate attachment.

Salt the grated pumpkin and set aside in a colander over the sink for 1 hour.

Rinse the pumpkin and wring dry using your hands. Try and catch and reserve the juices as they're squeezed out.

Transfer the pumpkin to a wide, non-stick frying pan. Add the ground ginger, cinnamon, turmeric, honey and butter to the pan, as well as 2 tablespoons of the reserved juices extracted from the pumpkin. Cook over medium-low heat for 45 minutes to 1 hour, until the jam has thickened and caramelised to golden. Remove from the heat and set aside until required.

FOR THE FRICASSEE DOUGH

Place the flour in the bowl of a stand mixer and create a well in the middle. Add the sugar, yeast and tepid water to the well and leave for 15–20 minutes for the yeast to activate and bubble.

Add the egg and salt to the bowl and, using the dough hook attachment, work the dough until it comes together. Add the vegetable oil and continue to work the mix until incorporated.

Turn the dough out, transfer it to another bowl, and shape it into a rounded ball covered with clingfilm. Set aside somewhere warm to prove for 2 hours, during which time it should double in size. Knead the dough again thoroughly, by hand this time, before dividing in two. Roll each half into a long log and cut each one into 6 pieces. Roll each piece into little oblong-shaped balls, each one weighing approximately 60g, and place them on a well-greased parchment-lined baking sheet or tray. Set aside, on a baking tray covered with clingfilm, for a further 30 minutes to rise once more.

Heat enough sunflower oil to deep-fry the dough balls, in a deep saucepan over medium until sizzling hot or to 160°C when probed with a thermometer. Gently lift the dough balls using a palette knife or slotted lifter, being careful not knock out the air or to lose the integrity of their shape. Deep-fry in batches, 3–4 at a time, until golden brown. Using a slotted spoon, transfer the fricassee to some kitchen paper to absorb any excess oil. Set aside until required.

FOR THE CAPER, PRESERVED LEMON AND TOMATO SALAD

Combine the capers, preserved lemon, tomatoes and shallot in a small bowl. Dress with the olive oil and lemon juice, and season with salt and black pepper to taste. Add the parsley just before using.

TO FINISH THE PORK BELLY AND SERVE

Cut the pork belly into 1cm thick slices, roughly the same length as the fried dough balls. Heat a cast-iron or heavy-based pan over medium heat and sear the pork belly on both sides until just warmed through.

Assemble the sandwiches by spreading a layer of harissa on the base, followed by some pumpkin jam and black olives. Lay a slice or two of pork belly on top, followed by a few slices of egg, and spoon the caper and preserved lemon salad over the whole thing. Serve immediately, then sit back and enjoy the labour of your love.

BERBER & Q SHAKSHUKA

I was first introduced to shakshuka by some Israeli travellers I met on the west coast of Australia many moons ago. It was a mediocre version at best, cobbled together with a paucity of random ingredients assembled like something off *Ready, Steady Cook*. At the time and place I was in, both physically and mentally speaking, it was a sign of travelling prowess and status if you could put together a meal for less than the price of a pack of gum.

Shakshuka means 'a mixture' in Tunisian Arabic, a reference possibly to the concept of mixing together whatever ingredients you have sitting in your larder or fridge. As good on a cold wintry night as it is for breakfast, this is what I cook when I can't be bothered to leave my house and go to the shops. But I also love the endless possibilities to create and innovate with a dish that's rooted in such simplicity. I'm always experimenting with it, such that it's rare for me to cook the same shakshuka twice.

SERVES 2–4

100ml extra virgin olive oil

1 red onion, finely chopped

2 garlic cloves, minced

1 red pepper, diced

1 tbsp smoked paprika

½ tbsp dried chilli flakes

1½ tbsp hot red pepper paste (biber salcasi), or tomato paste

100ml water

400g tinned tomatoes (best quality, such as San Marzano)

1 tbsp honey

4–6 eggs

SERVE

small handful of basil leaves, ripped

1 spring onion, green parts only, finely sliced

extra virgin olive oil

80g feta, crumbled

100g Tahina Aioli (page 264)

pita bread, warmed on the grill

Warm 50ml of olive oil in a cast-iron or heavy-based wide pan and sweat the onion over medium heat until translucent but not coloured.

Add the garlic and continue to cook for a few minutes, before folding through the red pepper. Cook until the pepper has softened, then season with the paprika and chilli flakes.

Stir through the red pepper paste and fry for a minute or so, before adding the water to loosen the paste to a thickened sauce-like consistency.

Fold the tomatoes through the sauce, season with salt and black pepper, and add the honey for some sweetness to cut through the acidity of the tomatoes.

Stir well and pour the remaining oil into the sauce to give a glossy finish. Turn the heat down to low and let the sauce simmer for 45 minutes to an hour, to reduce and intensify in flavour, during which time the excess surface oil will take on a glorious deep-red colour and become infused with the flavours of all the ingredients in the pan.

Make 4–6 wells in the sauce and gently crack the eggs in one by one, being careful not to break the yolk. Season each egg yolk with salt and pepper, cover the pan, and cook for 3–5 minutes over medium heat, during which time the trapped steam generated should cook the egg whites through, leaving the yolks still runny.

When the eggs are cooked through, remove the pan and garnish with basil leaves, spring onion greens, a drizzle of extra virgin olive oil (it's difficult to have too much) and the crumbled feta. Serve immediately with tahina aioli and warm pita bread.

CAMPFIRE MOROCCAN PANCAKES
WITH POACHED QUINCE, RAISINS & SWEET LABNEH

This calls for two types of semolina, to provide textural contrast, but if you can't find the extra-fine then substitute more fine semolina. You can use pears instead, just adjust the cooking time.

SERVES 4

SWEET LABNEH
500g full-fat natural yoghurt (or Greek yoghurt)
50g icing sugar
grated zest of 1 lemon
pinch of salt

POACHED QUINCE
2 quince
acidulated water (juice of 2 lemons mixed with 1 litre water)
500g caster sugar
500ml water
8 cardamom pods, lightly crushed
4 small cinnamon sticks
pinch of saffron
30g raisins

MOROCCAN PANCAKES
2 medium eggs, lightly beaten
350ml full-fat milk
70g plain flour
50g extra fine semolina
100g fine semolina
1 tsp sugar
pinch of salt
1½ tsp baking powder
½ tsp dried yeast
butter, for greasing

TO SERVE
handful of blueberries
icing sugar, to dust
picked mint leaves, ripped

FOR THE SWEET LABNEH
Combine the ingredients in a small bowl. Transfer to a muslin cloth, or double-layered J-cloth, tie a knot at the top using some kitchen string and hang overnight from the kitchen tap, to drip into the sink below.

FOR THE POACHED QUINCE
Peel, core and quarter the quince, transferring them immediately to a bowl filled with acidulated water to cover. This will stop the quince from discolouring.

Warm the sugar, 500ml of water, aromatics and saffron in a saucepan over medium heat, whisking to dissolve the sugar. Bring the stock to a gentle roll and simmer for 10 minutes to form a stock syrup.

Drain the quince quarters and add to the pan. Bring to the boil before lowering the heat back to a very gentle simmer and poaching the quince for 35–45 minutes. Try not to overcook the quince; they should be tender without falling apart. (Keep a watchful eye on them as the cooking time draws to an end.) Remove the quince from the liquid with a slotted spoon and transfer to a suitable storage container. Increase the heat to high and reduce the liquid by about two-thirds, until thickened. Turn off the heat and add the raisins to the pan to soften in the residual heat. Leave to cool to room temperature, then return the poached quince to the syrup and keep covered and refrigerated until required.

FOR THE PANCAKES
Ensure the eggs and milk are at room temperature before starting. Combine the ingredients in a stand mixer using the whisk attachment until smooth. The batter will also come together nicely using a whisk and a strong hand.

Set aside, in a warm place for a minimum of 1 hour, or preferably 4–6 hours, for the yeast to prove. The batter will bubble and should almost double in size.

Heat a wide heavy-based frying pan over medium heat on the stovetop, or a cast-iron pan on a campfire. Grease the pan with a knob of butter and ladle in roughly 2 tablespoons of batter for each pancake. Cook, on one side only, until the underside has lightly browned and the batter has all but dried. The pancake should be completely pockmarked, almost like an crumpet in appearance. Flip and cook for 1–2 minutes on the other side. Keep warm covered with foil, or in a very low oven (50°C) whilst you cook the rest.

TO SERVE
Serve the pancakes warm with the poached quince, fresh blueberries, a generous drizzle of stock syrup, some sweet labneh and a dusting of icing sugar. Finish with the ripped mint leaves strewn over the top.

CHAPTER 06

DESSERTS

ORANGE BLOSSOM
& LABNEH CHEESECAKE
WITH TAHINI CRUMB

This is not a traditional cheesecake in the sense that it's not baked. We whip the cream and labneh together and only bake the crumb. It still tastes amazing though.

If plums are not in season, sub them out for a fruit that is. Poached quince would make an excellent alternative.

SERVES 8
GENEROUSLY

ORANGE AND LABNEH
CHEESECAKE
500g Labneh (page 261)
300ml double cream
20ml orange blossom water
scraped seeds of 1 vanilla pod
grated zest of 1 orange
200g caster sugar

TAHINI CRUMB
100g unsalted butter
100g plain flour
100g caster sugar
50ml tahini paste

POACHED PLUMS
8 plums, destoned and quartered
250ml water
200g caster sugar
1 cinnamon stick
1 vanilla pod

FOR THE ORANGE AND LABNEH CHEESECAKE
Combine all of the ingredients together in a large bowl and whisk until the cheesecake mixture is thick and holds its shape. Spoon into 8 nice glasses and put in the fridge to set.

FOR THE TAHINI CRUMB
Preheat an oven to 170°C/150°C Fan/Gas mark 3½.

Rub the butter, flour and sugar together with your hands until you have fairly chunky crumbs. Add the tahini and mix through gently.

Spread the mixture on a baking tray lined with parchment paper. Bake in the oven for 10 minutes, stirring it up with a wooden spoon every 5 minutes or so to encourage it to form a crumb. Remove from the oven and cool.

FOR THE POACHED PLUMS
Bring the water to the boil in a saucepan over high heat and add the sugar, cinnamon stick and vanilla pod. Bring back to the boil, slide the plums in carefully, avoiding any splash-back that might cause you to burn, and cover with a piece of parchment paper pressed to the surface. Turn down the heat to medium-low, and let the plums gently simmer for 5 minutes until cooked through but still just firm – al dente, so to speak.

TO FINISH THE CHEESECAKE
Once the cheesecake mixture has sufficiently chilled, garnish with a poached plum and some tahini crumb sprinkled over the top.

BAKED PEACHES
WITH SWEET LABNEH

Peaches come into their own towards the back end of summer and hang around until early autumn. This is such a simple dessert, perfect if you're trying to impress on a first date but you lack the dessert skills to do so otherwise.

SERVES 6

6 peaches, halved and stoned

60g vanilla sugar, shop-bought

1 cinnamon stick

2 star anise

180g Sweet Labneh (page 222), or crème fraîche

Preheat an oven to 180°C/160°C Fan/Gas mark 4.

Lay the peach halves cut-side up in a roasting tray, sprinkle with vanilla sugar, throw in the cinnamon stick and star anise and add enough water to come to 0.5cm up the tray. Bake in the oven for 15–20 minutes, until the peach halves are softened but still retain some shape. They should be caramelised and coloured at the edges, yet not fall apart.

Transfer the peaches to a serving platter, drizzle with the juices that have collected in the tray and serve with sweet labneh if using, or crème fraîche as a substitute.

MOROCCAN DOUGHNUTS (S'FENJ)
WITH MOLASSES-ROASTED BLACK GRAPES

S'fenj are Moroccan doughnuts, often served plain for breakfast with mint tea. We jazz them up a bit with the addition of roasted grapes bound by a sweet molasses glaze. They'd still be good for breakfast though, especially so with mint tea.

SERVES 6

DOUGHNUTS (S'FENJ)
1 tbsp active dried yeast
1½ tbsp caster sugar
250–300ml lukewarm water
440g plain flour
1 tsp salt
vegetable oil, for deep-frying

ROASTED BLACK GRAPES
500g seedless black grapes
50ml pomegranate molasses
2 tbsp light brown sugar

SERVE
300ml crème fraîche
handful of flaked almonds, toasted
few mint leaves, torn
icing sugar, for dusting

FOR THE S'FENJ

Combine the yeast, sugar and a few tablespoons of lukewarm water and stir to activate the yeast. After a few minutes it will start to froth and bubble.

Place the flour in a large bowl, add the activated yeast on one side of the bowl and the salt on the opposite side. Start to gradually add the remaining water, a few tablespoons at a time, and knead the mixture as you do. Keep kneading the dough for 10–15 minutes, until you have a thick, sticky, sponge-like dough. (You may not need to add all the water to achieve the desired consistency.)

Transfer the dough to an oiled bowl, cover loosely with a tea towel, or place inside a plastic bag, and set aside to rise for 2 hours.

FOR THE ROASTED GRAPES

Whilst the dough is rising, preheat the oven to 150°C/130°C Fan/Gas mark 2. Put the grapes in a large roasting tray, drizzle with pomegranate molasses and sprinkle with the brown sugar. Roast the grapes for roughly 15 minutes until just starting to wilt but still slightly firm. Remove from the oven and allow the grapes to sit and cool in their juices.

TO SERVE

Heat the oil in a deep saucepan to 180°C (use a thermometer to test the heat).

Knock the dough back, oil your fingers and proceed to form small dough balls about the size of a plum. Use your thumb to punch a hole through the middle of each ball, stretching them out a little at each end to elongate their shape, before gently dropping the dough into the oil, being careful to avoid any splash-back. Deep-fry the s'fenj for 3–5 minutes or until golden brown on both sides, turning occasionally to ensure they colour evenly all over.

Lift the s'fenj from the oil using a slotted spoon and transfer to kitchen paper to absorb any excess oil.

Serve the s'fenj still hot, with some roasted grapes spooned over the top along with the juices, a dollop of crème fraîche, some flaked almonds and torn mint leaves strewn over the top. Finish with a generous dusting of icing sugar.

BAMBA MOUSSE
WITH SALTED CARAMEL, SESAME TUILE

I am indebted to Vicky Heafield, our brilliant head chef at Berber & Q Shawarma Bar, for helping me with large swathes of this chapter. Vicky has a natural instinctual flair for cooking, none more evident than when it comes to desserts. The genius of this belongs entirely to her. Bamba, an Israeli snack best described as a peanut-flavoured Wotsit, are available in most major supermarkets.

SERVES 8–10
GENEROUSLY

CHOCOLATE GANACHE
500ml double cream
130g cooking chocolate, 70% cocoa solids
pinch of flaked sea salt (such as Maldon)

SALTED CARAMEL
40ml water
165g caster sugar
250ml double cream
pinch of flaked sea salt (such as Maldon)

BAMBA MOUSSE
550ml double cream
60g peanuts, toasted
25g Bamba
2 egg whites, at room temperature
100g caster sugar

SESAME TUILE
30g unsalted butter, melted
30g plain flour
1 egg white
60g caster sugar
5g sesame seeds

SERVE
pinch of ground sumac

FOR THE CHOCOLATE GANACHE
In a heavy-based, medium-sized saucepan, bring the cream to the boil, making sure to keep an eye on it as it can boil over very quickly. Pour the cream directly over the chocolate in a bowl, add the salt and whisk until silky and smooth.

FOR THE SALTED CARAMEL
Put the water and sugar in a saucepan over medium heat and swirl it with your wrist to combine – never stir.

In a separate pan, slowly warm the cream. Once the sugar has caramelised to golden brown, slowly pour in the cream, carefully as it may spit. Once it's fully incorporated, add the salt and let it bubble away over low heat for 10 minutes.

FOR THE BAMBA MOUSSE
Bring 200ml of the cream to a gentle simmer over a medium-low heat. Add the roasted peanuts and Bamba, turn the heat off and let it infuse for 15 minutes. Pour the infused cream through a sieve and push through any melted Bamba pieces. Leave it to cool to room temperature.

Once the mixture is cool, add the infused cream to the remaining 350ml of cream and whip it into soft peaks, using a whisk and a strong wrist.

Beat the whites until you have firm, stiff peaks, using a stand mixer with the balloon whisk attachment, or else by hand with a whisk. Slowly rain the sugar into the whites until the meringue is silky smooth. Fold into the Bamba cream.

FOR THE SESAME TUILE
Preheat the oven to 180°C/160°C Fan/Gas mark 4 and line a baking tray with parchment paper. Place the melted butter and flour together in a bowl and whisk to combine. In a separate bowl, whisk the egg white and sugar together. Add the egg white mixture to the butter mixture and combine.

Smear thin layers of the mixture onto the paper, on the prepared tray, in whatever shapes you like. Secure the baking paper to the tray by dotting some of the mixture onto the underside at the corners and sticking it down. Sprinkle the sesame seeds over the top and bake for 5–6 minutes.

TO FINISH THE BAMBA MOUSSE
In some nice see-through Kilner jars (or similar), add about 2.5cm of the chocolate ganache, followed by about half that of salted caramel. Top with a good helping of the Bamba mousse and add sumac and a sesame tuile.

CARDAMOM & ROSE MALABI
WITH BOURBON-SOAKED CHERRIES

Malabi is similar in taste and preparation to a panna cotta. It's said to originate in Turkey but I've only ever had it on the streets of Jaffa, the old Arab quarter in Tel Aviv. There, it is served with sickly sweet, artificially coloured rose syrup and desiccated coconut. It's one of my favourite streetfoods.

We always have malabi on our menu, served with an array of fruit compotes that vary according to season. I like to add some nuts for much-needed crunch. Bourbon-soaked cherries are delicious on their own, but here they are the perfect garnish, a boozy hit of fruit to cut through the creaminess of the malabi.

SERVES 6–8

BOURBON-SOAKED CHERRIES

150ml water

150g caster sugar

1 star anise

1 cinnamon stick

few strips of orange zest

½ vanilla pod (seeds scraped and reserved for the malabi, see below)

300ml good-quality bourbon

250g cherries, pitted

CARDAMOM AND ROSE MALABI

1.25 litres full-fat milk

scraped seeds of ½ vanilla pod

150g caster sugar

seeds of 6 cardamom pods

90g cornflour

2 tbsp rose water

SERVE

3 tbsp green pistachios, toasted and roughly chopped

3 tsp desiccated coconut

FOR THE BOURBON-SOAKED CHERRIES

Combine the water and sugar in a small saucepan, add the star anise, cinnamon stick, orange peel and vanilla pod and heat to a gentle simmer, making sure all the sugar is dissolved. Reduce the heat to low, and simmer the syrup for 10–15 minutes, until thickened and infused. Whisk in the bourbon and continue to simmer for a further 5–7 minutes over a very low heat.

Place the cherries in a Kilner or suitable sterilised jar and pour the bourbon syrup, along with the aromatics, over the top. Seal and set aside, refrigerated, for 3–5 days before using. The cherries will improve with flavour over time, and can keep for up to a month.

FOR THE MALABI

Heat 1 litre of milk, the vanilla seeds, sugar and cardamom pods in a saucepan over medium-low heat and bring to a simmer. Let the milk tick over gently for 15 minutes to infuse.

Mix the remaining cold milk with the cornflour in a small bowl and then add this to the infused milk, whisking gently but continuously. The malabi will start to thicken. Once it has thickened to the consistency of thick custard (about 1½–2 minutes), remove it from the heat, whisk in the rose water and strain the mixture through a sieve. Pour the malabi into moulds (I like to use small Kilner jars or suitably sized glasses) and leave in the fridge to set until firm (about 3–4 hours should suffice but overnight would be preferable).

TO SERVE

Reduce the cherry liquor in a small saucepan over high heat until thickened to a glaze-like syrup consistency that will coat the back of a spoon. Remove the malabi from the fridge, spoon 3–4 cherries on top, followed by some of the bourbon liquor glaze and garnish with pistachios and desiccated coconut.

KUNEFE

Antepliler Kunefe is a small joint on Green Lanes that I go to as often as I can for Turkish çay (tea) and, you guessed it, kunefe. I implore you all to try kunefe at least once in your life. It's a dessert made from semi-soft cheese sandwiched between kataifi pastry crisped in a pan until the cheese starts to melt whilst simultaneously being soaked in sweet syrup. Admittedly I haven't made it sound all that appetising, but it's one of those things in life for which words cannot do justice.

SERVES 4

250g caster sugar

400ml water

1 tbsp lemon juice

300g shredded kataifi pastry, shop-bought

100ml clarified butter

340g crumbled Turkish white cheese (Peyniri) or grated mozzarella

60g finely ground pistachios

Place the sugar and water in a saucepan over low heat, allowing the sugar to dissolve. Add the lemon juice and simmer for 20–25 minutes to reduce the syrup by about 40%, until such time as the mixture has a consistency akin to maple syrup and coats the back of a spoon. Remove from the heat and set aside to cool.

Pulse the kataifi pastry in a food processor (if available) for a few seconds or chop it down by hand into smaller pieces using a knife.

Liberally brush four individual 16cm cast-iron pans with clarified butter and distribute half the kataifi evenly across each one. Top the pastry with the cheese before adding a final layer of the remaining kataifi. Press the mixture down with the palm of your hand or a flat kitchen utensil and cook over medium-low heat for 5–6 minutes, until the pastry crisps up and is golden brown on its base and the edges and the cheese starts to ooze. Continue to press the mixture down with the back of a flat utensil as it cooks.

You will need to flip the kunefe to crisp up both sides, which is the only technically difficult aspect of this dish. If technically confident, you can use a slotted spatula or flipper to gently lift and flip the kunefe, much as you would a pancake or fried egg. (Alternatively, use the foolproof method of placing a plate over the kunefe and giving it a quick flip to turn it out.) Top up the base of the cast-iron pans with some more clarified butter and slide the turned kunefe off the plate and back into the pan to continue cooking for a further 5 minutes until golden brown all over.

Pull the kunefe from the heat and pour the cooled syrup over the top of each one, evenly distributing it all over and across all four pans.

Serve immediately, piping hot, garnished with a generous mound of finely ground pistachios placed in the centre.

WALNUT & CLOTTED CREAM BAKLAVA

Gurel Muhidinov is a Turkish chef of notable distinction who has worked with us for several years now. He has two main culinary passions: working our intensely hot grill section and making the most delicately perfect baklava. He's a master at both. Yin and yang and all that. This is his recipe.

MAKES ABOUT 30

200g walnuts, toasted

½ tsp ground cinnamon

100g vacuum-packed ready-to-eat chestnuts

400g caster sugar

400ml water

1 tsp orange blossom water

46 sheets of filo pastry (3 x 400g packets)

350ml clarified butter

150g clotted cream

SERVE (OPTIONAL)

clotted cream

handful of dried rose petals

Blend the walnuts in a food processor to a coarse crumb, or chop. Transfer to a bowl and stir in the cinnamon. Crumble the chestnuts in your hands to a chunky rubble and add them to the blitzed walnuts. Mix well to combine.

Preheat the oven to 190°C/170°C Fan/Gas mark 5.

Place the sugar and water in a saucepan and heat gently to dissolve the sugar. Turn the heat up to medium-high and bring the syrup to the boil. Reduce the syrup by about 40 per cent, until the mixture is the consistency of maple syrup. Remove the pan from the heat, then allow to cool slightly before stirring in the orange blossom water. Set aside to cool completely.

Grease a 35cm x 25cm and 3.5cm deep roasting tray with butter. Trim the filo pastry to fit the tray.

Add your first sheet of filo pastry to the tray, brush it with clarified butter, then repeat with 15 further filo sheets, placing each on top of the last and brushing each sheet before adding the next. Spread a layer of clotted cream over before adding a further sheet of filo pastry, brushed again with clarified butter. Sprinkle the walnut mixture evenly over the top and then proceed to add a further 30 filo sheets, one at a time, brushing each sheet with clarified butter as you lay it down on top of the last.

Place the tray in the oven and bake the baklava for 25–30 minutes, until golden brown. Remove from the oven and immediately pour the cooled syrup evenly over the entire tray whilst the baklava is still piping hot. Set aside to cool to room temperature.

Slice the baklava and serve with some clotted cream and a garnish of a few rose petals (optional) strewn over the top.

PUMPKIN & URFA CHILLI SUNDAE
WITH DULCE DE LECHE ICE CREAM & APPLE

Everybody loves a sundae. This is a sundae for grown-ups. But I think your kids will love it, too.

SERVES 6–8

DULCE DE LECHE ICE CREAM
1 tin condensed milk, labels removed
315ml full-fat milk
50g soft light brown sugar
250ml double cream

BURNT PUMPKIN CARAMEL
600g pumpkin
200ml double cream
large pinch of urfa chilli flakes
2 sprigs of thyme
120ml water
400g caster sugar

APPLE COMPOTE
20g unsalted butter
1 cinnamon stick
1 star anise
1 vanilla stick, seeds scraped out and retained along with the empty pod
4 cooking apples, peeled and diced into small cubes
50g soft light brown sugar

FOR THE DULCE DE LECHE ICE CREAM
Fill a deep saucepan with plenty of water and bring to the boil over high heat. Carefully lower the tin of condensed milk into the boiling water, ensuring that it's fully submerged, and reduce the heat to a gentle simmer. Boil the tin of condensed milk on a low heat for 2½–3 hours, topping up the water as it evaporates. The tin of condensed milk must remain fully submerged at all times.

When the time is up, remove the tin from the water and set it over a wire rack to cool to room temperature. Don't open it until completely cool, since it may spit out steaming hot dulce de leche, which will leave its mark, believe me.

Once ready, put the dulce de leche in a small saucepan with the milk and brown sugar over medium heat and bring to the boil, stirring until the sugar dissolves. Cool the liquid down. Meanwhile, whip the cream to soft peaks and fold it through the now-cooled milk mixture. Place in the freezer until set.

FOR THE BURNT PUMPKIN CARAMEL
Preheat the oven to 210°C/190°C Fan/Gas mark 6½. Peel the skin off the pumpkin and cut it into 5cm chunks. Roast the chunks in the oven for about 15 minutes, until coloured and tender all the way through. Transfer to a food processor and blend to a smooth purée, about 3–4 minutes.

Whilst the pumpkin is roasting, bring the cream, urfa chilli and thyme to the boil, then remove it from the heat and infuse for 12–15 minutes.

Concurrently, heat the water and caster sugar in a cast-iron pan over medium-low heat, stirring gently until the sugar has dissolved, about 2–3 minutes. Turn the heat up to medium. As the water evaporates the sugar will begin to caramelise, changing from a light brown to a golden caramel, about 5–7 minutes. Watch it constantly, you don't want to take it too far. Once it has a lovely, medium golden colour, whisk in the infused cream immediately and reduce to medium-low. The caramel will foam and bubble up around the edges – knock this back with a spatula. Gently whisk until smooth with no lumps.

Remove the caramel from the heat and fold through the pumpkin purée. Set aside. You can serve it runny and warm, or let it set and serve it more chewy.

FOR THE APPLE COMPOTE
Melt the butter in a pan and add the cinnamon stick, star anise, vanilla seeds and scraped vanilla pod. Once the butter starts to brown, add the apples and brown sugar. Cook for 2–3 minutes, until the apples are tender.

TO SERVE
Scoop a few dollops of ice cream into a bowl, and add plenty of the apple and lashings of the caramel. Try to build it into layers.

CHAPTER 07

LARDER

CRISPY CAPERS

MAKES 120G

200g capers, drained and rinsed
vegetable oil, for deep-frying

Heat the vegetable oil in a large, deep saucepan over medium heat until it reaches 180°C when probed with a thermometer.

Deep-fry the capers for 1–2 minutes until crisp and slightly curled up at the sides. Lift the capers from the oil and transfer to kitchen paper to absorb any excess oil. Serve immediately.

●●●

CRISPY SHALLOTS

MAKES 30G

4 large shallots, thinly sliced
500ml extra virgin olive oil, for deep-frying

Heat the olive oil over medium-low in a large, deep saucepan until it reaches 120°C when probed with a thermometer. In the absence of a thermometer, test the oil with a few slices of shallot. They should bubble gently as they fry, not aggressively or too fast.

Once the oil is at the correct temperature, throw the shallot rings into the pan and continue to move them around intermittently as they fry.

Continue to cook the shallots until they turn a lovely golden brown, roughly 10 minutes or so, give or take.

Lift the shallots from the oil and transfer to kitchen paper to absorb any excess oil, then season with salt to taste. Store in an airtight container for 3–5 days.

CHILLI PANGRATATTO

MAKES 150G

½ a ciabatta or sourdough loaf,
   preferably stale, crusts removed
50ml olive oil
3 garlic cloves, minced
1 tbsp dried chilli flakes

Blitz the bread in a food processor to rough crumbs.

Heat the olive oil in a shallow frying pan over medium heat until shimmering, and fry the bread, along with the garlic and chilli flakes, until golden brown.

Transfer the pangratatto to some kitchen paper to soak up any excess oil, and season with salt and black pepper to taste. Store in an airtight container for 3–5 days.

• •

ANCHOVY & LEMON PANGRATATTO

MAKES 300G

400g ciabatta or sourdough loaf,
   preferably stale, crusts removed
50ml olive oil
2 garlic cloves, minced
3–4 anchovy fillets, finely chopped
½ tsp dried chilli flakes
40g pine nuts, toasted
grated zest of ½ lemon
small handful of parsley

Preheat the oven to 180°C/160°C Fan/Gas mark 4.

Rip or cut the bread into crouton-size pieces and toss them in a small bowl with the olive oil, garlic, anchovy and chilli flakes. Toast the bread in the oven for 5–7 minutes until golden brown. Leave to cool.

Blitz the pine nuts, lemon zest and parsley in a food processor to a rough crumb-like consistency. Add the toasted ciabatta and continue to blitz until combined. Check for seasoning. The anchovies should provide sufficient saltiness, but add some more salt accordingly if required.

Store in an airtight container in a cool place, for up to 3 days.

DUKKAH

This Egyptian mix consists of spices, nuts and dried herbs that are dry-roasted and pounded to a coarse texture. The combinations are practically endless – feel free to add whatever spices, seeds or nuts you like. Dukkah keeps indefinitely, and is great on most grilled meats, vegetables and fish.

● ●

PECAN & ROSE DUKKAH

MAKES ABOUT 350G

200g pecans, toasted
80g pumpkin seeds
50g sunflower seeds
2 tbsp pesticide-free dried
  rose petals
3 tbsp fennel seeds
2 tbsp coriander seeds
3 tbsp sesame seeds
2 tbsp flaked sea salt

In a food processor, pulse the pecans with the pumpkin and sunflower seeds to rough crumbs. Retain some texture by ensuring it's not overprocessed. Remove and set aside.

Process the rose petals to a rough powder.

Use a mortar and pestle to grind the fennel and coriander seeds. In the absence of a mortar and pestle, a spice grinder can be used.

Mix all the ingredients with the sesame seeds in a bowl, and season with the salt. Store in an airtight container for several months, or even longer.

PISTACHIO DUKKAH

MAKES ABOUT 275G

150g pistachios, toasted
6 tbsp coriander seeds, toasted
50g cumin seeds, toasted
handful of pesticide-free dried
  rose petals
3 tbsp sesame seeds, toasted
3 tbsp nigella seeds
1½ tbsp flaked sea salt

Blitz the pistachios in a food processor to coarse crumbs. Don't process the nuts for too long. The idea is to retain some texture.

Use a mortar and pestle to grind the coriander and cumin seeds. In the absence of a mortar and pestle, a spice grinder can be used, but once again, don't overgrind the seeds to a fine powder. Retain some texture and crunch by just pulsing them a few times.

Process the rose petals to a rough powder and combine in a bowl with the pulsed pistachios, coriander and cumin seeds, as well as the sesame and nigella seeds. Season with salt to taste and mix well. Store in an airtight container in the larder for several months.

HAZELNUT DUKKAH

MAKES ABOUT 200G

60g hazelnuts, toasted
10 tbsp coriander seeds, toasted
50g cumin seeds, toasted
6 tbsp sesame seeds, toasted
1½ tbsp flaked sea salt
1 tsp coarse ground black pepper

Blend the hazelnuts in a food processor to coarse crumbs. Don't process the nuts for too long. The idea is to retain some texture to the dukkah, with some larger pieces intermingled with smaller ones.

Use a mortar and pestle to grind the coriander and cumin seeds. In the absence of a mortar and pestle, a spice grinder can be used, but once again, don't overgrind the seeds to a fine powder. Retain some texture and crunch by just pulsing them a few times.

Season the dukkah with salt and black pepper and store in an airtight container in the larder for several months.

RUBS

Barbecue rubs are the cornerstone of any great barbecue joint and often a well-guarded family secret. We have a whole range of rubs that we use at Berber & Q, usually determined by the meat we're smoking. Our Mechoui Rub is intended for lamb, but works brilliantly with chicken as well. The same goes for our Shawarma Rub, and it can be used for certain cuts of beef. It's a solid all-rounder. Use these as a base and let your imagination do the rest.

• •

EVERYDAY CHICKEN RUB

MAKES ABOUT 75G

2 tbsp ground sumac

1 tbsp Aleppo chilli flakes or use
   1 tsp dried chilli flakes

1 tbsp garlic granules or powder

1 tsp ground turmeric

2 tsp salt

1 tsp coarse ground black pepper

2 tsp ground coriander

2 tbsp soft dark brown sugar

Put all the ingredients in a small bowl and mix well.

SHAWARMA RUB

MAKES ABOUT 160G

5 cardamom pods

3 cloves

¾ tsp fennel seeds

10g coriander seeds, toasted
   and ground

20g cumin seeds, toasted and
   ground

¼ tsp dried chilli flakes

10g ground allspice

¼ tsp ground white pepper

18g table salt

25g soft dark brown sugar

2 tsp ground cinnamon

¾ tbsp ground ginger

1½ tsp ground turmeric

pinch of cayenne pepper

grated zest of 1 lemon

Toast the cardamom pods, cloves, fennel seeds, coriander seeds and cumin seeds over medium heat in a heavy-based pan until smoking and fragrant. Set to one side and cool.

Blitz the toasted aromatics with the chilli flakes to a coarse powder, then combine with all the remaining ingredients. Transfer the rub to an airtight container where it will keep well, sealed, for up to 5 days.

All the rubs below follow the same method:

Just blitz all the ingredients together in a food processor or spice grinder to a fine powder, transfer to an airtight container and store for up to 2 weeks.

• •

TURKISH COFFEE BEEF RUB

MAKES 265G

20g Turkish coffee (or good-quality ground coffee beans)
25g chilli powder
30g smoked paprika
90g soft dark brown sugar

20g flaked sea salt
50g caster sugar
15g garlic granules or powder
10g ground cumin
large pinch of cayenne pepper

BERBER & Q PORK RUB

MAKES 300G

25g curry powder
40g chilli powder
30g smoked paprika
80g soft dark brown sugar
40g flaked sea salt
35g caster sugar

20g garlic granules or powder
10g ground cumin
¼ tsp ground fennel
1 tsp cayenne pepper

GAME BIRD RUB

MAKES ABOUT 220G

1 tsp ground cumin
½ tsp ground turmeric
¼ tsp garlic granules or powder
¼ tsp dried chilli flakes
½ tsp dried oregano

1 tbsp soft light brown sugar
½ tbsp flaked sea salt (such as Maldon)

MECHOUI RUB

MAKES 240G

80g ras al hanout
50g ground coriander
40g ground cumin
30g sweet paprika
20g garlic granules or powder
20g flaked sea salt

CHAPTER 08

PICKLES & SAUCES

PICKLES

Pickles are commonplace across the whole of the Middle East and North Africa, and an important component of American barbecue culture, served as a foil to cut through rich and fatty meats. There's not much we haven't tried to pickle at Berber & Q, and the recipes here are a collection of our most popular ones. We make our pickles in a few different ways. It's really a case of trial and error to see which method works best for a given ingredient. We choose a cold or a warm brine solution, which is either poured over the raw ingredient or heated together with it. In all cases, the pickle benefits from time spent on the refrigerator shelf, enabling the flavours to intensify.

• •

PRESERVED LEMONS

MAKES 2 LITRE JAR

10 unwaxed lemons
1kg salt
2 or 3 bay leaves
2 tbsp coriander seeds
1½ tbsp fennel seeds
2 cinnamon sticks
2 star anise

Wash and scrub the lemons to remove any dirt or impurities from the skin, and top and tail each one, just enough to remove the protruding nib.

Cut each lemon lengthways from top to bottom making a cross, but don't cut all the way through – the idea is that the lemon holds together at its base.

We like to put our lemons in a freezer bag at this point and freeze them for up to 48 hours, as we find it speeds up the preservation process quite significantly, from 3 months to roughly 1 month, but you can skip this step if you're not in any kind of rush.

Once thawed (if freezing) gently ease open each lemon and rub a generous amount of salt into the flesh of each one, packing them into a Kilner jar, or similar, one-by-one as you work. It's important that you press the lemons and pack them in quite tightly on top of one another – really squeeze them into the jar – and add more salt to surround each lemon as you go.

Repeat the process with each of the lemons, layering the rest of the aromatics through the jar at random intervals.

Twist or clip the lid closed, and store in a cool and dry place for 1 month (if the lemons had been frozen first) or 3 months if not. A larder or spice cupboard usually does the trick. Remember to turn the jar intermittently, checking back on the lemons every week or so.

The high concentration of salt and acidity from the lemon juice will preserve the lemons, rendering the skin down to a soft, gummy texture that makes a fantastically versatile garnish to most dishes.

QUICK-PRESERVED LEMON PICKLE

MAKES 30G

zest of 3 lemons, cut into very
    thin strips
juice of 3 lemons

Put the lemon zest strips and juice in a pan and set over medium-low heat. Cook for 12–15 minutes until completely softened but still holding shape. The lemon juice should be on a gentle, rolling simmer as opposed to an aggressive boil. Be careful not to overcook the lemon skin, as it will fall apart and disintegrate into unmanageably small pieces. The idea is to have long strips of softened, tender zest still intact.

Transfer the lemon zest with any remaining juice to an airtight jar and keep, refrigerated, for up to 1 month.

PICKLED POMEGRANATE SEEDS

MAKES 1 LITRE JAR

300ml pomegranate juice
380ml red wine vinegar
160g caster sugar
1 cinnamon stick
1 star anise
1½ tbsp coriander seeds
1 tsp rose water
350g pomegranate seeds, about
    2 pomegranates

Bring the pomegranate juice, vinegar and sugar to the boil in a pan over high heat, along with the cinnamon stick, star anise and coriander seeds, stirring occasionally, until the sugar has dissolved. Remove from the heat and stir through the rose water.

Cool the brine to room temperature and leave to infuse for 4–6 hours or preferably overnight.

Place the pomegranate seeds in a sterilised Kilner jar and decant the liquid over a sieve to cover the seeds. Seal the jar and store, refrigerated, for 3 days before using. Keeps for up to 1 month.

PICKLED RED CHILLI

MAKES 500ML JAR

200ml water
200ml white wine vinegar
60g sugar
1 tsp salt
1½ tbsp coriander seeds
1 tbsp cumin seeds, toasted
2 bay leaves
12 red chillies, thinly sliced

Put all the ingredients except for the red chillies into a pan and bring to the boil over medium-high heat, stirring occasionally, until such time as the sugar and salt have dissolved.

Remove the brine from the heat and drop the sliced chillies into the pickle liquor. Set aside to cool, then transfer to a sterilised jar. Leave to cool. Refrigerate for 3–4 days before serving, during which time the pickle will intensify in flavour. Kept unopened, this pickle will keep for several months, but once opened should be eaten within 2 weeks.

PICKLED CABBAGE & GRILLED OKRA

| MAKES 2 LITRE JAR |

200g okra

1½ tbsp olive oil

1 head of cabbage, quartered, cored and cut into 2.5cm squares

2 tbsp salt

6 whole red chillies

500ml white wine vinegar

1.2 litres water

4 bay leaves

1 tsp ground turmeric

1 tsp ground cumin

¾ tsp paprika

¼ tsp chilli powder

½ tsp coarse ground black pepper

Prepare a barbecue for single-zone direct grilling (page 17). Toss the okra in the olive oil and season lightly with a touch of salt. Blacken the okra on both sides over high heat, until cooked through, roughly 1 minute per side.

Sprinkle the cabbage with salt and place in a colander. Use a weight such as a large bowl filled with water, or some extra large tins from your larder, to press the cabbage down and leave to drain and soften for 1–2 hours.

Transfer the salted cabbage and charred okra to a sterilised Kilner jar or similar vessel. Layer the chillies intermittently within the jar, pour in the vinegar and water and add the remaining spices.

Seal the jar and store, refrigerated, for 3–5 days before using. This pickle will keep for up to 1 month if left undisturbed, but should be eaten within 2 weeks once opened.

PICKLED RED ONION

| MAKES 500ML JAR |

200ml red wine vinegar

3 tbsp caster sugar

1 tbsp salt

2 bay leaves

1 cinnamon stick

2 tbsp coriander seeds

1 red onion, very finely sliced

Heat the vinegar, sugar and salt in a small saucepan over medium heat, until dissolved. Add the bay leaves, cinnamon stick and coriander seeds, and set to one side to cool to room temperature.

Transfer the sliced onion to a sterilised jar. Pour the vinegar over the top and seal the jar. This pickle can be used within a few hours, but, as with all pickles, will benefit from having more time to souse. Refrigerated, this keeps for up to 3 weeks.

BREAD & BUTTER PICKLES

MAKES 1 LITRE JAR

4 baby cucumbers
2 onions, thinly sliced
30g salt
400ml cider vinegar
225g soft light brown sugar
10g ground turmeric
3 cloves
1 tbsp coriander seeds
2 bay leaves
½ bunch of roughly chopped dill

Wash the cucumber and cut to 3mm rounds.

Layer the cucumber slices with the onion slices in a colander and sprinkle with the salt. Cover with clingfilm or parchment paper and use a heavy weight, such as a large bowl filled with water, or some extra large tins from your larder, to press and extract the water from the cucumber. Leave for at least 2 hours.

Wash the cucumber under running water to remove any excess salt, then place atop paper towels and pat dry.

Put the vinegar, sugar, spices and bay leaves in a saucepan over medium-high heat, stirring until the sugar dissolves. Bring to the boil, add the cucumber and onions and cook over medium heat for 3–4 minutes, until the cucumber has just started to change colour. Remove from the heat, add the chopped dill and transfer to an airtight container or sterilised Kilner jar. Set aside and allow to cool. Keep refrigerated for 3–4 days before using, though the longer you can leave them the better they will taste.

PICKLED CAULIFLOWER

MAKES 1 LITRE JAR

2–3 whole dried red chillies
1 head of cauliflower, broken into florets
250ml water
200ml white wine vinegar
1 tbsp salt
1 tsp ground turmeric
1 tbsp coriander seeds
½ tbsp cumin seeds
2–3 sprigs of dill

Toast the chillies in a heavy-based or cast-iron pan over medium heat until smoking and fragrant, about 2–3 minutes.

Put the cauliflower in a sterilised Kilner jar, and cover with the water and vinegar. Throw the toasted chillies into the jar, along with the salt, turmeric, coriander and cumin seeds and dill.

Seal the jar and place in a dark, cool spot in your house such as a store cupboard or larder, until such time as the cauliflower has taken on the colour of the turmeric, about 3 days, give or take. Transfer the pickle to the refrigerator, where it will keep for at least 2 weeks if not longer.

PICKLED TURKISH CHILLI

MAKES 1 LITRE JAR

500g Turkish chilli peppers

250ml water

350ml white wine vinegar

200g caster sugar

1½ tbsp salt

pinch of sweet paprika

2 garlic cloves, finely chopped

2–3 sprigs of thyme

Pierce each chilli 4 or 5 times with a small bamboo skewer or toothpick. Bring the water to the boil in a saucepan over high heat and cook the chillies for 3–5 minutes, just until they start to soften. Lift the chillies from the pan and pack them tightly into a sterilised Kilner jar suitable for pickling, making sure to retain the liquor in the pan. Add the vinegar, sugar, salt and paprika to the pan and bring to the boil over high heat, stirring occasionally until the sugar has dissolved, about 2–3 minutes, then set aside to cool.

Stuff the garlic and thyme into the jar, and pour the cooled pickling liquor on top, ensuring the chillies are fully submerged. Seal the jar, and store it on a shelf for 10–12 days, turning regularly, after which time they should be ready to eat.

This pickle will keep, sealed, for at least a month, but once opened it should be kept refrigerated and eaten within 5 days.

MIXED HOUSE PICKLES

MAKES 3 LITRE JAR

1 head of cabbage, quartered, cored and cut into 2.5cm squares

4 tbsp salt

800ml water

360ml white wine vinegar

120g caster sugar

1 tsp yellow mustard seeds

½ tbsp cumin seeds, lightly toasted

1 tbsp Harissa (page 259) or shop-bought

1½ tsp ground turmeric

2 or 3 large carrots, peeled and thinly sliced

3 baby cucumbers, cut into 0.5cm rounds

1 head of cauliflower, broken into florets

2–3 bay leaves

Put the cabbage squares in a colander and sprinkle with half the salt. Press down using a weight such as a large bowl filled with water, or some extra large tins from your larder, and allow the cabbage to soften for 1–2 hours.

Heat the water, vinegar, sugar, mustard seeds, cumin seeds and remaining salt in a saucepan over medium heat, stirring occasionally, until the sugar and salt have dissolved.

Take the pickling brine off the heat and add the harissa and turmeric. Stir the brine well and decant over the cabbage, carrots, cucumber and cauliflower in a large pickling jar with a resealable lid.

Add the bay leaves and allow to cool to room temperature for 45 minutes to an hour, during which time the flavours will infuse and intensify. Seal the jar with the lid.

Store the pickles in the refrigerator, tightly sealed for up to a month. It will be ready to use after 3 days.

YEMENITE DYNAMITE (S'CHUG)

MAKES ABOUT 500G

30g mixed red and green bird's eye chillies, stalks removed

7–8 garlic cloves, roughly chopped

4 cardamom pods, crushed, husks discarded, seeds only

small handful of picked mint leaves

1 handful of picked flat-leaf parsley

½ bunch of coriander including stalks (ends trimmed off)

juice of 1 lemon

100–150ml extra virgin olive oil

Blitz the chillies in a food processor with the garlic, cardamom seeds and a bit of oil for a minute to make a rough paste.

Add the mint, parsley, coriander and lemon juice, and continue to blitz.

Start to gradually pour in the oil, until you get the right consistency. It should be coarse, but not too dry.

Season with salt and pepper.

The sauce is best eaten fresh and should be made daily where possible. However, it can be refrigerated and kept for up to 3 days.

• •

BLACKENED CHILLI KEBAB SAUCE

MAKES ABOUT 750G

5–6 Scotch bonnet chillies, thinly sliced

1 tsp salt

1kg red peppers (6–7 peppers)

250g large red chillies

50ml white wine vinegar

50g caster sugar

Put the Scotch bonnet chillies in a storage container and sprinkle with salt. Set aside to ferment for 3 days, during which time the chillies should start to break down and noticeably change in composition to a softened mass.

Once the Scotch bonnets are ready, blacken the red peppers and red chillies on or under a grill, or simply on the naked flame of your stovetop, until blistered and blackened all over. Transfer to a bowl and cover with clingfilm immediately so that they sit in their own steam for 10–15 minutes, which should help to loosen the skin for peeling. Peel the peppers and remove the stalks and seeds, then roughly chop them.

Warm the vinegar in a small saucepan over medium heat, then add the sugar and stir to dissolve. It should be the correct balance of sweet and sour.

Transfer the fermented Scotch bonnets, the chopped peppers and chillies to a food processor and blitz with the vinegar mixture until smooth. Season with salt to taste, decant into a bottle and refrigerate until required. The sauce should keep for 4–5 days, if not longer.

FERMENTED GREEN CHILLI KEBAB SAUCE

MAKES ABOUT 150G

8 green chillies, finely sliced

2 tbsp salt

2 tbsp white wine vinegar

½ tsp Ultra-Tex (optional), ordered online

Salt the sliced green chillies and transfer to a storage container with a tight-fitting lid. Set aside in a cool, dark cupboard for 2 days to start the fermentation process. The chillies will soften as they ferment.

Cover the chillies with water and return to the cupboard for a further week, during which time the chillies will noticeably change in texture and colour as they breakdown. A scum or mould may form at the surface during this time. Don't be alarmed; simply remove the mould with a spoon. You will also see bubbles rise to the surface over time or become trapped within the sliced chillies. This is supposed to happen and is proof that the fermentation process is working.

After a week to 10 days, drain the chillies and transfer to a food processor. Add the remaining ingredients and blitz to form a smooth sauce. You shouldn't require any further seasoning since the chillies have already been salted, but check and adjust according to taste. Similarly, don't be afraid to add more vinegar if the sauce is too salty. If you are able to get hold of any Ultra-Tex, you can stir it into the sauce. It will produce a beautifully viscous sauce with a great textural consistency.

Bottle and refrigerate until needed. The sauce will keep for several weeks.

• •

KEBAB SALSA (ACILI EZME)

MAKES ABOUT 350G

3–4 tomatoes, roughly chopped

30ml sherry vinegar

100ml olive oil

2 red peppers, blackened on the grill, peeled and deseeded

2 shallots, finely diced

4 red chillies, finely diced

3 green chillies, finely diced

4 garlic clove, minced

grated zest of 1 lemon

2 tsp dried chilli flakes

½ tsp ground cumin

2 tbsp chopped flat-leaf parsley

2 tbsp finely chopped coriander

2 tbsp lemon juice

1 tbsp Harissa (page 259) or shop-bought

Put the tomatoes, vinegar and 30ml of olive oil in a bowl and season with salt and black pepper. Allow to marinate for up to 2 hours.

Transfer the tomatoes to a chopping board and finely chop, along with the red pepper, to the consistency of a rough salsa.

Add the shallots, chillies, garlic, lemon zest, spices and herbs to the chopped tomatoes, and stir well to combine.

In a separate bowl, whisk the lemon juice and harissa together with the remaining olive oil until well incorporated.

Pour the dressing over the finely chopped vegetables and mix. Season well. The salsa will keep refrigerated for up to 1 week.

HARISSA

MAKES ABOUT 250G

8 dried red chillies
1 red pepper
1½ tsp caraway seeds
1 tsp cumin seeds
1 tsp coriander seeds
8 garlic cloves, roughly chopped
1 tbsp salt
120ml olive oil
2 tbsp smoked paprika
1 tsp cayenne pepper
40g tomato paste
120ml water
1½ tbsp lemon juice
extra virgin olive oil, to seal

Put the chillies in a bowl and cover with just-boiled water. Leave to rehydrate for at least 6 hours. Drain, cut off the stalks, deseed and roughly chop.

Blacken the red pepper on a barbecue grill, or directly on the gas flame on the stovetop, until charred and softened, then transfer to a bowl. Cover with clingfilm and leave to cool. Peel, quarter and deseed the pepper, removing any remaining white membrane, and chop into small dice. Set aside until required.

Toast the caraway, cumin and coriander seeds in a pan over medium-high for a few minutes until fragrant. Blitz in a spice blender until finely ground.

In a large mortar and pestle or food processor, crush the garlic with the salt until a rough paste forms. Work in the spice mix and add a tablespoon of olive oil as well as the paprika, cayenne pepper and rehydrated chillies and mix.

Heat the remaining olive oil in a heavy-based wide pan over medium heat. Add the garlic, spice mix and red pepper, and fry, stirring frequently, to infuse the oil without burning. Add the tomato paste and mix, followed by the water. Simmer over medium heat for 12–15 minutes, until almost all the water has evaporated and the harissa becomes dry, and looks dark and caramelised.

Transfer the mix to a food processor, add the lemon juice and blend to a coarse, textured paste. Check for seasoning and add salt if needed. Store in a sterilised jar, covered with extra virgin olive oil, refrigerated for up to 2 weeks.

ROSE HARISSA

MAKES ABOUT 175G

8 dried red chillies
4 dried red peppers
1½ tsp caraway seeds
1 tsp cumin seeds
1 tsp coriander seeds
4 garlic cloves, roughly chopped
1 banana shallot, roughly chopped
1 tbsp salt
80ml sunflower oil
2 tbsp smoked paprika
1½ tbsp sherry vinegar
1 tsp pesticide-free dried
  rose petals
½ tsp rose water
extra virgin olive oil, to seal

Put the dried chillies and red peppers in a bowl and cover with just-boiled water. Leave to rehydrate for at least 6 hours. Drain, cut off the stalks, deseed and roughly chop.

Toast the caraway, cumin and coriander seeds in a pan over medium-high for 4–5 minutes, until fragrant and smoking. Blitz in a spice blender until finely ground.

Place the rehydrated chillies and peppers in a food processor with the spice mix, garlic cloves, shallot and salt and blitz to a paste.

Heat the oil in a wide heavy-based pan over medium heat. Add the paste to the pan, along with the paprika, and cook for 15–20 minutes, stirring frequently, until caramelised and jam-like in consistency.

Pour in the vinegar, stirring to deglaze the pan, then transfer to a food processor and blitz with the rose petals and rose water to a coarse, textured paste. Check for seasoning and add more salt if necessary.

Transfer to a sterilised jar, cover with extra virgin olive oil to seal, and keep refrigerated for up to 2 weeks.

FILFELCHUMA

MAKES ABOUT 300G

4 dried red chillies

1½ tbsp cayenne pepper

3 tbsp sweet paprika

½ tbsp ground cumin

1 tsp caraway seeds

12–15 garlic cloves, roughly
chopped

1 tbsp salt

2 tbsp lemon juice

120ml sunflower oil

olive oil, to cover

Put the chillies in a bowl and cover with just-boiled water. Leave to rehydrate for at least 6 hours. Drain, cut off the stalk, deseed and roughly chop.

Toast the cayenne pepper, paprika, ground cumin and caraway seeds in a pan over medium-high for a few minutes until fragrant and smoking.

If you have a mortar and pestle big enough, work the garlic with the salt until paste-like in consistency. In the absence of a mortar and pestle, use a food processor. Add the spices, rehydrated chillies and lemon juice and work to combine. Gradually add the oil until the desired consistency is achieved. The filfelchuma should form a thick, rough paste with a texture comparable to pesto.

Transfer the sauce to an airtight container or sterilised Kilner jar or similar storage vessel and cover with olive oil. The sauce will easily keep for up to 4 weeks in the refrigerator.

• •

CONFIT CHILLI SALSA & CHILLI OIL

MAKES ABOUT 150G

12 red chillies, stems trimmed and
discarded

4 sprigs of thyme

5 large garlic cloves

2 bay leaves

olive oil, to cover

Preheat the oven to 150°C/130°C Fan/Gas mark 2. Place the chillies in a deep casserole or baking dish, along with the herbs, garlic and bay leaves and add oil to cover. Tightly cover with tin foil and roast for 45 minutes to 1 hour, until the chillies have softened but not dried out. Remove and allow to cool.

Once cool, remove the chillies from the pan (reserving the chilli-infused oil for later use) and chop them as finely as you can. Spoon the chillies into a sterilised Kilner jar, season with salt and cover with oil. Refrigerate for up to 1 week.

Store the excess chilli oil in the fridge, and drizzle it over dishes to add heat.

• •

CONFIT GARLIC & GARLIC OIL

MAKES ABOUT 450G

4 large garlic bulbs, cloves
separated and unpeeled

2–3 sprigs of woody herbs of your
choice, oregano, lemon thyme,
rosemary

2 bay leaves

500–600ml olive oil, to cover

Preheat the oven to 150°C/130°C Fan/Gas mark 2.

Place the garlic in a deep 25cm cast-iron pan or roasting tray, along with the herbs and bay leaves. Add enough oil to cover. Tightly cover the pan with tin foil and roast for 45 minutes to 1 hour, until the garlic cloves have caramelised and softened. The flesh should ooze out of the skins with the lightest of pressure.

Transfer to a sterilised Kilner jar or similar storage vessel. Keep, covered in oil, refrigerated for up to 2 months.

Retain the excess oil for drizzling over everything. You can never have enough garlic in your life.

WHIPPED FETA

MAKES ABOUT 375G

200g feta
160g crème fraîche
1 heaped tsp Dijon mustard

Soak the feta in a bowl of water for roughly 15 minutes to remove any excess salt. Drain and repeat.

Blitz the feta in a food processor with the remaining ingredients, pulsing until smooth and well combined.

- -

LABNEH

MAKES ABOUT 250G

500g full-fat natural yoghurt
1 tbsp salt

Season the yoghurt with the salt and mix well in a bowl.

Spoon the yoghurt into a muslin cloth – or several J-cloths overlaid on one another – and hang, if possible, or else set the cloth in a colander or strainer with a bowl underneath to collect the whey. I like to tie the cloth in a bundle affixed to the spout of my kitchen tap, enabling the whey to deposit in the sink below.

Hang or strain the labneh for as long as the desired consistency demands. 12–24 hours will yield a labneh with quite a loose and creamy consistency, whereas any longer will produce a drier and more crumbly-textured result.

- -

LEMON YOGHURT

MAKES ABOUT 125G

100g full-fat natural yoghurt
grated zest and juice of 1 lemon
1 garlic clove, minced
20ml olive oil
1½ tsp salt, or to taste

Combine all the ingredients together in bowl and stir well. Adjust the seasoning according to taste.

- -

TOUM (GARLIC SAUCE)

MAKES ABOUT 450G

200g (about 60) garlic cloves
40ml white wine vinegar
40ml lemon juice
2 egg whites
350ml vegetable oil
1 tsp salt, or to taste

Blitz the garlic in a food processor with the vinegar and lemon juice until finely chopped. Pour in the egg white and pulse to combine.

With the machine running, gradually pour in the oil in a slow-but-steady stream to emulsify. Continue blitzing until the sauce has emulsified and thickened, with a consistency similar to double cream. It should be silky smooth and pungent.

Season with salt to taste. Store in an airtight container or jar in the refrigerator, where it will keep for up to 1 week.

TAHINA SAUCE

MAKES ABOUT 220G

100g tahini paste
1 tbsp lemon juice (optional)
1 garlic clove, minced (optional)
100ml iced water

Pour the tahini paste into a bowl and add the lemon juice and garlic (if using). Gradually whisk in the iced water, bit by bit, as you pour.

The tahini will thicken at first to a very coarse paste, but will loosen to form a thick sauce with the consistency of honey as you add more of the iced water. Season with salt to taste.

Alternatively, you can blitz the tahini in a food processor or whisk together using a stand mixer, adding the water gradually to combine.

• •

TAHINA CORN REMOULADE

MAKES ABOUT 250G

200g sweetcorn kernels (fresh or frozen)

150ml mayonnaise or aioli, preferably homemade (page 264)

50ml tahini

2 tbsp gherkins, finely chopped

1 tbsp capers, drained, rinsed and chopped

1 tbsp finely chopped flat-leaf parsley

1½ tbsp pickle brine (preferably from a jar of sweet pickled peppers)

1½ tbsp lemon juice (if not using homemade mayonnaise)

1 garlic clove, minced

1 shallot, very finely chopped

½ tsp smoked paprika

pinch of cayenne pepper

1 tsp Harissa (page 259) or shop-bought

Put a heavy non-stick frying pan over high heat and throw in the corn kernels. Sauté for 2–3 minutes until softened and lightly blackened. Remove from the heat, cool, then combine two-thirds of the kernels in a bowl with the remaining ingredients. Retain the remaining corn kernels for garnishing.

TAHINA GRAVY

MAKES ABOUT 325ML

125ml tahini paste
250ml chicken gravy, best quality
  and shop-bought
1 tbsp soy sauce
2 tsp maple syrup

Put the raw tahini, gravy, soy sauce and maple syrup in a saucepan and bring to a gentle boil over medium-low heat, whisking well to incorporate.

Cook until thickened to the desired consistency. Season with salt and pepper to taste.

· ·

RED CHILLI VINEGAR

MAKES ABOUT 260ML

250ml white wine vinegar
1½ tbsp Aleppo chilli flakes (also
  known as pul biber or red
  pepper flakes) or use smoked
  paprika
1 tbsp dried chilli flakes
1 tsp coriander seeds
3 slices of lemon
½ tbsp date syrup or runny honey

Put all the ingredients into a bowl and whisk to combine.

Store in a small Kilner jar or similar storage container for 3 days before straining through a fine-meshed sieve and returning to the jar for later use.

The vinegar will keep almost indefinitely.

· ·

HERB SALAD

MAKES ABOUT 120G

50g flat-leaf parsley leaves
20g picked mint
20g picked dill
bunch of chives, cut to 2.5cm
extra virgin olive oil, to drizzle

Combine all the herbs together in a bowl and, just prior to serving, drizzle with olive oil and season with flaked salt and a pinch of coarse black pepper.

HERB OIL

MAKES ABOUT 200ML

small handful each of picked basil, dill and flat-leaf parsley leaves
200ml olive oil

Combine all the herbs with the olive oil in a food processor, ideally one designed for making smoothies or crushing ice.

Blend the herbs for 4–5 minutes until as smooth as possible. Transfer to a muslin cloth and hang to drip through a sieve, with a storage vessel positioned below to collect the oil. It should be a dark, vibrant green. Keeps for 3–4 days.

• •

BASIC AIOLI

MAKES ABOUT 300G

3 egg yolks
4 garlic cloves, grated
1 tsp salt, plus extra to taste
250ml extra virgin olive oil
juice of ½ lemon

Put the egg yolks, garlic and salt into a food processor and blitz to combine.

Gradually pour in the olive oil, slowly but steadily as the machine is running, until the mixture has emulsified to the consistency of a thick mayonnaise. Add the lemon juice and season to taste with salt.

• •

HARISSA AIOLI

MAKES ABOUT 150G

100g Basic Aioli (above)
50g Rose Harissa (page 259) or shop-bought

Put the ingredients in a bowl and stir to combine.

• •

TAHINA AIOLI

MAKES ABOUT 350G

10 Confit Garlic Cloves (page 260)
220g Tahina Sauce (page 262)
100ml Garlic Oil (page 260) or extra virgin olive oil

Blend the confit garlic cloves with the tahina sauce in a food processor until combined, then gradually pour in the garlic oil to emulsify. The tahina sauce will lighten and take on the more aerated consistency of an aioli. This is a particularly great accompaniment for grilled fish.

ONFIT GARLIC
EMENITE DYNAMITE
RED CHILLI VINEGAR
CHILLI
ACLI EZME
10/7
LLOTS

CHAPTER 09

COCKTAILS

Danny Varley, Berber & Q Bar Manager, master of all trades, jack of none, was our very first signing for Berber & Q. We hired him on the back of a DJ set that he'd posted on Soundcloud which we found whilst trying to investigate his credentials. True story. Sometimes, rarely, the best decisions are made with no rational foundation. These cocktails are all his, and we're indebted to him not just for his contribution to this chapter, but for his contribution to our restaurant. He's as good at drinking cocktails as he is at making them. Also a true story.

TOP SHELF

It seemed only fitting to start with the first ever drink I thought up for Berber & Q. It's always been a policy of mine when creating a menu to have one damn good bourbon sour. The Top Shelf came about because I really wanted to infuse a drink with the aromatic Moroccan spice mix ras el hanout (the name is Arabic for 'head of the shop', the closest to the English expression 'top shelf'), not least because it reminded me of Ras al Ghoul of Batman fame. It turned out that we didn't have any ras el hanout but had plenty of the Turkish equivalent baharat. I made the substitution and the drink was born.

SERVES 1

50ml Four Roses bourbon
12.5ml Somerset Cider Brandy
25ml lemon juice
25ml maple syrup
1 egg white
ice cubes

GARNISH
orange peel twist
pinch of baharat spice

Combine all the ingredients in a cocktail shaker and 'dry shake' (without ice) for 10 seconds, then add some ice and shake again.

Strain the drink over ice into a large tumbler or whisky glass.

Garnish with an orange peel twist and a pinch of baharat spice in the centre.

SCAMMED IN MARRAKECH

If you visit the Medina in Marrakech, Morocco, you'd do well not to be subjected to some kind of scam or grossly overpriced spice purchase. If you're bartering skills are not up to scratch then it's likely you too will be 'scammed in Marrakech'. You're not alone, which is why this drink was created to share with your fellow Medina novices. It's a great pre-meal drink and follows a similar path to the ever-popular Negroni, if with a little more sweetness. Easy to make in big batches, you can decant it into bottles and store in the fridge. It's non-perishable and will last for ages.

SERVES 2

70ml Broker's gin or other dry gin

50ml Lillet Rouge sweet vermouth or other sweet vermouth

30ml Clement Creole Shrubb orange liqueur

50ml cold water

GARNISH
ice cubes
orange blossom water

Mix all the ingredients together in a container, decant to a small bottle or flask and cool in the fridge or freezer before serving.

Fill two small tumblers with ice, garnish by lightly spraying the ice with orange blossom water (we use a small atomiser), and pour the cocktail over the ice as required.

• •

LAVANTA MAZGAL

Another attempt to make mezcal accessible and appealing to the masses was this, the Lavanta Mazgal. The name is Turkish for 'lavender loophole'. I think it has a nice ring to its name. The herbal notes of the Kamm&Sons aperitif take the edge off the intensity of the mezcal, producing a floral, slightly sweet and refreshing sour taste whilst still retaining the depth from the mezcal.

SERVES 1

35ml Pierde Almas Puritita Verde mezcal

12.5ml Kamm & Sons British Aperitif

12.5ml lime juice

25ml lavender syrup

1 egg white

ice cubes

sprig of lavender

Put all the ingredients in the shaker, and dry shake (without ice) for 10 seconds. Then fill with ice and shake again. Double strain the cocktail into a coupette to get a clean frothy top.

Using a pipette, carefully garnish 4–5 drops of lavender bitters in a semicircle shape around the centre of the drink. Then, use the stick end of a lavender sprig to sweep the droplets in towards the centre. Carefully de-flower the lavender sprig and place the flower in the centre of the drink.

KRAAK & SUMAC

Mezcal can divide opinion. At Berber & Q, we're obviously big on our barbecue and smoking so there was always going to be room for an alcohol that inherently is very deep and smoky in flavour, such as mezcal. The Kraak and Sumac was a little laborious to make quickly on a busy night, but I assumed the mezcal would put some people off. How wrong I was. The fresh pineapple and coriander drew in a lot of people and it was easily our biggest selling drink of summer 2016.

SERVES 1

20g pineapple
3 sprigs of coriander
12.5ml agave nectar
25ml Del Maguey Vida mezcal
25ml Cabrito tequila blanco
ice cubes
12.5ml lime juice
pinch of sumac

First of all, muddle the pineapple with 2 sprigs of coriander and agave syrup, then add the mezcal and tequila, fill the shaker with ice and shake.

Coat the rim of a tumbler glass with a little lime juice, then cover with sumac, garnished with a pineapple chunk on the rim.

Fill the glass with ice, strain over the cocktail, add a sprig of coriander and serve.

- -

LEBANEEZA

There has to be room for at least one long, refreshing fruity drink on our menu. This was the first one we came up with – it's nice and simple yet ticks the boxes for something summery that goes down easy. This would be a good one to whip up a big batch of at your next barbecue.

SERVES 1

DEMERARA SUGAR SYRUP
50ml water
50g demerara sugar

SAFFRON-INFUSED RUM
pinch of saffron threads
700ml bottle white rum

LEBANEEZA
50ml Saffron-infused Rum
  (see above)
20ml Demerara Sugar Syrup
  (see above)
75ml grapefruit juice
ice cubes
grapefruit segment and sprig
  of mint, to garnish

FOR THE DEMERARA SUGAR SYRUP
Your standard simple syrup recipe, just add the equal parts sugar and water to a pan, bring to the boil and then simmer for 10 minutes. Let it cool before making your drink.

FOR THE SAFFRON-INFUSED RUM
It's just a delicate small pinch of saffron added to a bottle of white rum, and left to infuse over 24 hours. This will keep indefinitely.

FOR THE LEBANEEZA
Put all the ingredients in a cocktail shaker. Add the ice, shake and strain into a tall or 'long ball' glass.

Garnish with a grapefruit segment and a sprig of mint.

HAGGERSTONED

The name preceded the drink on this occasion, and whilst trying to keep it green in colour (for obvious reasons), the idea was to create a boozy liquid version of a pistachio baklava. A sweet concoction that works brilliantly after dinner, it now has a permanent home on our dessert drinks menu due to popular demand. It's possible to painstakingly create homemade pistachio syrup, or 'orgeat', but only the shop-bought Monin can create that eye-catching colour.

SERVES 1

50ml Cabrito tequila blanco
12.ml green Chartreuse
25ml Monin pistachio syrup
20ml lime juice
3 dashes of orange bitters
ice cubes

GARNISH
orange peel twist

Combine all the ingredients with the ice cubes in a cocktail shaker and shake for 30 seconds.

Strain the drink over ice into a rocks glass.

Garnish with an orange peel twist.

• •

JAFOOLEY OLD FASHIONED

This was the first entry from our right-hand man and now bar manager over at Shawarma Bar, Malcolm Lunan. Some of the best classic cocktails have remained favourites for decades because of their simplicity, so when trying to create a Berber & Q version of the old fashioned, it definitely worked out that less equalled more. Replacing the traditional sugar with date syrup made for a simple and very popular drink with a Middle Eastern twist.

SERVES 1

20ml date syrup
3 dashes Angostura bitters
5ml warm water
50ml Buffalo Trace bourbon
ice cubes

GARNISH
orange peel twist

Stir the date syrup and bitters together with the warm water in a tumbler, then add the bourbon and some ice. Stir for 1–2 minutes, adding more ice as required, to ensure the cocktail is well mixed and chilled.

Garnish with an orange peel twist.

HABIBI FUNK

I loved finding out about the word 'habibi'. It's a very popular word in Arabic and can mean a lot of things, a good friend, a love, baby, sweetheart, etc. Habibi Funk was born as a nod to a record label we discovered, showcasing some weird and wonderful sounds spanning 1970s and 1980s Arabic funk and jazz. The drink is strong and fragrant and a much better gift than a bunch of flowers for your habibi. Say sorry with spirits, or raise a glass to underground musical talent.

SERVES 1

HABIBI LIQUEUR
10g coriander seeds, crushed
75g dried hibiscus flowers
75g dried rose petals
20ml sugar syrup
700ml bottle decent vodka

HABIBI FUNK
35ml gin
25ml Contratto Aperitif
25ml Habibi Liqueur (see above)
ice cubes
viola flowers, to garnish (optional)

FOR THE HABIBI LIQUEUR
Combine all the ingredients in a sealed container and leave to steep at room temperature for 3 days, giving it a shake every now and again. After the time has elapsed, strain the liqueur and decant back into a bottle.

FOR THE HABIBI FUNK
Put the three ingredients along with ice in a mixing glass and stir to slightly dilute for 20–30 seconds. Strain the cocktail into a rocks or old fashioned glass to serve.

We like to garnish this one with a couple of viola flowers.

• •

GUY BERBER

This simple short is one for fans of the cosmopolitan. Named after our favourite DJ and Israeli export, Guy Gerber. I think since its departure from our cocktail list, there's always been at least one drink reference to Mr Gerber, all in the hope that one day he'd come and visit us and possibly taste one of the drinks. We're still waiting, Guy...

SERVES 1

40ml Chase vodka (or your
   favourite vodka)
20ml Cointreau
15ml pomegranate juice
12.5ml lime juice
ice cubes

GARNISH
orange peel twist

Combine all the ingredients with ice in a mixing glass and stir for 30 seconds to ensure they are well mixed and chilled.

Double strain the cocktail into a coupette glass and garnish with an orange peel twist.

OUR TEAM

I have always pursued new food experiences relentlessly.

I map out my visits to foreign cities by where I plan to eat, rather than by the sights. Everything in between is just filler really. I relish an enjoyable meal in a good restaurant as much as I'm frustrated by time wasted in a bad one. A good restaurant can transport you to a different culture, country or era. It's where I go to unwind and luxuriate over great food and a glass of wine. It's a place to meet friends, to share past memories or celebrate special occasions. It is a creative expression of thought and detail, from the food to the music, the uniform of the staff to the crockery the customers eat from.

I love to sit in a busy and well-run restaurant watching all its moving parts working harmoniously, together in tandem – a living, breathing organism. Every position is critical, from the kitchen porter to the grill chef, the barman to the maître d'. Each has a vital role to play.

When done right, a restaurant is a place in which guests leave their worries at the door without being told to do so, and go back out into the world feeling that little bit better about life.

This is what hospitality has come to mean to me through the course of my years, first observing it and since providing it. It's what we set out to achieve with every service we conduct.

The hospitality we provide is only ever as good as the team we have around us who are providing it. We have been extremely fortunate and privileged to be surrounded by some amazing people who we consider to be part of our extended family. The energy, drive, dedication, passion and integrity of our team, across all levels and departments, play an enormous role in generating the spirit of Berber & Q that I believe contributes significantly to our success. We owe a huge debt of gratitude to so many of them, past and present.

ON FIRE

Nostalgia is such a powerful emotion, often stirred or awoken by a smell, or sound, taste or sight.

For me, the smell of burning wood has always been captivating. I spent every summer school holiday from the age of 9 onwards in Canadian cottage country, with my very dear and oldest friend David Sischy and his family. They had a large property holding along the shores of Muldrew Lake, near the town of Gravenhurst, Muskoka. A no-frills, rustic set-up, but to us it was our paradise.

By day we would swim, canoe and play beach bats and by night we would gather around the fire pit, carefully build and tend to our fire and barbecue. Our menu featured different cuts from different meats: strip loin, T-bone steaks, soy-marinated short-rib, tandoori chicken and lamb chops.

It was here that I first fell in love with barbecue, outdoor cookery and the unmistakable smell of burning wood. I also learnt and honed some basic fire skills. I've been learning ever since.

I think in many ways Berber & Q, as is often the way with paths we choose in our adult life, was an attempt to reconnect with my youth.

ON TRAVEL

I'm yet to meet a food lover who isn't also obsessed with travel and the edible discoveries that it promises. Berber & Q would not exist if it weren't for low-cost travel. Mattia and I have spent endless hours pounding streets, extensively exploring the grill houses of Istanbul, the food stalls of Jemaa el Fna in Marrakech, the Shipudim in Tel Aviv and the barbecue joints of southern America.

It's all about the stalls discovered by accident down the side alley of the Carmel in Tel Aviv, the small restaurant hidden along a cobbled backstreet in Istanbul or the street cart you stumble across whilst wandering lost in Marrakech's medina.

Ah, the medina. It's the merguez sausage from Stall 32 'Chez Hassan', bursting with fatty harissa-tinted oils and doused in its own juices, served simply with Moroccan country bread to mop up the flavours, accompanied by the sensory overload of Jemaa el Fna at dusk. Or the first time you discover mechoui alley, a narrow strip of the market lined with street-hawking traders who have been serving the same single perfected product for hundreds of years, passed down from generation to generation. Large hunks of slow-cooked lamb on display, the smell of burning embers rising up from the pit built beneath the storefront, in which whole animals are cooked, and then served on scrap paper with little more than some cumin salt and harissa as garnish.

These moments stay in our memories. They amount to far more than just an enjoyment of taste. They draw in all the senses – sight, sound, smell – and the emotions.

Berber & Q is an attempt to transport our customers back to those experiences of sensory overload, if only for a brief moment. The kitchen has been deliberately left open to facilitate the visual of smoke rising from our grill and smoker, to see the hustle and bustle of the kitchen, to hear the sounds that emanate, and to enable the smell of escaping aromas. The lights are kept dim, and the music loud. The restaurant's produce is left on display, as if for sale. The intention is for our customers to feel, even in just some small way, as if they were sitting at one of the food stalls in Marrakech at night, right in the heart of the action. The food is a critical aspect of our restaurant, but these other environmental factors play a role in the overall experience. Berber & Q would not be the same without them.

10 9 8 7 6 5

Ebury Press, an imprint of Ebury Publishing,
20 Vauxhall Bridge Road, London, SW1V 2SA

Ebury Press is part of the Penguin Random House group of companies
whose addresses can be found at global.penguinrandomhouse.com

 Penguin
Random House
UK

First published by Ebury Press in 2018
www.penguin.co.uk

A CIP catalogue record for this book is available from the British Library

Design: Noa&Hila Design in collaboration with Maru Studio

Photography: James Murphy, except for pages 27, 244, 245, 276 and 277
by Tom Bowles

Illustrations: Nick Powell

ISBN: 9781785035289

Printed and bound in China by C&C Offset Printing Co., Ltd

Berber & Q is far more than the sum of its parts, and I am hugely indebted to a cast of wonderful people who have contributed to this book and our restaurant, often both.

My founding business partners, my eldest brother Paul and dear friend Mattia Bianchi, without whom I'm just a lost little boy with a dream of one day owning a restaurant. Josh Talmud (aka Josh 2), the fourth musketeer, who joined shortly afterwards, but without whom we'd soon lose our way. These three work tirelessly in the shadows, making me look far better than I actually am, whilst letting me take all of the credit for our achievements publicly. Our restaurant, and subsequently this book, is as much about them as it is about me, and I will be forever grateful for their individual and collective diligence and passion for what we do.

Nick Lander, for giving me my break, when many wouldn't have done the same. My career owes you a debt of gratitude for this and for your ongoing support.

Our photographer James Murphy and the rest of his brilliant crew, for capturing our food so perfectly, and making all of us look better in print than we do in real life.

Louise McKeever, Lizzy Gray and the rest of the team at Ebury, for believing in this book from the get-go and for your trust, hard work and support throughout the process.

Hila Ben Navat and Noa Schwartz, our designers, who built us our identity. Judith Pearson, Phoebe Lewis and Amy Cook, who built us our look, and Dan Bardiger and his team of oversized builders who built us our restaurants.

Dom Fraser, her husband Marcus Baines Buffery and everybody else at Fraser Communications (of which there are now too many to mention, but I'll single out Nancy Brownlow), who work extensively behind the scenes to tell the world about Berber & Q. They've been with us from the start and are the catalyst for so much good.

For all the chefs and kitchen porters who have ever worked under or for me with diligence and integrity, I owe enormous thanks. It's not an easy job, and it doesn't pay well, but your hard work has been the backbone of so much of what's been achieved. To this end I'd like to single out Attila Bordas and Lukasz Wojcik who have been with me from the beginning and stayed the course of time. Ever dependable, they've never let me down and it's been an honour to have them by my side.

Hernan David Gietzinger (aka Mopito) for your help on this book, and for your friendship through the years. As loyal as they come.

Our investors, who dug deep into their pockets when logic might have dictated otherwise, because they believed in our potential. Without them there is no Berber & Q. Logic isn't everything, belief is. I got that from a Chinese fortune cookie so it must be true.

To all of our wonderful team at Berber & Q, who we consider part of our extended family, for bringing the vibe every single night and for doing what you do. It would be wrong for me to single out any individuals, since it is our collective teamwork that defines us.

And to our customers, all of our regulars, who have taken us into their hearts and make us what we are, thank you.

The life of a chef and restaurateur is far from straightforward. It is both all consuming and emotionally challenging. On a personal level, I am eternally grateful to so many for the love and support bestowed upon me, often at times when it is needed most.

To my friends, who I won't mention individually but you know who you are, who stay by my side, through thick and through thin, no matter how long it takes to sometimes hear from me.

To Navah, without whom I'd never have made it this far. You bore the brunt of my negative energy and tried so hard to turn it into something more positive.

Lois Gishen, one of my biggest fans, who never forgets my birthday.

Ruthie & Nev Sischy, for taking me in every year. So much of what I do now has been shaped by my cherished summers spent on Muldrew Lake.

My older brothers Paul and Rob, who've always had my back, I couldn't ask for anything more. Even though I once did when I was 12. I didn't mean it.

Sarah, for your counsel, continued support, ongoing tolerance and our beautiful daughter. Thankfully she got your looks.

My parents, David and Evelyn, for your endless dedication, generosity and thoughtfulness. An often-thankless task. Know just how thankful I really am. And yes mum, the restaurant was busy last night.

Little Delilah, whom I love with all my heart, may you read this book one day and be proud. x